SEE IT HAPPEN

BY THE SAME AUTHOR

The Defence of Madrid
The Red Army Moves
The Road to Trieste
The Race for Trieste

SEE IT HAPPEN

The Making of ITN

GEOFFREY COX

THE BODLEY HEAD
LONDON SYDNEY
TORONTO

British Library Cataloguing
in Publication Data
Cox, Geoffrey
See it happen: the making of ITN.
1. Independent Television News
2. Television broadcasting of news –
Great Britain
I. Title
070.1'9'0924 PR1992.3.G7
ISBN 0-370-30950-2

Printed in Great Britain for
The Bodley Head Ltd
9 Bow Street, London WC2E 7AL
by The Pitman Press, Bath
Set in Baskerville by
Rowland Phototypesetting Ltd
Bury St Edmunds, Suffolk
First published 1983

To all who have shared
in the building of ITN

Acknowledgements

My chief sources have been my own recollections, my diaries, and the ITN film registers, script records and press cuttings, to which the ITN management has given me generous access. I owe much to the recollections and records of those who shared in these events, and in particular to Aidan Crawley, John Cotter, Martin Gray, Cyril Page and Robert Verrall. Bernard Sendall, who was Deputy Director-General of the ITA throughout the period covered by this book, gave me invaluable advice despite the pressure of his own massive task as official historian of Independent Television. David Warner, Film and Tape Library Manager of ITN, Jim Green, Head of ITN News Information, Jon Lane and Richard Lindley helped me greatly with illustrations, as did the *TV Times* Picture Library and John Emery of the *Daily Mail*. Mrs Scott and Mrs Planer, Mrs Gumpert and Mrs Miles worked miracles in turning my handwriting into typescript.

I am grateful to Hamish Hamilton Ltd for permission to quote from Edward Behr's *Anyone Here Been Raped and Speaks English?* and to Bernard Levin for permission to draw on his early television criticism.

The photographs on pages 6 (bottom), 13 and 16 (bottom) are reproduced with the kind permission of Popperfoto; all the others belong to ITN.

Contents

I
Picture Power

In the early hours of Tuesday 30th January 1968 the Vietcong and the North Vietnamese for the first time carried the war into the heart of the major cities and towns of South Vietnam. In the darkness they moved out of their hiding places in the forests and villages and rice paddies, and struck into the streets of more than a hundred areas which until then had suffered at most random rocket fire. The attackers gained almost complete surprise. It was the time of Tet, the Vietnamese New Year, which in previous years had been marked by a truce. In Saigon in particular the Vietcong got right to the heart of the city, and even seized for a time the ground floor of the American Embassy.

The next night the American public saw on their television screens exceptionally vivid filmed reports from the streets of Saigon, Da Nang and Hue, newsfilm reeking with authenticity. The fighting had broken out in areas where the camera teams of the American television networks were based: cameramen, recordists and reporters were in the thick of the battles from the outset. Into the homes of television viewers throughout the world, but particularly into the homes of people in every corner of the United States, was to pour for the next six weeks a stream of reports of front-line fighting which had almost the impact of live broadcasts.

For those who viewed this film night after night in the cutting rooms of television news, some of these scenes remain in the mind like personal recollections – American boys, their faces taut under their steel helmets, crouched behind a sandbag barricade in a surburban street in Da Nang before going into an attack; unshaven young Marines, ammunition belts looped over their shoulders, stalking like movie cowboys through the shattered temple gardens of Hue; Vietnamese refugee children hunched amid American troops taking shelter from mortar fire on a road verge. Though the fighting in the jungles and open country had been extensively covered throughout the previous three or four years nothing had the impact of these reports of the Tet fighting as they came through, in colour, evening after evening.

The Tet offensive was, in strictly military terms of casualties inflicted and ground held or gained, a severe defeat for the North Vietnamese and the Vietcong. They were rapidly ousted from Saigon and most of the other urban areas. Only in a few places, most particularly in the ancient capital of Hue, did the heavy fighting last for some time. At the end of six weeks the American and South Vietnamese forces had regained control of all the attacked towns and cities, and the war had reverted to its former pattern of frontal attacks by the North Vietnamese in the North, and continual guerrilla harassment elsewhere. The Vietcong and Northern losses had been heavy, for at last they had appeared in groups large enough to provide a real target for American fire power. It was to be a matter of many months before they could mount another major offensive. Significantly, too, the people in the invaded areas had not risen to help the attackers. On the ground, in Vietnam, the American commanders had reason to claim that in this bitter New Year fighting the victory had been theirs.

But the wider reality was very different. Despite their losses, for the North Vietnamese and the Vietcong the Tet offensive was to prove a spectacular success, was in fact to be the decisive battle of the Vietnam war. For it struck a deadly blow at America's will to win. And it struck that blow through television. Though the invaders may have been forced to withdraw, though their losses were high, this was not the picture which lingered in the American mind. What stayed was the image of their first successes, and the image of the high cost to young Americans of countering these attacks.

The Tet offensive came at a moment when the American public had regained confidence that the war, terrible though it was, was grinding slowly towards an American victory. Two months earlier the American commander, General Westmoreland, had spoken of the low morale of the Vietcong. Now these guerrillas had appeared in the safest of the non-Communist areas, in the innermost parts of Saigon itself. Suddenly, powerfully, there was evidence before the eyes of the public that victory was far from certain. For the first time the American public faced the prospect that their suffering might be crowned by defeat. When Walter Cronkite, watching the first film of the attack in the newsroom of CBS in New York, exclaimed, 'I thought we were supposed to be winning this goddam war,' he spoke for tens of millions of Americans.

The impact of the pictures was the greater because the fighting was in confined city streets, where the cameramen could work alongside the front-line troops in a way which had seldom been possible in the intermittent battles of the jungle. Certainly the film caught the expression of American boys, of the boy next door, of the boy perhaps from this very home where the family was now viewing, with his face showing that unmistakable concentration of battle, or twisted in agonies of pain. It caught the look of boys acting in heroism, or in bafflement, or in frenzied excitement, or in grey, barely controlled fear. All of this was set against a background of the suffering of the civilians of these crowded towns and cities, a background of wide-eyed children and women and aged men fleeing with their bundles and tin basins and rickety hand carts from burning buildings whose yellow flames rose against the postcard blue of the Ektachrome film skies.

These were war pictures without parallel, and they were to show that television had become a news medium without parallel. For the first time in the world's history a people at war saw, in the peace of their own homes, the visage of front-line fighting. No censor had intervened here, as in the coverage of World War II, to ensure that only a few glimpses, if any at all, were seen of our troops being killed and wounded. No constraints of distance, or of logistics, or of official policy were to operate, as during the fighting in the Falklands, to inhibit the flow of these pictures to the screen. No patriotic commentary underlined the necessity of it all. Only the laconic voices of the reporters and the shouts of orders and the cries of the wounded were to be heard against the crunch of mortars and the crackle of automatic arms fire. The experience the American people underwent was unique, and suddenly became more than was bearable – or at least more than their leaders judged they could bear. Within six weeks of the first television pictures of the Tet offensive reaching the screen President Johnson swung American policy in Vietnam on to a new course. He announced that he no longer intended to stand for re-election as President that autumn, and he began the process of American de-escalation which was to lead to the Paris peace talks and America's ultimate withdrawal from Vietnam.

Other more recent manifestations of the power of television news abound. Its cameras provided irrefutable evidence of the massacres in the refugee camps of Beirut. The full scale and nature of the Soviet occupation of Afghanistan in 1980, which the Moscow authorities were then denying, was made plain in film of Russian tanks massed on the edge of Kabul airport, starkly clear against a background of snow-covered mountain ranges, in material snatched by a CBS cameraman as he was being hustled from the country. And from Bluff Cove in the Falklands came pictures which conveyed unforgettably both the heroism and the human cost of the Falklands war. In less than a third of a century television news has moved from its infancy to a position – at least within open democratic societies – of formidable power. We who were involved in its early development had faith in its future, but few of us realised the force we were in the process of unleashing.

2

From Radio to Television

Within Britain a major role in shaping this new journalism was played by an equally new journalistic enterprise, Independent Television News. ITN, as the British passion for initials soon dubbed it, was a specialist news organisation set up to provide the new commercial television system with a service of national and international news. It was brought into being for two main reasons. One was to give the mosaic of separate, regionally-based programme companies which made up the ITV network a strong central news service. The other was to meet the obligation laid on commercial broadcasting by Parliament that all news should be presented 'with due accuracy and impartiality'. This rule stemmed from the fears expressed during the debates on the Television Bill that a broadcasting system financed by advertising might produce either a yellow press of the air, filled with sensationalism, or be biased in favour of the advertisers and of the business interests behind the system.

To meet these requirements, and to share the high cost of news, the first four programme companies and the Independent Television

Authority, the body set up to regulate this new form of broadcasting, hit upon the idea of a specialist news company. This would be a subsidiary of the programme companies, but its Editor would be appointed only with the approval of the Authority, and would have to be dismissed if he lost that approval. The ITA would also have the right to attend all meetings of the Board of the news company – a right which the Director-General of the Authority has always exercised in person. A good name for the organisation, and for its service, was to hand – Independent Television News – and in February 1955 its formation was announced.

As their first Editor Independent Television News appointed Aidan Crawley, the presenter of the BBC programme 'Viewfinder' and unquestionably the leading figure of the time in British current affairs television. Crawley, an Old Harrovian and an outstanding cricketer, had been a journalist and documentary film-maker before the war. In 1939 he became a fighter pilot, was shot down over the Western Desert, and spent the remainder of the war in prison camps. In 1945 he won the marginal seat of Buckingham for Labour, and became a junior Minister. When he lost his seat in 1951 he had turned to television.

Though Aidan Crawley's Editorship of ITN lasted only fourteen months, in that time he set in train a revolution in television news in Britain. For eight years after television came back on the air in 1946 the BBC confined news on television to the format which had prevailed in pre-war days, in which a radio-style bulletin was read by an unseen announcer from behind a caption card. However, in one flash of brilliance in 1938 BBC Television had given a glimpse of what television news might be. On 30th September that year it had stationed an outside broadcast camera at Heston Airport when Neville Chamberlain returned from the Munich conference. Richard Dimbleby had provided a commentary as the cameras portrayed live the scene of the Prime Minister stepping from his aircraft holding aloft the piece of paper on which Hitler had written his promise not to go to war. But when the television service had sought permission to present the news in visual form in 1946, the Director-General, Sir William Haley, had been adamant in his refusal. This could give rise to the need 'to subordinate the primary functions of news to the needs of visual presentation'. The most he would permit would be the development of filmed newsreels 'if they are thought worth developing'.[1]

They were so thought, and a BBC 'Television Newsreel' unit was brought into being. Under the skilled leadership of Philip Dorté 'Television Newsreel' quickly became a popular and respected element in the Television Service's programmes. By 1952 the 'Newsreel' was appearing five days a week, with a round-up programme on Sundays, introduced by Richard Dimbleby. Throughout this time, however, the daily news remained strictly confined to a summary read by an unseen announcer.

This determination not to allow visual presentation to put at risk the great reputation won by BBC News during the war resulted not only from Sir William Haley's directive, but also from the adamantine resolve of Tahu Hole, whom Haley made head of BBC News in 1948. Born in New Zealand, Hole had been seasoned in the hard school of Australian journalism. During the war he had become a regular and acclaimed broadcaster from London of news analyses. His entry in *Who's Who* notes with some pride that he was often attacked by the Nazi propaganda department for his broadcasts, and that cards listing his activities were found in Gestapo headquarters after the fall of Berlin.

A very tall man, with a long, deeply-lined bloodhound face, Hole had the air of standing apart, as if from his great height he could see dangers and disasters which were not apparent to lesser men, but which, given the power, he could in his own inscrutable way deal with satisfactorily. His attitude could vary from geniality to a sombre, brooding gravity, a gravity emphasised by the black Homburg hat he wore – we all wore hats in those days – a hat associated with pallbearers as well as with statesmen. A powerful man filling a powerful position, he was not going to be hustled into putting at risk the reputation of BBC News by modifying the tried techniques of radio with the chancy ones of pictorial journalism.

Only in July 1954, under a new Director-General and with competition from the new commercial service on the horizon, did the BBC change their pattern and bring into being 'Television News and Newsreel'. In this the hard news of the day and the newsfilm appeared in a single programme, produced by the BBC News Division, under which the 'Newsreel' unit had now been placed. But the BBC were still so wary of the news appearing biased or opinionated that they kept their newsreaders out of vision. They relied extensively on still pictures and maps, and presented much of their film in a five-minute newsreel ghetto in the second half of the programme. Only three weeks before ITV came on the air in September 1955 did the

Corporation at last bring their newsreaders out from behind the caption card, and even then they did not name them. Night after night a series of figures to whom the public were not introduced appeared in the viewers' sitting rooms, read their pieces and departed unnamed.

This left the BBC open to attack on the flank where it might have seemed strongest, in its news services, and Aidan Crawley proceeded to mount that attack with vigour. His chief new weapon was the newscaster system. Under this Crawley had the news presented by men and women of personality and individuality, who not only read the news from the studio, but helped to gather and prepare it. To underline the difference of this approach he called his presenters 'newscasters', as distinct from the BBC's 'newsreaders'.

Crawley had hoped to find his first newscasters from the ranks of experienced newspaper or radio journalists, and invited me to be one of them. But I wanted to remain an executive, rather than become a performer before the camera, much though I had enjoyed the free-lance work I had done on the screen for BBC Television current affairs. After some 300 people had been tested, including actors and barristers as well as journalists, Crawley chose two newcomers to journalism, Christopher Chataway, then the transport officer for a brewery, and Robin Day. Chataway was very much in the public eye as an Olympic Games long-distance runner, whilst Day, after training as a barrister, was working as a producer in BBC Radio. Literally overnight Chataway established himself as a considerable screen figure, combining vitality with authority. Day came through somewhat more slowly, but soon demonstrated by his reporting with the cameras in the field that he had the makings of a very considerable journalist. Flanked by the first woman newscaster to appear on the screen, the South African-born Barbara Mandell, Chataway and Day within a matter of weeks established newscasting as a major development in television news.

Crawley had been such an important catch for the new system that he had been able to insist that the Editor should have complete freedom, within the requirements of the Television Act, to decide what should go into the news bulletins. Equally significantly, he had ensured that the Editor should also be the Chief Executive of the news company, responsible for the ultimate management of all its branches – engineering, accounts and administration, as well as for the editorial and film departments. This was a breach of the practice which prevailed in the programme companies, where a Managing Director was the Chief Executive, through whom the Head of Programmes was responsible to the Board. It was a change, too, from the Fleet Street practice, under which a Managing Director flanks the Editor as an equal and, at times, as an uneasy rival. Within ITN, which did not have to gather its own revenue or, as in Fleet Street, to buy newsprint and organise the complicated process of printing, distribution and sales, it made sense for the man responsible for programme-making also to be responsible for the technical and administrative tasks ancillary to that programme-making. The work of the Editor of ITN was greatly simplified by this concentration of power and responsibility which Crawley had achieved. Without it the hard battles of the years ahead would have been even harder.

In setting up ITN Crawley had had the assistance of Philip Dorté, who had left the BBC to join Norman Collins's company, ABDC Ltd. Within six months Crawley and Dorté had carried out a prodigious task of organisation, recruiting editorial staff, cameramen and recordists, technicians, engineers and administrators. Equipment was delayed – the last items were got into place as the first bulletin was being rehearsed – and for much of the time the newscasters had to practise delivering their bulletins in a crowded newsroom, where a wooden stand represented the camera and film was projected on to a wall. Yet from the first the new service was acclaimed by the critics and liked by the public. It was a bitter blow, therefore, for Crawley when, within a few weeks of the service going on the air, the programme companies, faced by acute financial difficulties, not only limited the funds for ITN but also cut back drastically the time allocated for bulletins. When in December 1955 these pressures reached the form of demands, made in particular by Howard Thomas, the Managing Director of ABC Television, the contractor for weekend programmes in the North and the Midlands, for bulletins to be shortened to a form which would have made them little more than radio in vision, Crawley put in his resignation. Only three months after the new service had come on the air it faced the loss of its first Editor.

This goaded the ITA into action, and they ruled that there must be a minimum of twenty minutes of news a day, and that this must contain a reasonable amount of film. The figure of twenty minutes seems to have emerged in a stormy interview which Aidan Crawley had with Sir Kenneth Clark, Chairman of the ITA (later to be Lord Clark of 'Civilisation' fame) and Sir Robert Fraser, the Authority's Director-General. In this Crawley, who was unaware of moves which the Director-General had been making behind the scenes to restrain ABC, accused Fraser of never intervening to support ITN. Clark countered by saying that he would insist upon there being a daily minimum of twenty minutes of news. When I asked him some years later what he had based that figure on, he said, 'I plucked it out of the air.' This ruling was to be the Magna Charta of ITN, giving it a secure foundation upon which to build.

Crawley withdrew his resignation, but the companies, finding that the Editor had won this battle, moved against him in the area where they were absolute masters, that of finance. They refused to accept his budget for the required twenty minutes of news, demanding drastic cuts (Crawley's clear recollection is that they wanted the expenditure reduced from £350,000 a year to £200,000 a year) and setting up a sub-committee of the Board to examine the operation and make recommendations about its cost. Crawley saw this as an unwarranted interference with his management, and he and his Deputy, Richard Gould-Adams, resigned. There was uproar in the press, questions in Parliament and demands that the ITA should take over ITN and produce the news itself.

It was therefore a somewhat storm-tossed craft on to the deck of which I sought to mount when Aidan Crawley's resignation was announced on 13th January 1956.

3

Risky Business

Only a lucky chance put me into a position to bid for the Editorship of ITN. On the afternoon of 12th January 1956, the day Aidan Crawley wrote out his second and final resignation, I was on my way into The Langham, the grey-brick former London hotel opposite Broadcasting House which the BBC had taken over as offices. I was due to attend a planning meeting for the BBC interview programme 'Press Conference', on which I appeared from time to time as a questioner. In the glassed-in doorway I met Robert Reid, the stocky Yorkshire broadcaster who had been a colleague of mine on the *News Chronicle* and who had been an outstanding reporter on the BBC's 'War Report'. He was in a hurry. 'I've just heard that Crawley has resigned, and I'm off to put in a bid for his job,' he said.

It was for me a fortunate meeting. I had in my pocket a letter which, once delivered, would have ruled me out of broadcasting for the immediate future. In it I had accepted a three-year contract as Deputy Editor of the *News Chronicle,* the paper of which I was then an Assistant Editor. It was a post which attracted me strongly because I believed that Michael Curtis, the *Chronicle's* new young Editor, and I could together save the paper. But with the ITN Editorship now suddenly in prospect I kept my letter undelivered.

Over the weekend I consulted a number of knowledgeable friends. They were unanimous in advising me that to give up a Deputy Editorship of the *News Chronicle* to enter the uncertain world of commercial television would be folly. There was substantial evidence for their point of view. The programme companies were losing money heavily. By the end of 1955 Associated Rediffusion had lost more than £2 million. ATV was on its way to losing £3 million in its first year of trading – a very big sum in those days. Within three months ATV was going to have to sell one third of its shares to the *Daily Mirror* group in order to keep afloat. Within six months Lord Rothermere was to become so disillusioned with television that he sold all but ten per cent of Associated Newspapers' half-share in Associated Rediffusion to his partners, Rediffusion. We were close to the time when, as the ITA were later to tell the Pilkington Committee, the ITV system was on the point of collapse. In Fleet Street the first walking wounded from this venture were back, with alarming accounts of amateurishness in high places, of alternating waste and meanness. If Fleet Street was a jungle, commercial television looked like a jungle on quicksand, a Florida swamp with more than its fair share of alligators.

Against this I could pit only my instinct, and my knowledge of the way television was sweeping America. I had appeared enough before the BBC cameras – just enough – to know that the lightweight film camera could be the journalistic instrument of the future. So I took the gamble, against all advice except that of my wife, who had no doubt that the future lay with television, and put in my application to ITN.

My anxieties were not lessened when, a few days later, I rang Sir Robert Fraser, whom I had known since his pre-war days in Fleet Street, and told him what I had done. He mused aloud in that quiet, unhurried voice which was to guide and steer, cajole and warn so many television executives and chairmen over the next fifteen years. 'We are having a hard time, but the audience is swinging over to us. Yes, I think the industry will survive.' Survive? That indeed shook me. Few of the industry's most vehement critics went so far as to predict its complete collapse. That the Authority itself might have even a shadow of doubt about the viability of the system in the long term had not occurred to me. Sir Robert's next remark gave me even more cause for concern. 'ITN is a nice little job,' he said. 'It's straightforward enough. All your copy tasting is done for you by the evening papers. It's above all a matter of boiling down the copy to get it into a small space. Anyone coming from Fleet Street is going to find that part rather cramping. But it's a nice little job.'

Little. That adjective struck a harder blow against my confidence than did the danger that the industry might collapse. Was I turning from the mainstream of national journalism into a minor tributary? Fewer than a quarter of the homes in the country at that time had television sets. Was I setting off on a laborious diversion, liable to find myself producing a nightly picture supplement to the news of the day, entertaining maybe, but not essential? Was I coming away from the fulfilling task of informing and influencing millions of people to something more meagre both in scope and impact?

Richard Gould-Adams, who had resigned as Deputy Editor of ITN along with Crawley, used words which strengthened these fears. 'The end product in ITN seems so slight,' he said. 'You work all day getting the film in, arranging interviews, boiling down thousands of words of agency copy to a few hundreds that wouldn't even fill one column of *The Times,* and all you have to show for it at the end are these two short bulletins, these two brief spurts on to the air.'

But I had taken the plunge, and delivered by hand my letter of application to ITN. As I neared the entrance of Television House at the foot of Kingsway a taxi drew up and a burly figure in a duffle coat, wearing horn-rimmed spectacles, with thick hair, and with his head held slightly backward and aloof, suggesting a mixed air of shyness and aggressiveness, paid off the driver and strode into the building. There was something familiar about his face. It took me a moment to realise that this must be Robin Day. He looked much bigger, more shaggy, broader in build and in manner than the dark, sharp, rather pedantic figure who came over on the screen. His striding figure exuded the gusto that every journalistic enterprise needs, and which conditions in the *News Chronicle* had so often conspired to stifle. If he was typical of the staff, ITN could survive.

The drab rear doorway, the brick-walled stairway to the first floor were not encouraging. But the hallway to ITN was bright and welcoming. The walls were a cheerful white; the strip lighting was sharply clear; the girl behind the simple reception desk was pretty, well dressed and cheerful. She was, I noted, typing in her spare time, which showed both a good sense of economy and of giving people a full job. It was a world apart from the more ponderous, more pompous entrance halls of Fleet Street newspapers, with their uniformed men commissionaires, their panelled walls, their grubby messenger boys, their scent of ink and oil from the machines of the newspaper factory which lay behind the scenes. These bright lights, this cleanliness spoke of the world of the camera. I felt as if I was stepping from London gloom into Hollywood sunshine. This, more than any reasoned calculation, strengthened my instinct that I had done the right thing.

4

A Varied Apprenticeship

I approached television as a newspaper man with fifteen years of national newspaper work behind me, but also with experience of broadcasting and of film-making. I had gained a footing in Fleet Street in 1935 as a reporter on the *News Chronicle,* immediately after I came down from Oxford, where I had been a New Zealand Rhodes Scholar. Eighteen months later the Spanish Civil War provided me with a lucky break. In October 1936 Franco's forces were advancing on Madrid in what seemed an unstoppable fashion. The *News Chronicle* was Franco's least favourite British paper. One of its reporters, Arthur Koestler, had already done a stint in a Burgos gaol. It seemed probable that any *News Chronicle* reporter whom the Nationalists found in Madrid would at the very least be held under arrest for some time. The paper was reluctant to have one of its stars, like Vernon

Bartlett or Philip Jordan, wasted in this way. So they looked around the newsroom for someone more expendable, and their eye fell on me. But Madrid did not fall, and I found myself one of only two Fleet Street men left in the capital, the rest of the press having withdrawn with the Government to Valencia. My reports led the paper day after day, particularly when Franco turned his Italian bombers against its streets, a foretaste of what a second world war might bring.

I returned to find myself with something of a reputation and the material for a book, which was published by Gollancz early in 1937 under the title of *The Defence of Madrid* – books were published in a matter of weeks in those days. This caught the eye of Arthur Christiansen, then at the peak of his fame as Editor of the *Daily Express*. He offered me the post of *Express* correspondent in Vienna, one of the pleasantest newspaper jobs at that period, for your bailiwick covered the varied and lively Balkan countries. I covered the 1938 Anschluss between Austria and Germany, and the Munich crisis from Prague. By 1938 I was promoted to the top *Daily Express* foreign post, that of correspondent in Paris. From there I covered the start of World War II, moved on to Holland for the invasion scares of the winter of 1939-40 – scares which were more real than we knew at the time – and to Finland for the Russo-Finnish Winter War. From Brussels in 1940 I reported the German invasion of Belgium, spending in the process an uncomfortable half-hour in the company of Hugh Greene, the future Director-General of the BBC, as part of Tournai was bombed to pieces around us. I moved on to Paris to report the fall of France, escaping finally from Bordeaux.

When I got back to an England awaiting invasion, I decided I had had enough of writing about wars, and that it was time to try fighting in them instead. I joined the New Zealand 5th Infantry Brigade, which had been diverted to Britain from the Middle East. My luck held, and I came unscathed through the campaigns of Greece and Crete and the Libyan offensive in 1941, which culminated in the battles of Sidi Resegh.

New Zealand is a small country and one of the advantages of smallness is that it can offer a variety of experience. This certainly came to me in 1942, when the New Zealand Government, having to build its first Diplomatic Service from scratch, took me from the desert, put me back into civilian clothes, and made me First Secretary at their newly-established Legation in Washington. Since the Minister in Washington, Walter Nash, was also the Minister of Finance in New Zealand, the Legation was entrusted to me as Chargé d'Affaires for surprisingly long periods. So it was that I found myself in my early thirties sitting as the representative of a sovereign nation at meetings of the Pacific War Council, headed by President Roosevelt, and at meetings of British Heads of Mission, on occasion chaired by Winston Churchill. I even signed a treaty on behalf of my country, appending my name to the document establishing UNRRA – the United Nations Relief and Rehabilitation Agency. We signed in alphabetical order, so I found myself signing for New Zealand just ahead of a young Mr Gromyko of the Soviet Union.

But it seemed right, since I decided I did not wish to remain a diplomat after the war, to see out the remainder of the war as a soldier. In 1944 I went back to the 2nd New Zealand Division at Cassino. In due course I was lucky enough to get back my old job as Chief Intelligence Officer to General Freyberg, under whom I served until VE Day found us in Trieste, one war won but another, the Cold War with Stalin's Russia, only too apparent on the horizon.

When I was demobilised I went back to the *News Chronicle*. I had been promised a post as a senior executive but, in the *Chronicle*'s exasperating way, I was asked to do a stint as a Lobby Correspondent in the interim. It was an interim which lasted eight years, but which brought me something invaluable for my ITN Editorship – a firsthand knowledge not only of British politics, but of British politicians. I came into Westminster with the wave of new men who entered after the 1945 Election, worked with them, grew to know them well, so that when they came to maturity and power in the Sixties and Seventies, they were familiar, and mostly friendly figures.

The Lobby had also brought another unforeseen advantage. The firsthand knowledge of politics it gave made me welcome at the BBC as a news analyst – the word 'commentator', with its implication of being an opinionated observer, being rigorously shunned. I quickly realised that one of the basic rules for broadcasting success is that you must not only be able, but available. So I stretched my working day at both ends to do early-morning analyses for Australia and New Zealand, and late-night ones for North America and Canada. I saw more dawns break over Portland Place on more wintry mornings than I like to recall.

I had also a chance in 1949 to gain experience as a scriptwriter on documentary films. 'This Modern Age', the monthly twenty-minute current affairs documentary which J. Arthur Rank launched to compete with the American 'March of Time', invited me to work part-time to help their chief commentary writer, the novelist J. L. Hodson. Hodson's fellow producer, Sergei Nolbandov, relished debate not only about commentaries but about the shaping of the films, and in many long sessions in the 'Modern Age' preview theatre I served a concentrated apprenticeship in film-making.

In 1954 I moved from the Lobby to the post of Assistant Editor. This involved me in supervising the production of the paper at night. I learnt then the hard task not only of deciding the values and significance of stories and of pictures, but of carrying your colleagues with you in those decisions. There is an art in guiding the minds of other men and women with strong views of their own, in winning the allegiance and tapping the skills and talents of people who, as often as not, have become journalists because they like doing things their way. There is an added art in doing all this against the clock, with an impatient head printer demanding that the page be closed. It was exhausting work, done into the small hours on a diet of sausage and mash and tea, carried out at unsocial hours, so that you saw your children only at weekends, when you were likely to be half stupefied by fatigue. But it was rewarding work. I came to know the pleasure of holding in your hand a paper fresh from the press with a front page of which you were truly proud, with a clean layout, eye-catching pictures, clear, well-phrased headlines above well-written stories. There was the added pleasure of watching the other papers in later editions switch to your lead story – provided your nerve held, and you had not meanwhile switched to theirs.

Even more importantly, I was able to offer in my application to ITN an ingredient then in very short supply – experience in front of the television cameras. I got my first chance to appear on screen during the tumultuous Labour Party Conference at Morecambe in September 1952, the first since the Bevanites had emerged as a force to be reckoned with. Like virtually all my colleagues in Fleet Street I did not then possess a television set. In the austere post-war years it seemed no more than a luxury gadget, a toy of the rich, the kind of thing which went with chromium-plated cocktail cabinets in lush sitting rooms in outer suburbia. But on a neighbour's set I had glimpsed an interview programme called 'Press Conference', which the BBC had recently launched, in which three or four journalists questioned someone in the news. When at Morecambe I got a telephone call from Grace Wyndham Goldie, Talks Producer for BBC Television, asking me to go to Manchester to take part in a 'Press Conference' interview with Morgan Phillips, Secretary of the Labour Party, I accepted with alacrity.

I drove across from Morecambe with another journalist making one of his first appearances on television – Malcolm Muggeridge. In the Midland Hotel a corner of the ballroom had been curtained off to make a temporary studio. Lights on tall metal stands shone on a table covered with green baize, and on the chair where, at right angles to us, Morgan Phillips was to sit. In the gloom behind the lights appeared a small host of men and women, the technicians and the studio staff. I was relieved to find that the days of yellow grease-paint were over and that our make-up proved to be no more than a dusting of powder. Then we took our places and the lights were fully switched on, plunging us into a glare like that of a Mediterranean terrace. Small lights on the top of the cameras glowed red; the Floor Manager, lines trailing from his headphones, swung down an arm dramatically to cue the first question, and we were on the air.

As journalism, the programme was scrappy and inadequate. We seemed to get in each other's way, to press none of our points home, to bring out no really new information. I was yet to learn that these are enduring characteristics of interviews conducted by a panel of journalists, as distinct from those where one interviewer can sustain and guide the pressure. But, inexpert though I was, I was also aware that in some indefinable way the programme was proving viewable. Much of this stemmed from the manner in which Malcolm Muggeridge and television fitted together instantly. He spent no time on the details of the Bevanite struggle. Instead, his voice ringing with mock earnestness, he put this question: 'Tell me, Mr Phillips, suppose I had all the right qualifications for a Labour candidate, how would I go about getting a constituency? Suppose I had been to a good public school and to Balliol, and had a private income, how could I find a seat to contest?'

Morgan Phillips coped skilfully with this bouncer. 'Mr Muggeridge,' he replied, 'you have the advantage of me. I have not been to a public school, or to Balliol, and I do not have a private income. But I do believe in the principles of Socialism – and that is the test by which Labour candidates are selected.'

Then, with astonishing rapidity, it was all over and we were sipping that most satisfying of all drinks, the one which follows a programme which has gone well, enabling us to share a moment of euphoria before beginning the long cold drive back to Morecambe.

Other chances to appear on 'Press Conference' followed. Among those we interviewed were Aneurin Bevan, Arthur Deakin, the last of the great right-wing leaders of the Transport and General Workers Union, and Archbishop (later Cardinal) Heenan. The Archbishop started off with a marked psychological advantage by telling us, just before we went on the air, that he had spent much of his time in the train from Liverpool praying for us, his interrogators. Under the guidance of a young producer, Huw Wheldon, I joined an equally young lecturer from the London School of Economics, Robert McKenzie, in tackling Sir Godfrey Huggins, the Prime Minister of Rhodesia. He wore a hearing aid, and countered any awkward questions about the colour bar by carefully failing to hear them.

When the national newspapers were off the streets for three weeks in 1955 the BBC gave Donald Baverstock, with whom I had worked in radio, the task of producing a nightly discussion programme on the air. This gave me the chance to learn how to put my own views forward on the air, as well as to seek those of others. It was followed in the autumn by invitations to help edit and to present the BBC's coverage of the Conservative and Labour Conferences – the first time both were covered by television cameras. In October I conducted the Budget interviews with the Chancellor of the Exchequer, R. A. Butler, at No. 11 Downing Street, and with Hugh Gaitskell, Leader of the Opposition.

I was fortunate to serve this apprenticeship before the television cameras under the sharp eye of Grace Wyndham Goldie, whose qualities of editorial leadership I rapidly came to respect. She had come into television from sound radio only four years previously. An alert, confident, slightly-built woman with wide-set eyes and a sharply quizzical look, Mrs Goldie's vitality proclaimed her Scottish origins. So too did her outspokenness. Her manner was forthright and direct, verging on the impatient and the imperious, as if there was not a second to waste in pursuing the opportunities opened up by this marvellous new medium.

This capacity to react quickly and clearly to a programme or performance is an essential quality in a television producer. What a performer before the camera, or a writer or designer or organiser behind it, wants above all is an evaluation, then and there, of his work. No audience has been within his sight or his hearing to provide a reaction as to how he has done. It is painful to be told, as you emerge from the studio with your adrenalin still racing like a millstream, that you did this or that wrong. It is even more painful, however, to meet no reaction, to be left to drive home through the dark streets, uneasy and uncertain about your work, wondering whether to take that silence as approval or disapproval. Grace Wyndham Goldie never left anyone in that sort of uncertainty. She would assess the show with a directness which was acceptable because it was so manifestly based on a desire to make good television.

One of these experiences before the cameras was etched sharply in my mind. The report of the last day of the Conservative Conference, a Saturday, was scheduled to go out at the peak time of 7.30 p.m. There had been an exciting atmosphere of show business about the Lime Grove studios that evening. For this occasion I had even been allotted a dressing room. Father Grove of 'The Grove Family', the soap opera of the day, had the room to one side of me; Glyn Daniel of 'Animal, Vegetable and Mineral', was on the other side. There was a healthy flow of adrenalin in my veins when I walked across the wide studio floor to take my place at the desk, ready for transmission.

I needed it. For suddenly, alone under the lights in the centre of this huge studio, I realised as never before how much the effectiveness of the next half-hour depended on me, and on me alone. In the unlit half of the studio I could see the gleaming dresses of the girls and the white evening shirts of the men of the cast of the next programme, 'Café Continental'. As I waited for the Studio Manager, earphones on head, to swing down his arm to cue me, I was aware of families settling down in their millions across the country in front of their sets, and I felt very much on my own. But the gods were with me and I found myself suddenly relaxed, alert, authoritative. By the time I had finished – and how short that time seemed – I knew that I had done not only a good, but a very good broadcast. As I hurried off the set a murmur of approval arose from the 'Café Continental' extras, and the Floor Manager gave me an enthusiastic thumbs-up sign.

That experience was, for me, irreplaceable. For I had learnt, isolated under those lights, the responsibility which falls on any performer who faces the camera alone. Later when I had to deal, not only with newscasters and interviewers, but with restive backroom journalists impatient with the way the front men were handling their copy or their ideas, I drew on the knowledge I had gained that Saturday evening.

5

The First Television Demagogue

One other experience had convinced me that television could revolutionise news coverage. This was the spectacle of Senator McCarthy in action before the cameras of the American networks in 1953, when he was at the peak of his power.

I spent six weeks in Washington that summer for the *News Chronicle*. The doings of Joseph Raymond McCarthy, the junior Senator from Wisconsin, dominated the headlines and obsessed the dinner tables of the American capital. His use of the post of Chairman of the Senate Investigations Sub-Committee to probe, harry and bully those he suspected of Communist sympathies was already making his name a synonym for character assassination and for the use of privileged defamation as a form of terror within a democratic society. Wariness of him, indeed fear of him, permeated Washington like a deadly virus. No one in Government service, no one with any links with Government service, however tenuous, was free of the thought that he might be the next to be affected, the next to be called to the witness stand in the big, high-windowed Committee Room of the New Senate Office Building. There he could be called to account for actions, friendships, thoughts dating back a decade or more, when he might have had contact, however slight or unwitting, with organisations in which Communists were active. Other Committees in Congress had previously sought to identify Communists and their fellow travellers, and in doing so had provided the element of truth upon which McCarthy's fabrications were based. But McCarthy's hearings were the first to be televised. He became the first demagogue of the television age, the first to be made and the first to be broken on the screen.

Through one sultry, humid Washington morning after another I sat in my bedroom at the Mayflower Hotel and watched the cameras depict the hunched, swarthy figure of McCarthy, with deep-set eyes and thinning hair, now in whispered consultations with his young counsel, Cohn and Schine, now swinging round to put a question to the witness in either deceptively soft tones, or with a whip-crack of hostility. Facing him, separated by only a few yards of floor space, would be the man or woman accused of links with Communism, links with the force which the United States was not only up against in the Cold War, but also with whom its troops were then battling in the mountains of Korea. For McCarthy was above all a phenomenon of the Korean War. His wildest accusations found an echo in the minds of people who might otherwise have spurned them, but who listened because they had sons or brothers or husbands risking death or disablement on those bleak, arid Korean mountainsides. McCarthy rose in power with that war. Once it had moved to stalemate and then armistice his power was to be undermined and abruptly destroyed.

But at this stage he seemed invulnerable. Relentlessly the cameras swung from the intent, sneering, grimacing face of the Senator to the tense, sad faces of the accused who, by their very appearance on this stand, were also his victims. Relentlessly the cameras pulled in to peer into eyes strained with sleeplessness or fear or agony of soul, or to the whispering lawyers or the swiftly-writing reporters, or the dark-shirted police guards. A terrible incongruity was added by the summer heat, which gave a festive air as the Senators took off their jackets and sat in their white shirts, whilst sightseers in brightly-patterned summer frocks or seersucker suits came and went from the rows of public seats. Amidst this the accused fought to preserve some shreds of reputation, knowing that their jobs, their careers, were all at risk. They knew that if the Senator succeeded in pinning on them the label of Communist, or Communist sympathiser, they might lose all opportunity of worthwhile employment; they would be shunned by their neighbours, either out of conviction or of fear, and would be lucky if they ended up with the anonymity of filling station attendants, or with a chance to slip abroad to Britain or to Mexico.

All of this was conveyed pitilessly by television into the homes of the friends and neighbours and acquaintances of those being interrogated. On television screens in the corner of rooms where housewives were dusting or preparing the children's lunch the spectacle flickered hour after hour. McCarthy, cool, unhurried, deliberate, his eyes never resting on the witness, but seeming to focus on a point just above his head, was portrayed facing a man who from time to time passed a hand over his sweating face, as if seeking to wake from some fantastic dream. Then the session would end, perhaps with McCarthy refusing – as I heard him once do – to provide information about the charges which would be brought the next day. 'I think we have the right to get information without the witness knowing what to lie about,' was his final retort. The image would fade from the screen; the commercials would come up; and the housewife would remember it was time to collect the children from school. It was a drama at once garish and ghoulish. Since those days I have been responsible for making thousands of hours of television, and I have watched countless hours more. Very little of it has struck me with such force as did those scenes from the Senate Committee Room in 1953.

6

Seeds to Nurture

Late in February 1956 I was asked to appear before a committee of the ITN, in a high-ceilinged office in Sidney Bernstein's Granada cinema headquarters in Golden Square. They probed me hard about whether I would bring a visual approach to the job, clearly concerned that I might tie its wings too closely to written journalism, in the way the BBC television news had tied theirs to radio. They also seemed very anxious to establish whether I wanted to go before the cameras myself, as Crawley had done on a number of occasions. He had, for instance, been the main presenter of the Party Conferences for ITN, paralleling the task I had undertaken for the BBC. It was clear that they did not want a second Editor who could establish his own constituency with the viewers, another screen figure who might be difficult to displace.

A week later I was asked to lunch with Captain Thomas Brownrigg, DSO, RN (ret'd), the General Manager of Associated Rediffusion, and Chairman of ITN. He seemed to take offence when I refused a pre-lunch drink. I explained that I never drank alcohol when I was negotiating on my own behalf, or that of anyone else. 'Well, I've had a damned hard morning and I'm having a pink gin,' he said dismissively.

But we got on firmer ground when he found that I had been one of the New Zealand troops whom the Royal Navy had evacuated from Crete after the island fell to the German airborne attack in 1941. He had been a senior staff officer to Admiral Cunningham, C-in-C Mediterranean at the time. 'If I had had my way, you would never have been taken off. We had already lost half the Mediterranean Fleet. It was madness to send in the *Arethusa* to take off one further lot. I was dead against it, but Cunningham would not listen. Said the Navy had never let the Army down.'

Finally he got around to offering me the job, but at a salary which I knew to be below that which they had paid Crawley and below what I knew the job was worth, and stretched my nerve close to breaking point by saying he would have to go back to the Board to see if they would increase the figure. (Later I was to note from the files that he had been told to offer me the higher rate from the start.) I passed one more week of anxiety (which would have been all the greater had I known that among the other applicants was Kenneth Adam, then Managing Director of *Picture Post* and soon to be head of BBC Television) before I learnt that the job was finally mine.

The *News Chronicle* insisted that I should work out at least six weeks of my period of notice, but I was able to use the time to study the ITN operation and to get to know its staff. It was only then, in early April, that I learnt that Christopher Chataway had resigned at the same time as Crawley, and was due to join BBC Current Affairs at the end of the month. It was a heavy blow. To the public Chataway was ITN. None of the other newscasters had made any comparable impact. With ITV having just opened in the Midlands, and about to open in the North, we would need every scrap of talent in the fight there for audience. There was also the danger, as I knew from Fleet Street, that when one key figure goes, other lesser but still valuable men and women will take alarm and follow.

The only practical course was to build anew around Robin Day, whilst we sought new talent. We were helped by a decision by ATV, who held the contract for weekdays in the Midlands and weekends in London, to close down an arts programme it had mounted on Sunday afternoons – a closure which brought Lew Grade's name into the headlines for the first time. 'High Grade or Lew Grade?' was the title of an article on this development by Tom Driberg in the *New Statesman*. Ludovic Kennedy had been among the programme's presenters, and when it was axed he walked down a couple of floors from ATV's offices in Television House and literally knocked on ITN's door. Crawley rang me to say he proposed to offer him a post as a newscaster. Did I agree? I did, swiftly, even though I wondered whether Kennedy, since he was primarily an interpreter of news rather than a reporter of it, might find the role too restrictive.

Meetings with other members of the staff followed, and with each my spirits rose. In Arthur Clifford I sensed immediately the imagination and urgency essential in a News Editor. The Film Manager, John Cotter, brought the cameramen and recordists to meet me in the George Hotel in the Strand, appropriately midway between Fleet Street and this new news centre in Kingsway. As one huge, quietly aggressive man after another filed into the bar I felt as if I was in the All Blacks' changing room before an international. Robin Day and I carefully sounded each other out over lunch in the Inner Temple, surrounded by young barristers who teased him, not without a touch of envy, at leaving the law for show business.

Once I began to study the bulletins closely, as a potential producer rather than as a casual viewer, I realised that newscasting was not the only new element which had emerged. There were at least two other trends I was eager to develop. One was the robust style of interviewing, a complete change from the deferential tone which had characterised much broadcast interviewing in the past. Robin Day had given a striking example of this on the night of Crawley's resignation, when he had interviewed Sir Kenneth Clark. There was no precedent for the head of a great public enterprise being questioned by an employee of one of the organisations he supervised, but Day 'hammered at Sir Kenneth Clark so hard that at one stage a definitely worried look came into Sir Kenneth's eyes'.[1] During Easter the technique of the probing interview had been carried a stage further by another ITN reporter taking his first steps into television, George Ffitch. He and a camera crew had been sent to cover the Communist Party's annual conference – the first the Party had held since, six weeks earlier, Khrushchev had set the pieties of Communism on their head by denouncing the dead Stalin as a traitor to the faith. In the past, had this conference been deemed worthy of coverage at all, it would have been covered by filmed excerpts of the speeches or, more probably, by a spoken report by a reporter. But Ffitch, microphone in hand, stalked up to the Party members waiting to enter the hall and asked them bluntly, 'What do you think of Stalin now?' Nor did he content himself with merely recording their replies. He pressed those who criticised Stalin to say why they had not done so earlier, and challenged the one man who stood up for the dead dictator to justify himself to his comrades. Today it might seem a routine enough line of questioning, though there are few modern reporters who could match Ffitch's swift and clear supplementary questions. At the time it represented a fundamental change, bringing politics alive in a new way, clarifying the issues by the sharp edge of the questioning.

A further development was the use of the cameras, and in particular the sound cameras, to bring news to the public more directly and with greater immediacy than was possible in the newspapers or in radio. This had been seen in a story in October 1955 which, routinely treated, would have been commonplace enough. Norman Dodds MP, the Labour member for Dartford, had watched from his suburban window Electricity Board workers laying a cable in the street outside. Their low rate of work and their high rate of consumption of tea led him to write a letter of protest to *The Times*. The newspapers and radio had reported the news in the orthodox way, with interviews with Mr Dodds and with the workmen. But ITN set up a camera and microphone in the men's canvas shelter, and persuaded Norman Dodds to argue out his case there with the workmen. The film story opened with a shot of one of the men making tea in a zinc bucket of water boiling over a primus stove. Then, as Maurice Richardson commented in the *Observer*, 'Dodds confronted the tea makers, led by their foreman, Percy Diamond, for five minutes of furious disputation which made any organised free speech programme seem like kiss-in-the-ring.' In the *Manchester Guardian*, Bernard Levin wrote:

> 'Here at last was pure television, television as it ought to be and yet might be. The people were real and recognisable; there was an intelligent man and a less intelligent man and a still less intelligent man and a member of Parliament. And the first three were very angry with the last and let him know it in several ways. They argued. They shouted, they banged on the table; and the camera looked at them and at the tea Mr Dodds had accused them of drinking to excess, and at their workaday clothes, while they for their part looked at each other and did not spend their time gawping into the cameras for Aunt Cissie to see. For five minutes the screen looked in on life and came alive with an immediacy and a degree of reality that for the rest of the week it never even suggested.'

Other examples had followed of this practice of thrusting the cameras into the heart of the news, and of sending reporters out to question people caught up in it. Striking Smithfield porters arguing their case in rich Cockney slang; Teddy boys protesting at the way American servicemen were getting away with their girls; London slum-dwellers arguing with the Minister of Housing for a faster rate of slum clearance – and the Minister arguing back; flower-sellers in Piccadilly Circus giving their views on the visit of Bulganin and Khrushchev; all of these brought life onto the screen with remarkable freshness and force.

The Easter bulletins had contained another instance of the way the cameras could not only bring news directly to the public, but could portray it in human terms – for most news is, after all, about people. One of the hardiest of Fleet Street's hardy annuals had long been the regular crop of spring weddings, as couples sought to gain the tax advantage of marrying before the financial year came to an end. In the papers this tended to produce an array of fashionable brides walking on their bridegroom's arm from St Margaret's, Westminster or from St George's, Hanover Square, or at least from a pretty church in Esher or Sunningdale. But Arthur Clifford changed the scene to a church in Hackney, where Lynne Reid Banks interviewed a series of newly-married East Enders on the church steps. Cheerfulness and gusto poured from them in vintage Cockney accents. One bride's cry, ''Ere, can't you wait even a few minutes?' as her husband responded with vigour to the cameraman's suggestion that a kiss would add to the picture had echoes of the Edwardian music-hall in its heyday.

Class barriers were more marked then, and this report brought onto the screen people whose day-to-day lives had not often in the past been thought worth reflecting on the air. It gave a new meaning to the journalistic concept of the human interest story. In Fleet Street the term meant stories which were interesting because they were of the unusual, the abnormal, the exceptional. But here the cameras were making fascinating viewing out of ordinary everyday life, bestriding the gaps between the classes – and making compulsive television out of it. Whether the story was hard news or not did not seem to me to matter. It was life, conveyed by the camera with honesty and without condescension, adding interest and humanity to the bulletins in a way I was determined should be continued.

7

Opening Sequences

My first week at ITN was one in which we were accused of faking the news, suspected of running a blue film show, and in which a cameraman was eaten by a crocodile. Whatever other limitations this new medium might have, monotony was not one of them.

Indeed the first story I had to grapple with on 7th May 1956, when I took over the Editorship, might have been specially designed to embarrass the news service of a commercial broadcasting channel. At the morning editorial conference, when the half-dozen department heads and senior production staff gathered, clipboards on knee, around my desk in a corner of the big first floor room which served as Editor's Office, Board Room and Conference Room, the top story on the news list was a statement the Minister of Health was to make that afternoon about possible links between smoking and cancer. It was the first of such inquiries into an issue which had been highlighted by the death in 1952 of King George VI from lung cancer. Two years earlier, in the Committee stage of the Television Bill, this topic had been cited as the kind of news which a commercially financed broadcasting system could not be trusted to handle fairly. One of the most vociferous opponents of the Bill, Sir Leslie Plummer, the Labour MP for Deptford (later to be a Director of Granada Television) had argued that the programme companies should not be allowed to provide a news service, which should be done by the ITA. He had posed the question of whether an ITV news producer would organise a programme announcing or discussing whether smoking has any direct relation to cancer of the lung. 'Of course not,' was his assessment.

Though cigarette advertisers were amongst the few supporting ITV in those lean days, the Minister's statement posed a less difficult problem than at first appeared. I knew from my experience in Fleet Street that, quite apart from any question of journalistic ethics, there is no practical point in trying to appease advertisers by trimming your editorial copy. What they want is not nice words in the editorial columns – though they will take any on offer – but large numbers of readers or of viewers for their advertisements. Only once had the advertising department of the *News Chronicle* sought to influence my presentation of news. That had come when, after seeing an early edition, they had asked if there might not be another place on the front page for a story about a daring bank robbery than immediately alongside an advertisement for a High Street bank headed 'Safe as a Bank'. So I ruled that we would carry the Minister's statement, together with any comments the tobacco industry or the doctors might offer.

The film list for the day made clear at a glance on what a tight financial rein ITN was held. Only two sound film units were on duty, and the main sound-on-film story on offer was an interview with the Governor of Kenya, Sir Evelyn Baring, about a visit Princess Margaret was due to make to East Africa, which would be her first major public activity since the breakdown of her romance with Group Captain Townsend. Other items showed only too clearly their cinema newsreel parentage – a trade fair in Paris; the annual blessing of the tulip fields in Lincolnshire as the crop came into bloom; the opening of the tomb of an Egyptian princess outside Cairo. It was hardly a list which offered much promise of turning news into pictures.

This thin diet was, however, to be spiced by a dash of controversy involving ITN itself. The editorial conference had been over only a few minutes when the News Editor, Arthur Clifford, was back in the room, accompanied by a tense-faced, bespectacled young man called Roger Balaam. He was a schoolteacher who had done a fortnight's relief work for ITN as a scriptwriter, and had been conveniently available when the newsroom needed to interview a teacher about reports of indiscipline in London schools. Balaam had confirmed that there had been considerable indiscipline at the East London school at which he had taught. The interview had been supplemented by shots of children pouring out of the front door and down the steps of the school, and by a tumultuous interview with a bobbing, laughing crowd of them outside, in which they all declared themselves firmly in favour of keeping the cane. Although Balaam had talked with his back to the camera, he had been recognised, and the LCC Education Committee had now informed him that he was struck off their list of relief teachers.

Today a great clanking machinery of industrial tribunals and redundancy laws and union consultants and rights of appeal would come into action. The one thing we could do was to allow Balaam to defend himself on the air, and so we arranged for him to be interviewed by Robin Day on the late bulletin. I had little doubt that his story would stand up, for only a few months earlier I had edited for the *News Chronicle* a series of articles about the growing indiscipline in inner London secondary modern schools.

Despite the shortage of film we had adequate early bulletins and a surprisingly strong bulletin for the main evening news, which in those days went out at 10.45 p.m. The trade fair and the tulip ceremony provided some pleasant if not very newsworthy pictures. The interview with Sir Evelyn Baring about Princess Margaret's tour was on a topic of keen interest. Another interview with the world cruiserweight champion, Archie Moore, rated as news to a public not yet sated with the sight and sound of sporting personalities. We had an action story close at hand, with Waterloo Station packed with commuters held up by a signal failure. A mass meeting of BOAC workers, protesting against the appointment of a part-timer as Chairman of the Corporation, provided first-hand coverage of an industrial dispute, still then a relative rarity on film. A Miners' Gala in Edinburgh was all the more pictorial for being held in driving rain and howling winds. Agency film from Vienna of Soviet- and American-made tanks appearing side by side in the newly-equipped army of neutral Austria was of interest to a Britain filled with wartime veterans. Motor cycles swerving and skidding in a speedway contest – one of the few sports we were then free to cover – were reasonably exciting to watch.

What made the bulletin, however, was the strength of the newscasting. Robin Day was due to present the programme, having hurried back to Kingsway after hearing in the Commons the statement on smoking and cancer. The draft of the story prepared by the sub-editor had been straightforward. 'The Minister of Health, Mr Turton, told the Commons this afternoon that so far two known cancer-producing agents had been identified in tobacco smoke, but he added that it has not been proved that smoking directly causes lung cancer,' was its opening sentence. I was reading this when there was a knock at the door and Robin Day's intent face peered round at me. Could he discuss a point of presentation? Did I think he would be right to personalise the cancer story so as to make it read, 'After lunch today I stubbed out my cigarette and went into the House of Commons Press

Gallery to hear – with some apprehension – what the Minister of Health had to say about smoking and cancer.'?

It was for me the best moment of a long day. This was exactly the popular yet informed touch which I saw as the key to the presentation of news. When the bulletin came on the air this opening gave it a directness which at once caught attention. The interview with Roger Balaam provided a dramatic – indeed a melodramatic – close. His eyes glaring with strain and nervousness, Balaam swung round to the camera and declared, 'I told the truth.' It was news in a direct and personalised form which no other form of journalism could have provided.

We had not heard the last of the Balaam affair. The Chairman of the LCC Education Committee retorted that the film sequences showing 'an unruly mob at a London school' had been 'arranged for the television cameras'. Newspaper placards outside Television House proclaimed 'Mob Scenes Staged by ITV' and 'Teacher Sacked after TV Show was TV Scriptwriter'. The LCC told the press that 'a group of boys were induced, in breach of school rules, to run down a staircase normally reserved for fire escape purposes to give the effect of an undisciplined and unruly mob'. Today such complaints would either be shrugged off by the broadcaster, or would make their way through the series of committees and tribunals established to deal with allegations of media misdoings. For the young news service of ITN in 1956 they were dangerous. We had so far been the one part of Independent Television free from the scorn and antagonism heaped on the system by a hostile press. If our product became suspect it would take weeks to repair the damage. Fortunately I knew the subject, and was sure the ITN report was firmly based. So we stood our ground, but gave the complaints full rein on the air, re-running our film to enable viewers to judge for themselves. We also gave Balaam a further chance to confirm his story, which the film librarian duly recorded as 'Live Spot. Roger Balaam standing by the truth again.' But we could do no more to protect him for his outspokenness. The LCC stood adamantly by their ban, and we had no post we could offer him. A month later he was stoking boilers at the Temperance Hospital at Euston.

The Balaam case had taken up so much of my time that I was not greatly pleased when the next morning another distraction arose. It came in a telephone call from Captain Brownrigg, whose office was just three floors above mine in Television House. His tone was severe.

After a brief inquiry about how I was settling in he asked, 'Are you aware that your film editors are using your preview theatre at lunch time for blue film shows?' I was not so aware. 'I think you will find it is so,' he continued, 'and I look to you to put a stop to it.'

It was certainly not a problem I relished. I hardly knew where the preview theatre was. Was I to go up quietly at lunch time, fling open the door and catch them in the act? For all I knew in the film world such activities might be commonplace, might be regarded as a custom and practice to which a blind eye was turned. It was not the kind of issue on which I wanted my first contact with the film editors to be based.

I consulted Norman Dickson, the big Scot who was the General Manager of ITN. He dealt with it promptly. That lunch time he went up to the theatre and found just such a film show in progress – being run not by our film editors but by a group from Brownrigg's own staff on Associated Rediffusion. Dickson warned them off in no uncertain terms. I had some pleasure in passing that information on to Captain Brownrigg.

The third event, that of the missing cameraman, was so macabre and so extraordinary that at first I simply disbelieved it. Among the few pieces of foreign film expected my first day was a report, due to be filmed by a freelance stringer cameraman working from Nairobi, of a drive by British troops in Kenya against the Mau Mau rebels. On the first evening the Assistant Film Manager, Freddie Partington, told the conference that there were difficulties with the film and it would not arrive that day. Though Partington had come to ITN from Paramount News, he bore no resemblance to the aggressive, bustling executives one associated with the camera newsreels. He was a quiet, rather diffident man, with prematurely grey hair, who might have been a librarian or a backroom scientist. That this unassuming manner hid great determination and shrewdness was something which I was to learn only over the months ahead. When the next evening the film had still not arrived I showed some impatience. On the third evening Partington met my inquiries with the words, 'Well, there are some difficulties. I don't think we are going to get the film after all.' I sensed inefficiency, and asked with some asperity, 'What sort of difficulties?'

Partington looked disconcerted, and blushed with anxiety. 'Well,' he said nervously, 'great difficulties. Unusual difficulties.' This exasperated me. 'What are they?' I insisted. 'What are you holding back?' Partington took a deep breath. 'Well, sir,' he said, 'the cameraman has been eaten by a crocodile.'

My first reaction was that I was being subjected to some form of sardonic joke, some test which the film industry applied to newcomers. But indeed Partington was telling no more than the truth. The boat in which the cameraman, an East Indian Kenyan, had been crossing a flooded river had overturned. He had been swept away, and had either been drowned or, more probably, had fallen victim to the crocodiles which infested the river. Certainly his body was never recovered. Of the many strange events which occurred within ITN in those early years, this was amongst the strangest, as well as the most tragic.

8

Kingsway Pioneers

The editorial staff of ITN in May 1956 was, to say the least, compact. In addition to Robin Day and Ludovic Kennedy our total editorial strength was nineteen. Today the total is well over the hundred mark. We had two news editors, three reporters, eight sub-editors and six scriptwriters. This would have been far too small a team to produce three bulletins a day on weekdays and two at weekends but for two factors. The first was that they were all able men and women, some very able, one or two brilliant. The second was that they were all prepared to tackle any editorial job. Scriptwriters would readily turn their hands from writing commentary to subbing stories for the newscasters or to voicing commentaries. On occasion they would rush out from the office to do an emergency interview. The sub-editors for their part frequently acted as reporters, whilst reporters would take over as relief news editors or do a stint on the subs desk. And all were prepared to work long hours, forgo their days off, even postpone their holidays, to keep the service going. This was possible only because of the attitude of the National Union of Journalists, then under the commonsense leadership of Percy Jarret. He knew that if ITN was to survive its staff must not stand on demarcation lines, few of which were in any event those days drawn with any sharpness. The rigidities of union practice today would have stifled ITN at birth.

The dominant figure in the newsroom was undoubtedly Arthur Clifford, who had held the post of News Editor since the previous November. He was a big man in every way, well over six feet tall, with a massive Viking head, a thick shock of hair, alert eyes and the bearing more of a boxer (which indeed he had been in his youth) than of a journalist. An East Ender, he had come into journalism by the traditional route for those without influence or higher education, as a tea boy and copy messenger for United Press, the American-owned news agency. He graduated to sub-editing, and after war service in the Coldstream Guards won a job in the BBC Radio newsroom. He came through quickly to be a chief sub-editor, and was one of the team sent off to Alexandra Palace to staff the first television news bulletins in 1953. There he saw the possibilities which television offered, and chafed at the way in which the BBC system, as it then worked, blunted these possibilities. When commercial television came along he determined to get into it.

That was not as easy a task as it might have seemed. Crawley's desk in ITN's temporary headquarters in Kingsway – which were, by chance, in the building in which John Reith had begun work as the General Manager of the British Broadcasting Company in 1922 – was piled high with applications from experienced journalists. The few posts available might readily be filled by others from Fleet Street before Crawley got around to seeing anyone from the BBC newsroom.

Fortunately Clifford had one friend already on the ITN staff – John Cotter, who had been a member of Philip Dorté's team at Alexandra Palace, and whom Dorte had brought across to ITN to head the camera teams. John Cotter carried in his bones the newsreel cameraman's belief in the unorthodox approach. One evening, when everyone else had left the building, he climbed out of the newsroom window onto a narrow shelf which led, seven floors above the street, along the outside of the building, and edged his way along this to Crawley's window. Once inside he found Clifford's application, and set it near to the top of the pile. Within a week Clifford had been interviewed and appointed Assistant News Editor. Within a couple of months the Chief News Editor had parted company with ITN, and Crawley had given Clifford his chance. This he proceeded to take with both of his large, confident hands, wading into the problems of each day's coverage with the same vigour with which he had come out of his corner in his boxing days in Simpson's Gymnasium in the Mile End Road.

Arthur Clifford had not only a clear idea of what he wanted to do, but also the force of personality to achieve it – a force all the more remarkable because under his tough exterior he was in fact a highly sensitive man. He wanted to use the cameras to bring the news more directly to the public, to let them hear and see for themselves the events and people who made news. Ideas welled up in him day after day, not just ideas of what to cover, but of fresh and original ways of covering it. He had a gift for approaching news stories not head-on, in a way which would give no depth or perspective, but from an angle which could bring out the story's light and shade. When the holders of the VC gathered in London for the first time since the war Clifford did not take the obvious step of asking them how they won their medals, of looking back to the war. Instead he sought them out and interviewed them at their new peacetime tasks, the farmer VC back at his plough, the sailor VC in his new role as a naval frogman, the shoe salesman VC back in his shop. When the Minister of Transport wanted to appeal on the eve of a Bank Holiday for motorists to drive more slowly Clifford avoided the hackneyed approach of an appeal from behind the Minister's desk. Instead he had him interviewed on the margin of the North Circular Road, with the holiday traffic thundering behind him. When Churchill's birthday came round he did not seek the birthday tributes of the great. Instead he sent a camera team out into the streets to find people with their own wartime memory of Churchill: the former Home Guard sentry who had been on duty when he visited coastal defences at Brighton; the present-day tobacconist who, as an air raid warden, had walked with him through the bombed streets of the East End; the woman factory worker who remembered him in her blacked-out munitions factory.

Myth already surrounded Clifford's name by the time I joined ITN, chiefly concerning the Homeric rages with which he would sweep aside constraints in his path. In one bout of exasperation he was said to have hurled a heavy typewriter out of the newsroom window, only for it to fall through the open window of the bank on the floor below, where a clerk found it on his desk, miraculously upright, when he returned from lunch. But I respected from the start Clifford's abounding creativity. We had many arguments, for it was his job to press his ideas to the limit, and mine to see that they did not overstep those limits. But far more often we were in agreement. We shared the view that even complex issues could be made interesting to a wide public if they were expressed in human terms, and that television offered a marvellous new way of doing this. We were both entranced by this new form of journalism, delighting each day in the chance to try out new ways of using it, sharing our anxieties when things went wrong, sharing our relief and pleasure when an idea came to fruition, or when we had hit upon some new technique.

Clifford had a remarkable gift for simile. He complained to me angrily one evening that changes made by a newscaster in the introduction to a film story had blunted the impact of the day's work of the reporter and camera team. It was too late for the copy to be further revised without throwing the newscaster off balance.

'Whether we like ot or not,' I argued, 'we are as dependent on the newscasters for getting our work across to the public as any Fleet Street journalist is on the printer. If the newscaster is on edge then the public is going to be put on edge too and all our other work spoiled as a result. It's like giving a grubby imprint to a well-written, well-subbed story.'

'I suppose you're right,' he sighed. 'I suppose we have to regard newscasters like showcattle. Rattle them just before the judges come round and they break out into a muck sweat and get marked down a couple of classes.'

Some years later, when we were colleagues again on Tyne Tees Television, Clifford was rightly infuriated when we learnt that the Network Committee, dominated by the big five companies, had refused to network a superb short documentary which we had made on the scenes in Sunderland on the day the Sunderland team, then in the Second Division, beat mighty Leeds in the Cup Final at Wembley. 'Those damn dog-food producing denizens of the Thames Valley,' he thundered. 'They don't know anything about the real people of this country.'

John Cotter, whose task as Film Manager was to translate Clifford's ideas into film, was short, muscular, cheerful and indomitable. His enduring quality was his resourcefulness. The son of a newsreel cameraman, he had inherited the belief that nothing should stop a camera team in search of a story, or a film organiser in laying one on.

On the News Desk Clifford was flanked by John Hartley, a sturdy, open-faced man who had given up a post as Senior Reporter on *The Times* to join ITN, and by three newcomers to broadcasting, Reginald

Bosanquet, George Ffitch and Lynne Reid Banks. Bosanquet was then twenty-three, a handsome figure, upright, self-possessed and quiet-voiced, given to hacking jackets and hand-made shoes, and wearing his hair, in those close-cropped National Service days, exceptionally long, though by later standards it was short enough. George Ffitch was a stocky, youthful-looking man, with keen grey eyes set wide in a square face, with a bearing which was at the same time cheerful and pugnacious. He had grown up in the outer eastern suburbs of London and had begun his journalism on the *Dagenham Times*. Highly intelligent, he had learnt Russian during his National Service days, and had graduated from the London School of Slavonic Studies. He had helped Robert McKenzie with his book on British political parties, the first notable landmark in the new discipline of psephology. McKenzie had turned down an invitation from Crawley to become a newscaster, and had suggested Ffitch as a potential reporter in his stead, so launching him on the broadcasting career which was to bring him to the leadership of Britain's first all-news radio station, LBC – the London Broadcasting Company.

Lynne Reid Banks had an equally sharp, questing intelligence, and an eager, alert manner. She was an actress turned journalist who, when sent to interview Aidan Crawley, had taken the opportunity to ask him for a job. Lynne and Barbara Mandell, who had become a reporter and scriptwriter after her afternoon newscasts had been axed during the first economy drive, provided a vitally important feminine element in our presentation at a time when reporting was seen predominately as a male preserve. We had another woman journalist behind the scenes, Jo Hodgson, who had come across from the BBC newsroom. In due course, she was to become Chief Sub, one of the first women in Britain to hold such a post.

Both the studio directors had worked with me on 'This Modern Age'. James Bredin had been a researcher there, and had gone to the BBC to become one of Grace Wyndham Goldie's team of young producers. Robert Verrall had been a film editor. With BBC Television's film unit he had prepared the telerecording of the Coronation in 1953 so skilfully and so swiftly that it had raced onto the screen in the United States the more elaborate efforts of CBS and NBC.

ITN's domains were as compact as its staff. On the first floor they were dominated by the newsroom, a big open-plan room, well lit by day by windows on two sides, and at night by strong but warm strip-lighting. From the windows the bustle of Kingsway could be seen, its shoppers and office workers a useful constant reminder of the people by whom our work would ultimately be judged. The film and technical areas had, as a precaution against fire, been set apart on the eighth floor at the top of the building. It was there that one became aware that this was indeed a new form of journalism. The telecine room, where film was transformed from a series of images conveyed by light to images conveyed by electronic impulse was, with its gleaming equipment and its white-coated operators, like something out of the as-yet-unrealised space age. The Debrie film-processing machine was equally impressive: hundreds of yards of film and of leaders, looped over spools and bobbins in a big glass tank, ran at top speed in spectacular fashion as material was developed, fixed, washed and dried.

The studio itself, the holy of holies, was disappointingly small, with a low ceiling only twelve feet above floor level, which posed severe problems for the lighting experts. Three cumbersome cameras, their grey lens shafts thrust out like the barrels of small cannon, and an overhead microphone boom like a small crane, crowded in on the newscaster. During rehearsals the adjoining control room would be a babel of sound, as voices crackled in from other technical areas with queries, or warnings of late film or of incomplete scripts; as the engineer talked to his fellows up and down the network; as the director gave instructions over his intercom to the floor manager or the cameramen. It seemed impossible that any programme could emerge from such chaos. But as the long second hand on the clock ticked down towards 10.45 p.m., and the production assistant began her count-down: 'Ten seconds to transmission . . . nine . . . eight . . .' order would suddenly reign. The director would call, 'Take two, cue grams,' the ITN title would show on the monitor, and our theme music, 'Non Stop', would begin its quick course, to be followed by yet one more curt order into the intercom, 'Take three, cue Robin,' and one more bulletin would be on the air.

9

News into Pictures

'See It Happen on ITN' was the slogan franked on the letter which had offered me the Editorship, and it was a slogan I was keen to see made into a reality. The use of the film camera to turn news into pictures was the new element television could bring to journalism. Yet when I came to scrutinise the ITN bulletins closely it became apparent that hard news on film was in short supply. Though the film list on my first day had been exceptionally scanty, the lists which reached my desk as the weeks unfolded showed that we were far from letting the viewers see the day's news. The vigour and freshness of the newscasting and the imaginative use of the sound camera for interviews and human interest stories hid the fact that our hard news coverage was at best patchy. During February 1956 film had been available on only four occasions to illustrate the lead story. Three of these had been no more than brief underlays, silent film brought up as background to the newscaster's words. For many important news stories the cameras had not been on the scene. We had had virtually no film of the mounting guerrilla war in Cyprus, where we faced an onslaught from the Eoka forces claiming union with Greece; of the continued search-and-destroy operations against other guerrillas in the jungles of Malaysia; of operations against the Mau Mau insurgents in Kenya.

It did not take long to discover the reason. We lacked hard news film because we lacked hard cash. Film coverage was where the shortage of funds bore hardest on ITN. The clamp on expenditure meant that the excellent network of freelance stringer cameramen which John Cotter had set up at home and overseas went largely unused. The budget for the year until September 1956 had provided only £20,000 for all stringer film coverage. This permitted the commissioning of only two stringer stories a day – and by May most of it had already been spent.

The bulk of our foreign news coverage had to come from the package of newsfilm which reached us from CBS in New York six days a week. This was not an agency service in the fullest sense, offering coverage of all the main stories, but consisted of copies of those stories CBS had shot for their own programmes. This made it not only American-orientated, but frequently meant that stories were some days behind the news. Coverage from Europe and the Far East had to go to New York, to be processed and edited there, before it could make its way back to us. We were still in the era of piston-engined aircraft and the Atlantic crossing took at least twelve hours. At best film of events on the Eastern seaboard of the States could reach us for showing the next day. Material from other parts of the American continent and from the rest of the world would not be available in under forty-eight hours. But for all this the CBS package was invaluable, for their television newsroom matched the high standards set by their radio news. And we could do something to supplement their service by gathering in, at low rates, material from the European cinema newsreels and, occasionally, from the newsrooms which the European television stations were in the process of establishing. This material was liable to lag after the event, but with skill it could be freshened up and given an impression of immediacy. A news report that Tito, on his first official visit to France, had visited Lille could sustain film of his cavalcade, escorted by French police on motor cycles, passing down the Champs-Élysées in Paris the day before. A shot of troops on routine patrol on Cyprus could help to illustrate a report of the latest bombing or shooting. Above all we could use our own staff cameramen to fill the gap, particularly within the United Kingdom. We had eleven of them, five equipped with sound cameras, the other six with cameras which could shoot only silent material.

Their key instrument was the Aurican Cine-Voice sound camera, a California-built instrument which recorded pictures and sound on 16mm film. It looked amateurishly small for its task, despite its triple lens plate, and had indeed originated as an amateur camera. The American networks, facing the need for a lightweight camera with which to cover the Korean war in 1950, had bought Auricans off the shop shelves, modifying them only with a larger magazine capable of providing ten minutes of running time. Yet the Cine-Voice was to become the great work-horse of the first twenty years of television news, as durable and as widely used as, in the field of aviation, the

Dakota had been in its time. Indoors, and for set-piece occasions, the Cine-Voice was used on a tripod. Outdoors it could be humped on one shoulder by the cameraman for covering swift-moving action. The sound recordist, whose apparatus was linked to the camera by a heavy insulated cable, could move with the cameraman to keep near the heart of the action – and they learnt to make such moves with remarkable swiftness and co-ordination.

For filming without sound we used the German-built Arriflex, an improved version of the cameras with which the German Army film cameramen had provided Dr Goebbels with so much masterly front-line material. We called the six cameramen who used the Arriflex 'silent cameramen': the BBC and the programme companies called their comparable operators 'mute cameramen' – a nice distinction for linguistic experts to ponder.

The problem with our camera crews in 1956 lay not with their equipment, which was then the best which money could buy, but with their numbers. By the time we had made allowance for holidays and sickness, and by the time we had rostered them to work a long day from early morning until nine at night, across a seven-day week, we could count on only two or three sound crews being available each day, plus up to three silent cameramen. To back up our crews only one film agency then existed in the United Kingdom, that of the Brennard brothers who covered, in silent film only, the comings and goings of the newsworthy through London airport. In Manchester one freelance cameraman possessed his own Cine-Voice, and we could call on silent coverage from other freelances at points across the British Isles. These included a chemist at Lerwick in the Shetlands who was always ready to hand his shop over to his assistant and dash out to film a shipwreck or a storm – all that those as-yet-undisturbed islands provided in the way of news.

But home stringer coverage, like that of foreign stringers, cost money. So too did the use of our own crews. We could not roam far on the £6,000 a year which represented our total budget for travel, even if petrol cost only the equivalent of 20p a gallon. I quickly learnt that one of the key decisions of the day was how best to deploy the cameramen, and above all the sound crews. It called not only for flair and decisiveness, but also for a mixture of diplomacy and ruthlessness. Crews and reporters had to be hurried and harried from one story to another. Often after a team had driven many miles, and had arranged an interview or a filming session at considerable inconvenience to all concerned, they would be told, when they checked in from a nearby telephone kiosk, to scrap the whole affair and hurry off to some more urgent story.

Despite all these limitations, we steadily increased the amount of hard news coverage in the bulletins, above all by using the silent cameramen as reporters on action stories, relying on their pictures rather than on a reporter's words. They relished the wider scope this gave them after the confines of cinema newsreels which had appeared only twice a week. It may not have been coverage in depth, but it was coverage in pictures. The bulletins became increasingly pictorial – more indeed than was often to prove the case later.

Few people at the time detected the gaps in our film coverage of hard news. Radio was still the main source of broadcast news, to which television seemed to be largely an illustrated supplement. Moreover our technique of using the sound camera to put chunks of real life on to the screen, as with the Norman Dodds story in 1955, made the bulletins highly acceptable regardless of whether we had managed to corral the day's news fully into pictures. When Arthur Clifford learnt that I found the coverage of the Hackney weddings very much to my taste he set about exploiting this vein of human interest material vigorously. On Whit Monday he sent George Ffitch and a camera crew to Southend to see if that traditional holiday place for London's East Enders had changed. Outwardly much was the same. The pier was crowded with strollers and fishermen; donkeys plied for hire on sands which soon became mud; there were fathers in braces and mothers in felt slippers. But the young wanted more than this. Men back from the war recalled in interview the sunny Mediterranean beaches they had fought on, and now wanted to camp on. The long columns of cyclists which had swept along the pre-war roads had shrunk to small groups, many of whom spoke longingly of the day when they might own a car. What had been a routine news story became a glimpse of social history – and indeed the social historians need not look beyond the ITN archives to illustrate the changing pattern of British life since 1955.

We found also that the sound camera could enable us to put into human terms issues and problems which were otherwise likely to be suffocated in the language of official reports or in the circumlocutions of official spokesmen. When yet one more report was published on the plan to drive a relief road for Oxford traffic through the meadows between the colleges and the Thames, we did not adopt the accepted practice of summarising the findings in words and mounting a discussion in the studio. John Hartley and a camera crew went off to Oxford and interviewed embattled dons and ambitious town planners under the elm trees of Merton Mall, the quiet avenue which would have been the first casualty of the new road. Today such ombudsman reports are commonplace, even if they have tended of late to be confined to regional news magazines or 'Nationwide'. At that time, if they appeared at all on television, they found their place only in the weekly news magazines.

Where we could combine social inquiry with human interest, the result could be very viewable. When the local authority in Slough forbade people to take dogs into parks except on leash, we found a rich crop of individualistic Britons ready to voice their protests. When the education authorities in Hertfordshire decided they must counter the sloppy speech of their school children, and appointed a special teacher for that purpose, we not only collected a wide sample of dialects and phrases, but interviewed the teacher. We tracked him down, not in the classroom, but alongside a milk float in a suburban street, where he was plying his second trade as a milk roundsman. Such human interest stories formed a lode which we mined strenuously, and which we had very much to ourselves until a year later, when the BBC's 'Tonight' programme set its prospectors loose in the same territory. In 1956 television had not yet tramped bare the by-paths of British life, nor yet helped to spread uniformity. Varied characters, varied scenes came freshly onto the screen, many of them a revelation to people in other places and other classes. In those early years television introduced the British people to one another.

Street interviews played an important part in this process. The technique of seeking the views of a random selection of passers-by had been used on radio from time to time in 'Radio Newsreel', and very occasionally by the cinema newsreels. ITN had adopted it as a way of sampling public reaction in November 1955 to Princess Margaret's decision not to marry Group Captain Townsend. Half-a-dozen interviews shot in the street outside Lancaster House had brought the man in the street literally to the screen, well supported by the woman in the street. From the summer of 1956 we increasingly utilised this technique. (Its later name, Vox Pop, had to wait until the classicists of 'Tonight' took it up.) It provided a sample, albeit a very random one, of what the public were thinking. We never sought to present this as a fair or accurate sample, but merely as a varied expression of views. We deliberately selected some speakers for, and some against, and made clear in the commentary that the outcome was not to be taken as a measure of public thinking.

Successful and popular though such sound film coverage could be, it was essentially away-page material and did not solve the problem of presenting fully the hard news of the day on television. Moreover, the silent camera, valuable reporting instrument though it was, lacked one important dimension. It captured only the sight of events, not their sound. Only on ceremonial occasions such as Trooping the Colour, where the cameras and the microphones could be placed in position beforehand, did we use the sound cameras to record the natural sound, as well as the picture. This was in accordance with newsreel practice, established in the days of the cumbersome 35mm cameras. Like the newsreels we backed our silent action film on the screen either with music or with dubbed effects from the sound library – cheering for football crowds, clapping for cricket, cheering and the rumbling of wheels for processions, indeterminate noises (called 'mush' in the trade) for more general scenes.

This system I took for granted until a report from Cyprus made me aware for the first time of how much the actual sound of an event could add to its impact and authenticity on the screen. Towards the end of May 1956 a riot in Nicosia was captured at considerable length by the sound cameras of CBS. Their film began with shots of a march, headed by Cypriot schoolgirls in white blouses and dark skirts, chanting for union with Greece and carrying the banned blue and white striped flag of Greece through the narrow streets of the old town of Nicosia. The camera had recorded not only the blazing eyes and defiant looks of the girls, but their shrill cries of '*Enosis*, *Enosis*'. The CBS reporter had been on the spot with the camera crew and had spoken his commentary as if at a live outside broadcast. 'Here come the troops,' he said urgently as a platoon of the Royal Lancashire Regiment, riot shields in hand, their faces set and tense under their steel helmets, their boots sounding sharp and insistent on the cobbles, mounted the steep roadway. There was a sudden click as they unhooked their batons and broke into a charge. One girl seized back a Greek flag which the police had taken and held on to it as a soldier tried to wrench it from her. Then suddenly there was the crunch of an explosion. 'A grenade,' said the commentator, 'a policeman has been wounded.' And in the middle of the street a burly Cypriot gendarme, in shirt and black shorts and flat black cap, was huddled and writhing. A Red Cross jeep raced into the street and two soldiers lifted the policeman onto its tailboard. His knee was a mass of blood, pitch black on the film. Pain struck him as he was lifted and he gave out a short howl like a wounded forest animal. The camera zoomed in on his smashed leg and on his face taut with agony.

Here indeed was news as it happened. The natural sound of the chanting crowd, of the marching troops, of the wounded officer, intermingled with the words of the reporter, gave an authenticity and force to the material which I had not known in any film I had ever seen on television. To me that CBS report was a revelation of what the sound camera could achieve.

Two months later a chance arose for us to adopt the same technique. On Tuesday 24th July 1956 the main item on the film schedule at the morning conference was the strike at the Austin works at Longbridge. We had a sound crew on the job, with John Hartley as reporter, Stan Crockett as cameraman and Bill Best as recordist. They formed a strong, assertive and quick-witted group. Our coverage the day before had been along accepted lines – some silent footage of pickets outside the factory gates, interviews with Union leaders and with the Austin public relations officer. But the situation that Tuesday morning looked nastier. The strike was not unanimous and some workers and lorries were forcing their way through the pickets at the main gates. Police, mostly on foot, but with half-a-dozen mounted men in reserve, were present in force. In mid-morning a lorry approached the gates. The strikers formed up to halt it.

Normally such a scene would have been filmed with a silent camera. But at that moment the crew were on the outskirts of the crowd, preparing to use the sound camera to interview strikers. Suddenly the mounted police moved into the midst of scuffles which had broken out around the lorry. Hartley, Crockett and Best, held together by the quarter-inch insulated cable which linked the microphone to the camera, thrust their way through the crowd towards the scene of action. John Hartley moved in front, holding out the microphone to pick up the sound as the mounted police reached the crowd around the lorry. Struggling to keep up with him, Crockett filmed the scene from the sound camera on his shoulder.

When we viewed the film that evening I knew we had something special. The clatter of horses' hooves, the half bantering, half menacing shouts of the pickets – for we were a long way then from the grim visages of flying squads of secondary pickets – the curt orders of the police, the roar of the lorry engine revving up, the clang as the factory gates shut behind it all gave not only vividness but authority to the story. It gave, too, an added element of truth. 'Mounted Police Charge Strikers' ran the headlines on the evening papers. These words were accurate enough in themselves, but they conveyed an inaccurate impression of a cavalry charge, of horses thundering into the midst of ranks of strikers, whereas the film showed the careful if frightening manœuvring of the police horses into the midst of the pickets. Cheerfulness as well as anger came across in the shouts of the strikers. It had the ring of real authenticity. We had achieved for ourselves what CBS had done in Cyprus two months earlier. This was truly a case in which we were able to let the public 'see it happen'.

Our coverage was noted within the BBC. Robert Dougall has told how 'this fresh visual approach' impressed him and his fellow news-readers at Alexandra Palace. He quotes the *TV Mirror*, a popular weekly of the time: 'The BBC treated the subject with scrupulous fairness. A few brief newsreel shots were supplemented by long carefully modified verbal reports of what the people involved had said and what the management and unions were going to do. Factual, but to the great majority of people, dull. The ITN version consisted largely of lively gripping film shots of the picket lines outside the factories (the part which, let's face it, has the greatest appeal for the mass of the public) backed by a simple lucid commentary giving the main facts'.[1] In those few minutes Hartley, Crockett and Best had carried the coverage of news on television in Britain a major step forward. Though our chances of using the technique were for many months ahead to be limited by a shortage of cameras, the shooting of natural sound to accompany action film was now established as a key element of the new journalism.

We did not, however, at this stage put the sound camera to what is today its commonest use – as a means for the reporter to recount into camera, against a background which symbolises or illustrates the story, his report of an event. That came later, when recording techniques improved. For the moment the reporter's task was seen as less that of amassing and reporting the facts than of doing one specialised task – interviewing. Facts for stories were, for the most part, taken from agency copy, though extra information might be telephoned through by the reporter or recorded on the cameraman's dope sheet. But reporters were not encouraged to linger on the scene to delve more deeply. Their role was to get back into the car with the camera team and hurry to the next location to provide yet another interview, leaving a dispatch rider to rush the film back to Kingsway.

10

Newscasters

Christopher Chataway made his last newscast for ITN four days before I took over as Editor. His going was a severe loss. Yet it was remarkable how soon this breach was repaired. Robin Day soon developed a trenchant authority and – to my surprise – a touch of wit and humour which had hitherto lain unseen. Ludovic Kennedy proved an ideal counterpart to Day. Darkly handsome, with a natural warmth, and an easy clarity of speech, he soon proved himself popular both with the viewers and the critics. He brought to the screen the confidence not only of an Old Etonian, but of a man with a good war record in the Navy, in which he had served on the Arctic convoys to Russia. This was particularly apparent in his capacity to take in his stride the technical breakdowns which were a hazard of those days. In his first week with ITN the film suddenly broke half-way through a story, leaving the screen blank and flickering. Newscasters wore no hidden earpieces then through which instructions could be relayed. But Kennedy was not troubled. 'It looks as if the film has broken,' he told the viewers. 'Oh, well, I expect they will want me to read a bit more news.' And he picked up the next story from the desk without any sign of flurry or embarrassment.

Ludovic Kennedy did not parade his very genuine interest in social reform, which was to find expression in the book he wrote about the Rillington Place murders, a book which did much to prevent a return to capital punishment in Britain. Glamour also attached to Ludovic Kennedy, through his marriage to Moira Shearer, then at the peak of her fame as a ballerina and as a film star. I feared that in those days of more sharply-defined class shibboleths Kennedy's unmistakably upper-class bearing might lessen his appeal to our largely working class audience. This might have been the case had he not lacked all sense of class consciousness and had he not rapidly proved himself to be a clear, authoritative and relaxed presenter of the news, whose impact was all the greater for being in contrast to Robin Day's sharp-edged urgency and emphasis.

When Chataway had first told me in April that he was resigning he argued that the public could quickly tire of men and women they saw daily on the screen. 'People's faces wear out,' he said. The reverse in fact was to prove the case. The public have showed a remarkable loyalty to those who become familiar figures on their screens – as witness the anguish caused when Reginald Bosanquet finally left ITN. But the counterpart to this is the speed with which the public forget those who are no longer before them, the eagerness with which they transfer their support to new faces. 'Out of sight, out of mind' is one of the many old adages whose truth has been underlined by television.

We made much play, in stressing the differences between ITN newscasters and BBC newsreaders, that the newscasters were men (or women, for Barbara Mandell still broadcast some of the early evening and weekend bulletins) of personality. But the key to the system was that the newscasters wrote the news in their own words, and took as full a part as they could in the shaping and evaluation of the bulletin. They attended the editorial conferences, and could – and did – voice views about the film as well as about the words. This was important, because the effectiveness of newscasting depends above all on the power to communicate – or, to be more exact, the power to communicate news. This power is reinforced if the newscaster is truly interested in the news of the day, and knowledgeable about it. If he has helped to prepare, and above all to gather it, those qualities are the more likely to show through. It was important, therefore, in these formative years to ensure that the newscasters were fully enmeshed in the process of making the bulletins.

This gave rise to the question of the proper editorial limits of the newscaster system. How far, in deploying the personality by which we set such store, was the newscaster entitled to express his own opinions on the air? How far into the field of comment should he carry his interpretation of the news? This was a new problem for me. In Fleet Street news and comment were never sharply divided into separate compartments. If it was in the nature of the newspaper correspondent to interweave with the facts of the story some of his personal reactions to those facts, that was accepted and acceptable. It applied not only in the popular papers. The great *Times* reporters of the Thirties – Norman Ebbutt, Douglas Reed, de Caux – and men like G. E. R. Gedye and George Steer of the *Daily Telegraph*, had left no one in any doubt about what they thought were the rights and wrongs of the events they described. C. P. Scott's dictum that comment is free, facts are sacred, was not seen as incompatible with a report which interwove facts and comment, provided the facts were scrupulously accurate.

I was now, however, working under the Television Act, which behoved me to ensure that the news should be presented 'with due accuracy and impartiality'. I saw this as an advantage rather than a constraint. Impartiality, if it was interpreted actively, and not passively, could be a means both of protecting our independence and of strengthening our power to gather and interpret news, to arrive at the truth. It was a safeguard against pressures not only from the Government or other people of power, but also against the views and whims of the programme companies who owned us. When I first read, in the Lobby Correspondents' room high above the Thames at Westminster, Clause 3 of the Television Bill of 1954, with its requirements about the accuracy and impartiality of the news, my determination to get into television increased. These few words could free a television News Editor from the proprietorial pressures which were then widespread in Fleet Street – much wider than is the case today. They could give him the freedom to create something new in popular journalism.

Impartiality could also strengthen ITN journalistically if we applied the principle actively, if we interpreted it as placing on us the positive responsibility to seek out all sides of an issue, rather than confining our role to making a fair selection of facts and arguments which reached us from other sources. The BBC's early, and prestigious, reputation for news in the Thirties had rested not on the news it had covered itself but on the fair and objective way it had selected and presented the news reaching it from the agencies. Indeed the names of the agencies from which the news was drawn were chanted like a litany: 'from the Press Association, Reuter, Associated Press . . .' at the start of each bulletin. Before 1939 the Corporation originated little news of its own, and even after the war moved cautiously into direct news gathering. But my training and instincts were those of Fleet Street, where news was not something which came along the agency conveyor belt – valuable though the agencies were both as guide and support – but was something you had to hack from the coal-face yourself. Within the highly sensitive area of public broadcasting, such direct news gathering was helped rather than hindered by the requirement of impartiality, for the need to give all sides justified asking difficult and probing questions.

At the same time the heart of the ITN operation was the newscaster system, which called for the news to be given in robust and human form, in adequate depth and perspective. We wanted the newscasters to be men of personality: yet a key element in any personality is the strength of his opinions. It was easy to decide that, in pursuit of impartiality, analysis and interpretation were all right, but expressions of opinion were not. It was another matter to determine, in the constantly changing pattern of daily news, exactly where that line should be drawn. Was it right for a freelance broadcaster (I tried out a number of new faces on the 5.55 early bulletin we did for the London area) to modify an item which had reported that 'in Cyprus we are continuing to practise stern measures' into one which said 'in Cyprus we are, for better or for worse, continuing to practise stern measures'? I thought so when I read the words in the script, and passed them. But on the air they sounded not only like comment, but like comment we were trying to smuggle in by the back door. Almost every bulletin posed a problem of this kind, as we sought to personalise and clarify the news, and yet keep it fair. One of Napoleon's maxims about war – 'It is a simple art: all lies in the exercise of it' – quickly proved to be true also of television journalism. In exercising it in those early days the newscasters played a cardinal role, not only in their work on the screen, but in the discussions and debates off screen in which we built up our own case law in the new visual journalism.

11

A Hard Look at Politics

One of the new techniques which ITN had begun to develop, the probing interview, was to revolutionise not only political journalism, but politics itself. Until this time people had been largely dependent for their information about the political scene on the impressions of others – of Gallery and Lobby correspondents, of political columnists, of cartoonists and still photographers. It was through their eyes, their pens, their lenses, that the public gained their knowledge of the people who ruled them – or sought to rule them. Few people, even those ardently interested in politics, had a chance to meet or study at close quarters the leaders of political parties, or of the trades unions, or of the Church. They saw at most a distant figure striding through crowds, or glimpsed on a public platform. Still photographs or shots in a cinema newsreel could provide an outward impression of a man or woman in the news. But these did not convey a first-hand impression. To learn what the great, or the would-be great, were really like you had to rely on what an inner circle of writers and reporters vouchsafed to you.

Radio had added one further highly significant dimension to this study of politics and of politicians. It had provided a directness of spoken, if unseen, contact between the leaders and the public. It was through the radio that the British people felt that they knew Churchill not only well, but very well, because his words had conveyed not only his ideas but the man himself. Television now offered a further major step forward in the political process. It could bring the politicians into every sitting room in the land, could provide for the first time a chance for the citizen and the voter to scrutinise closely those who would be their leaders. People could now not only look at politicians, they could stare at them in close-up, could have the means of forming their own opinions about them on the evidence of their own eyes and ears. So long as the television cameras were not admitted to Parliament, the interview was the best way in which television could bring this new, sharper view to bear. It had, however, to be an informed, questing, challenging interview, capable of testing and portraying the politician's personality as well as his policies. Otherwise this powerful new medium would merely be a passive platform, a way of enabling you to see people better, but not necessarily to know them better. A new style of questioning was needed to complement the electronic picture, if television was to convey to the public a fully-rounded view of people in the public eye. The rigorous interviewing style of ITN met that need.

To utilise it we had, however, had to gain acceptance among those who were interviewed. Not all of them by any means favoured this new approach. How new it was can be seen from an article by George

Scott in the *Manchester Guardian*. He began with the text of an imaginary interview from pre-ITN days:

'Sir, would you say that your visit to Timbuktu was worth while?'

'Oh yes, I would definitely say my visit had been worth while. Yes, definitely.'

'Ah, good. Could you say what topics you discussed, sir?'

'No, I'm afraid I couldn't do that. These talks were of a highly confidential nature, you understand, and you wouldn't expect me to reveal anything which might prejudice our future relations.'

'No, of course not, sir. Well, sir, you must be very tired after your talks and your journey – may I ask, sir, if you are going to take it easy for a while now – a holiday perhaps?'

'Ah, if only one could. But you know a Minister in Her Majesty's Government can never take it easy, never rest, not really you know. *They're* waiting for me now.'

'Well, thank you very much, sir.'

'Thank *you* very much.'

That, Scott concluded, 'in essential caricature, is the kind of BBC airport interview we used to see on our television screens not so many years ago. I for one say thank goodness things are not what they used to be.'

This is indeed a caricature, but it was the over-statement of a true fact. Before competition existed, broadcast interviews were not only very much rarer than they are now, but they tended to take place on the terms of the man or woman interviewed, not on those of the interviewer. Ministers and other public figures claimed the right to decide in advance what questions they would be prepared to answer, and were often able to establish this right. They frequently regarded themselves as conferring a favour on the broadcasters by agreeing to be interviewed at all. The view that the broadcaster, since he represented the general public, had the right to put any question which might be in the public mind was not one which found favour in Whitehall.

This was certainly the case in the last interview I did for BBC Radio before I joined ITN. It was with Mr Selwyn Lloyd, and was the first interview he had given since being made Foreign Secretary. Because of this the BBC had agreed that the questions should be submitted to him in advance, and his officials arrived at Broadcasting House on the night with the questions and answers beautifully typed on thick grey paper which would not crackle and so give the game away when we read our parts from this script.

But that afternoon a new question had arisen. Burgess and Maclean had surfaced in Moscow for the first time. This was clearly an issue which would be in the public mind, and on which the Minister should be questioned. But Selwyn Lloyd and his officials were insistent that no such question could be added at this short notice, and in any event no answer was ready. I insisted that at the least the Foreign Secretary could repeat on the air what he had said in the Commons that afternoon, the text of which was in the evening papers. With great reluctance Mr Lloyd agreed, and the report in the *Evening News* was added in handwriting to the papers in front of us. On the air the Foreign Secretary, perhaps because of these changes, misread his answer on trade with Canada, and emerged furious from the studio blaming me for spoiling the interview by these last-minute changes.

Such rigidities, and the pat-ball style of interviewing which George Scott parodied, were now being eroded by the advent of competition and by the inherent nature of television, a more candid medium than radio or print. Under the eye of the camera artificiality and reticence were much more readily apparent. Within BBC Television, in programmes like 'Press Conference' and 'Viewfinder', a more vigorous style of questioning was encouraged. This trend had been stimulated by the recruitment in the early Fifties of three former MPs as interviewers – Aidan Crawley, Christopher Mayhew and Woodrow Wyatt. They were accustomed to the cut and thrust of Parliamentary debate, and instinctively applied a more rigorous approach to the questioning of public figures. This style Aidan Crawley had brought into ITN, and when I took over the Editorship I readily confirmed the rules he had laid down. Foremost amongst this was the insistence that a list of questions should not be submitted or agreed in advance, and that the interview should not be rehearsed. This change made it an interview on the broadcaster's terms, not those of the person questioned. It affirmed the principle that within our democracy the broadcasters were probing issues on behalf of the public at large. It also had advantages as a technique. An interview in which the questions were not known or rehearsed in advance tended to be much fresher and have more immediacy and impact, indeed more truth, than one where the answers had been worn flat with repetition.

It was a technique which had to be fought for. Many politicians disliked it; all public relations officers detested it. Its acceptance had certainly not been acknowledged by the spring of 1956. Again and again throughout the ensuing months Arthur Clifford and I would have to argue the issue out with yet one more Ministry, one more firm, one more trade union, all of whom wanted questions to be submitted in advance.

We were helped by the fact that the television age was also the air age. We were still a couple of years away from jet travel, but even in that era of piston-engined aircraft London Airport had become the gateway through which Ministers and diplomats passed, as they increasingly used aircraft to supervise and exercise Britain's power, then still widespread and strong. From 1956 onwards the VIP lounge at Heathrow, with its improbable background of patterned curtains, which gave it the look of the sitting room of a pretentious seaside boarding house, became a setting in which public men (for there were then few women in posts of prominence) expounded their policies, and in which television interviewing stretched its fledgling muscles. Gradually, too, Ministers came to appreciate, or at least to accept, the value of the short interview which was all that television, by contrast with radio, had space for. R. A. Butler, that master of the cryptic utterance, was one of the first to do so. 'Anyone with anything worth saying can say it in three minutes,' was his response when I told him that that was all we could allocate to him when we interviewed him during Suez.

In June 1956 one interview confirmed my faith in the probing television interview, not only as a revolution in political journalism, but as excellent viewing. It was conducted by Robin Day with ex-President Harry S. Truman, then on his first visit to Europe since giving up the Presidency. For a man who prided himself on not being an intellectual, the ex-President had taken what in those days was an unusual step and had written a book about his days in the White House. Oxford University had invited him to accept an honorary degree and Mr Truman was combining his journey to receive that degree with publicising his book in Britain. The only minor cloud on this otherwise clear horizon was that a Somerville don, Miss Anscombe, was seeking signature to a petition opposing the conferring of the degree. She argued that since it had been on President Truman's orders in 1945 that the atomic bombs had been dropped on Hiroshima and Nagasaki, he was no man for Oxford to honour. This was one of the first stirrings of protest in Britain against the bomb.

The Americans had tested their second H-bomb at Bikini only a couple of weeks before Truman arrived, without the explosion arousing much interest, let alone protest.

Robin Day told me he proposed to raise, in his opening question, the issue of the Oxford protest. In the broadcasting climate of the time this was an iconoclastic move. It might be thought discourteous both to the man and to the office he had held. Tradition demanded that such a question – if it were to be put at all – should come later, after the ex-President had been able to play himself in with some less provocative questions on, for instance, Korea, where the war had been followed only by an armistice, not by a peace treaty. That was the type of issue the BBC and the press were likely to raise when they interviewed Truman – and they did. Were we not just indulging in stunt journalism by putting the Oxford protest first?

Perhaps. But there were good arguments for doing so. It was a new issue, which might produce new information – and that was what we were in the business of providing. It was an issue which the viewer could readily take in, whilst those other wider questions might well pass him by; and it was an issue which could be put simply and shortly and which might evoke simple and short answers, ideally suited to a news bulletin. So I agreed to Day's plan.

Once he settled down in his turn to face Mr Truman in a corner of Claridge's ballroom, Robin came swiftly to the point. 'Mr President,' he began, 'I understand that one reason for your visit is to receive an honorary degree at the University of Oxford.'

'That is so.' Truman looked pleased by the question.

'Are you aware, Mr President, that a lady at Oxford is campaigning against your receiving that degree because you authorised the dropping of the first atom bomb?'

Truman looked, for a brief moment, disconcerted. No, he was not aware of that.

The next question was nothing if not succinct. 'Mr President, do you regret having authorised the dropping of the atom bomb?'

The President's concentration seemed almost visibly to tighten. There was no delay in his answer. 'No, I do not. I made the decision on the information available to me at the time and I would make the same decision on the same information again.' He paused, and then, with a smile, 'But you can read all about it in my memoirs.'

Day was back immediately. 'Mr President, this programme is going out to people who cannot afford thirty shillings even for the memoirs of a former President of the United States. Won't you explain your reasons a bit further?'

Truman did, clearly and forcibly. It was marvellous television. Even today the copy in the ITN archives, drab though the picture quality is, in the black and white filming of the time, radiates vigour and interest. In the bulletin that evening it provided several minutes of sharp drama, demonstrating the qualities which were to establish Robin Day as the screen's best political interviewer. It produced something not only eminently viewable, but also provided information both about a key issue and about the character of this small, bespectacled man who had been such a truly big figure of our time. This had been accomplished by questions which went to the point and by an interviewer who listened to the answers, and based his supplementary questions on them, not just on further questions written out on his clipboard.

The Truman story firmly established the probing interview as an integral part of ITN's technique. I used to have it run through for later recruits as a model. Not only Day but George Ffitch and Reginald Bosanquet quickly became masters of the technique. It was something which politicians expected when they faced an ITN camera – and something which most of them valued as a step in the right direction for the democratic process.

12

Covering Sport

Sport, that essential component of popular news, proved a good deal more difficult to cover than I had anticipated. In television sport is not only the raw material for news: it is programme material in its own right, highly viewable action capable of pulling in huge audiences. The sports promoters and the sports producers were in no mood to allow television news, in the name of freedom of reporting, to pick the plums out of their cake by showing the winning goals, the close finishes, the winning hits. Their approach to television news was the same as that which the promoters had adopted towards the cinema newsreels – if newsmen wanted to cover sport, they could pay for it.

The issue first forced itself to my attention not because of a sports story, but because of a general news event placed within a sporting setting. The drive of the Royal family in their landaus along the course at Ascot before the day's racing has been for decades one of the most durable perennials of the newspapers and the newsreels. When early in the afternoon of 19th June 1956 I watched, on BBC Television's outside broadcast, the Queen and Prince Philip make their way up the course of the opening day of Ascot, a day of glittering sunshine, the scene seemed to me ideal for television. Then I recollected that coverage of this drive had not been on the film list we had discussed at that morning's conference. I checked with the newsroom. We were not covering the Royal drive because the Ascot authorities were adamant that their agreement with the BBC ruled out any filming by ITN on any part of the course. Though this was designed to protect the exclusivity of the racing coverage, in the view of the authorities it included any other news at Ascot. We had a camera crew and a reporter covering the Ascot fashions, but they were doing so outside the gates, not within the ground.

This seemed to me absurd. The Royal drive was a news story, and my first reaction was to help ourselves by telerecording it off the BBC's outside broadcast. But this proved technically impractical, and legally dubious. All we could do was, the next day, to station our cameras on the Heath which stretched opposite the stands, and which was theoretically open to the public. But the cameraman was spotted and within minutes the Ascot authorities were on to John Cotter, threatening to sue if we used the material and, even more ominously, to ban us from every race course in the country.

It proved to be an empty threat. We ran the material that evening, and no action followed. We had won that immediate battle. But the wider question of news access to sporting events remained. How could we win for our cameras the same freedom to report sport as was open to the newspaper reporter and the newspaper cameraman?

The cinema newsreels had dealt with this problem either by paying for the coverage rights – or by pirating them. When a rival newsreel bought the rights to a Wembley Cup Final, Movietone's star cameraman got on to the field disguised as the West Ham mascot and filmed the game through the end of the big mock hammer which he carried. When Paramount pirated a Test Match at the Oval by building a scaffolding tower overlooking the ground, the companies who had bought the rights tethered a big gas-filled balloon in front of the tower. Paramount riposted by trying to shoot down the balloon, and when that failed, managed to cut the cable holding it. Bill Hodgson, who was to become ITN's General Manager, recalled being sent down as a boy with the sandwiches for his cameraman father, who was lodged in a plane tree overlooking the Oval, helping himself to a share of another newsreel's exclusive. It was a contest which had its own rules – the most important of which was that no newsreel, however much its costly rights were impaired, sought to invoke the law – for indeed next week they might well be the contract breakers.

But it was a contest not open to us. In television, operating under Parliamentary franchise, supervised by public authorities, neither the BBC nor the ITA could be expected to stand aside in this way. There would have been questions in Parliament, an outcry against the offending camera crews, and in all probability legal action to halt such self-help. Moreover the pinched material was seldom equal in quality to that filmed legitimately. We had to find another route – and it was clear that ITN would have to find it. For BBC News was protected by the arrangements which their outside broadcast department, with its long tradition of sports coverage, had made to cover all the major sporting occasions of the year. The owners of Independent Television were less interested in sport, and in 1956 did not have the money to spend on it anyway. This tilted the balance against any knock-for-knock deal, under which ITV could have given BBC News access to the events which they broadcast, in return for BBC doing the same for ITN.

I could see only one answer to this problem. Television organisations would have to be given access to sporting events as of right, though the length of their coverage could be restricted to protect the programme interests both of sports promoters and of programme departments. This right should be written into the contracts made by the broadcasters with the sporting bodies. I put this idea to the programme companies, to the ITN Board, and through them to my opposite number on the BBC, Pat Smithers, Editor of BBC Television News. Smithers sensibly took the long view. He foresaw that the day might come when ITV had money enough to buy up exclusive rights to sporting fixtures. Nor did he, as a seasoned journalist, need any convincing on the principle of free access. He therefore won over the BBC hierarchy to allowing us to show two minutes of coverage in

Geoffrey Cox at the start of 'News at Ten', July 1967.

Two stories which set the pattern for covering not only the sight but also the sound of action news: a demonstration in Cyprus, May 1956 (*above*) and (*below*) the Austin car workers' strike, Longbridge, July 1956.

The Kingsway Pioneers, May 1956. Left to right: John Cotter, Film Manager; Ronald Reid, Head Cameraman; Geoffrey Cox; Arthur Clifford, News Editor.

Christopher Chataway, Britain's first newscaster.

Aidan Crawley, Editor of ITN 1955–56.

Robin Day (*above*) and Ludovic Kennedy (*left*), the team which firmly established newscasting as a new way of presenting broadcast news.

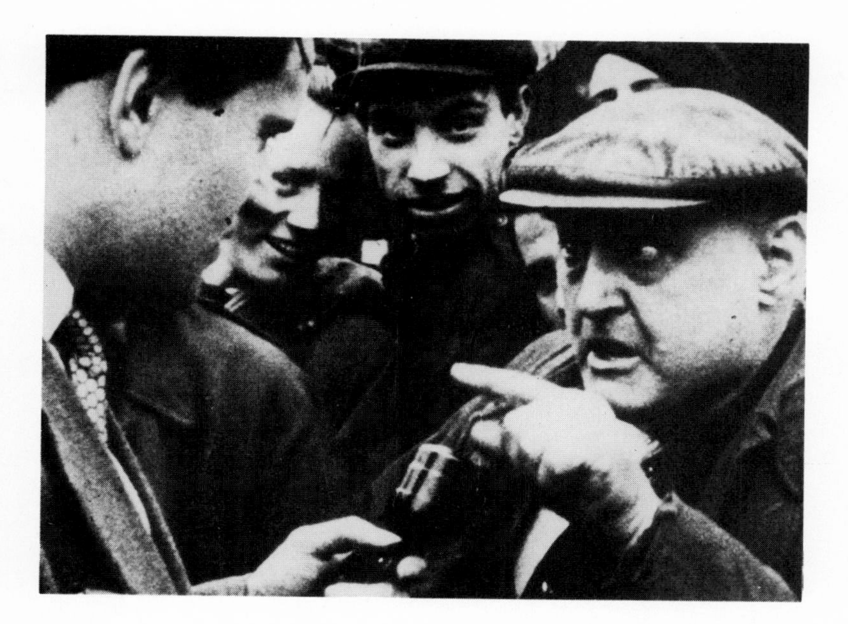

Reporters who broke new ground: Reginald Bosanquet (*above*) covers the engineering strike, 1958; Lynne Reid Banks (*left*), Britain's first woman television reporter; George Ffitch (*right*), master of the probing interview.

Suez and Hungary, November 1956—the big stories which provided the young ITN news service with its first big test. Robin Day interviews the British GOC, General Stockwell, against the background of Port Said harbour (*above*). Russian tanks re-occupy Budapest (*below*).

The cameramen who met the challenge of Suez and Hungary: Cyril Page (*left*) and Martin Gray.

To cover sport ITN had to fight entrenched interests.

The second wave of newscasters: Brian Connell (*above*), Huw Thomas (*left*) and Ian Trethowan (*right*), who became Director-General of the BBC 1977–82.

each bulletin of play in the remaining Test matches against Australia, provided we acknowledged that this came 'with the co-operation of the BBC Outside Broadcasting Department'. We secured similar access to the tennis at Wimbledon.

This was an important breakthrough which enabled us from then on to give regular coverage to the main events in the sporting calendar, instead of the haphazard reporting of any odds and ends of sport which might be accessible. We still faced considerable technical problems in covering with film cameras games which stretched over days, as with cricket, or over several hours, as with tennis. If you tried to film everything not only would it be outrageously costly, but you would expose much more film than you could process or cut in time for use. Estimating when the high spots in these games were likely to occur, and concentrating your filming on them, became a fine art.

Discussions of news access to sport rumbled on until, in the winter of 1959-60, the issue came to a head during the MCC tour of the West Indies. The West Indies Cricket Board sold exclusive rights in coverage of the tour to Eddie Carroll, a West Indian calypso singer, who was certainly not going to allow any news organisation to have access without paying. The BBC stood admirably firm and refused to buy any of Carroll's longer reports of the matches for showing in their sports programmes until BBC News and ITN were allowed to film short excerpts for their bulletins. They won the day, and Carroll gave us news access. This speeded up a final agreement between the companies and the Corporation. In January 1960 what amounted to a treaty was signed between the two broadcasters. Each agreed, in negotiating television rights for sporting events, to include a clause along the lines I had proposed to the ITN Board in 1956, to offer free access for news organisations to secure film coverage. Such coverage was to be brief, and to be shown only in regularly scheduled news programmes, not in longer sporting programmes. There was a great deal of haggling about what should be the proper length of such news items. In the end this came down to two minutes per bulletin for most events. For some the limits were shorter. On the Grand National only the finish and another fifteen seconds of the racing could be shown. For boxing matches, where the knock-out was by definition not likely to last, even with its preliminaries and aftermath, more than fifteen or twenty seconds, the scheme proved unworkable. No promoter was prepared to let those few seconds go for free. But by and large the agreement opened up sport to coverage by television news on much the same basis as by radio and newspapers. The battle which began on the day of that Ascot meeting in 1956 had proved worth fighting.

13

Newspaper of the Air

Our news values in 1956 were pitched between those of the popular and those of the quality papers. I set our goal as that of carrying the main stories which made the front page of the *Daily Telegraph* and the back page of the *Daily Mirror* – then a model of clear, sharp sub-editing – plus a dash of the flair and style of the *Manchester Guardian*. I believed people could take somewhat harder intellectual tack than they were being offered in the popular dailies, provided it was presented with clarity, gusto and a human touch, and provided serious and significant news was interwoven with lighter material. There was a didactic element in my approach. I saw the task of the journalist as being not merely to inform, but to widen and sharpen public interest in the big issues of the day, not by preaching at them or trying to guide their views, but by setting out the facts clearly and comprehensibly, breaking complex matters down into terms which could be readily understood. 'Say simple things to simple people,' A. J. P. Taylor was urged by his mentor at Oxford. I would have put this a little differently, if less elegantly, as 'Say things simply to ordinary people.' But the aim was the same. And in television we had now the great new instrument of film to help do this.

ITN had widened broadcast news values significantly from the moment when, in its first bulletin, it had reported on the progress of a crime trial at the Old Bailey. I extended this still further, for I set myself the aim of making a daily newspaper of the air, with its sport, show business, fashion and feature pages, its crime and human interest stories, as well as the hard news of the front page. It was to prove an over-ambitious scheme, for no bulletin lasting just under fourteen minutes a night could encompass all that. To provide a newspaper of the air needs a whole television channel, not just a news bulletin, and as the months went past we found ourselves forced more and more into the mould of a front page, with at best a glimpse of what the other pages might carry. But it was not a bad goal to set, for it broadened our ideas and our horizons.

We took fashion seriously, regularly reporting the London and Paris collections, engaging artists to sketch those models we were not allowed to film, avoiding the arch and condescending commentaries of the newsreels, treating these shows as news events which set changes of style for High Streets up and down the country. We widened coverage of the arts from the newsreels' traditional quick look at preview days at the Royal Academy to include interviews with Maria Callas and with Margot Fonteyn, and with some reporting on the theatre, the ballet (of which Lynne Reid Banks was a devotee) and on books. When Colin Wilson sprang to fame as author of *The Outsider* we interviewed him outside the bivouac tent in which he slept on Hampstead Heath. When we got a free ride to the Cannes Festival for Lynne, she interviewed not only starlets on the beach, but Jean Cocteau in his home. We even tried our hands at theatrical criticism. On the London first night of *The Caine Mutiny Courtmartial* a dinner-jacketed Ludovic Kennedy appeared in the late bulletin to give his appraisal. The newspapers warmed to the idea. One said we were 'leaping along with a string of ideas the BBC should have thought up years ago'.[1] But the item scared the programme companies (particularly those with theatrical interests) and the ITN Board insisted that such reviewing, if it was to be done at all, belonged within the magazine format of 'This Week'. Our experiment was to prove the only attempt to review plays on television until BBC 2's 'Late Night Line-Up' did so a decade later.

We treated film stars as news, as they undoubtedly were in those days when the star system operated not only in Hollywood but also in the minds of the public. Cinema-going was not yet undermined by television; film stars were glittering and remote figures, a world away from their counterparts of a generation later leading anti-war demonstrations in duffle coats and jeans. But we sought to treat the system with candour and humour, and to avoid being enmeshed in public relations fantasies. When Marilyn Monroe paid her first visit to London in the summer of 1956 we detached Robin Day from his duties as our Political Correspondent to interview her. Our cameraman at Heathrow had already added his own further dimension to the traditional coverage of a star's arrival. He had not waited until she stepped out onto the aircraft gangway, but had caught the moment as she paused inside the doorway to pull her already skintight dress just a shade tighter and composed her mouth into her celebrated pouting smile before she swayed down the steps.

Clifford had rightly detected that Robin Day had not a little of the showman in him, and could cope with Miss Monroe as effectively as he had done with Truman. Seated on a striped silk divan in a suite in the Savoy Hotel, her hands folded demurely in her lap, she gave an interview which was at one and the same time shallow and sincere, endearing and slightly self-conscious, a clear, deft performance which Robin matched by his own courtesy and touch of mischief. At the end of it we had produced a report which met the public desire to see in close-up one of its greatest stars, and yet had done so with an added touch of frankness which indicated that we were aware that this was all part of a carefully contrived world of fantasy.

Jayne Mansfield, that cruder imitation of Monroe, was also in due course interviewed by Robin. She gave him one good response, a reflection either of her own wit or that of her public relations men. Asked why she had as a pet a panther which she led on a pink ribbon, she smiled and cooed, 'Because I like pink.'

Such coverage today would no doubt be assailed as escapist, but it had its place in the bulletins of the time. We were not yet clear of the clutches of wartime austerity. Life was still for many people drab, luxuries were few. People had an appetite for colour and gloss which were not in their own lives. Such material also served other useful editorial purposes. It drew and held an audience for the more significant political, diplomatic, military and international news we had to offer. It gave the bulletins contrast, light and shade. And it served as a reminder, as did our human interest stories, that all of life was not confined within the stresses and disasters and horrors which form such a large part of news coverage.

One important element in our bulletin formula was not designed. It just grew. This was the tailpiece, the quip or brief light-hearted story with which the newscasters rounded off the bulletin. It was to become as much the trade-mark of the early ITN programmes as was the hard-hitting interview. The tailpiece developed from the interplay of the minds of three men – Robin Day and Ludovic Kennedy before the cameras, and the Chief Sub, Desmond Grealey, behind them. Day had the relish of a former President of the Oxford Union for a neatly turned and pointed phrase; Kennedy had an instinct for doing things with a flourish; Grealey an Irishman's sense of the droll. Since the best tailpieces owed their impact to their aptness in highlighting or off-setting some point in the major news of the day, it is difficult to convey their effectiveness. So many words are needed now to describe the setting the viewer at the time took for granted that the items can seem laboured. But some survive the strain of the years.

In the spring of 1956 the Dockers were an inescapable element in every gossip column and, often enough, on the front pages of the popular papers. Sir Bernard Docker, a prominent Midland businessman with a peculiarly woe-begone expression, was married to a petite blonde with a habit of backing into the limelight. They practised ostentatious spending in times grey with austerity, travelling in a gold-plated Daimler (the cost justified as publicity for the car) or moving about the Mediterranean in their yacht, their doings watched with apparent fascination by the mass public, perhaps because they were a reminder that hard times need not always be with us.

In April 1956 Lady Docker let it be known that she was dissatisfied with the seats allocated to her and her husband in the Cathedral at Monaco for the wedding of Grace Kelly and Prince Rainier. She threatened to leave before the ceremony.

'It remains to be seen,' Ludovic Kennedy added, 'whether anyone will stop them.'

Peter Black of the *Daily Mail*, a man who could see television in its social setting, wrote the next day: 'I imagine that a gasp and then a shout of laughter ran round the whole of ITV's network. This healthy irreverence for the gods of the mob is something new in TV journalism (the BBC ignored the story). It is very much worth having.'

Sometimes the touches had a more specialist appeal. All journalists are familiar with the expression commonly used to avoid contempt of court when an arrest is made. It runs, 'Later, a man was detained and is helping police with their inquiries.' When an Alsatian dog went beserk, broke away from its owner on the top deck of a London bus and terrorised the conductor and the other passengers, the bus driver coped with the problem by driving to the nearest police station, where a professional dog handler got matters under control. 'Later, a dog was detained,' the report concluded.

Robin Day's tailpieces tended to be more tightly integrated with the story of the day, to have a rare quality of sharing a joke with the audience. When the Grenadier Guards celebrated the three hundredth anniversary of their founding, Reginald Bosanquet rounded off an ITN report of their parade by interviewing the adjutant of one of the battalions. It was clearly not a process to the officer's liking, and a cold disdain impregnated his answers. One factor may have been Reggie's hairstyle. The camera, filming over his shoulder, emphasised the fact that, horror of horrors, his hair was long enough to overlap the top of his collar. It was a detail likely to catch the eye of every male viewer in those days of soldierly short back and sides. Robin summed up their probable reaction neatly. 'That's the news from ITN,' he said at the end of the bulletin, 'and,' he added in tones as incisive as that of the adjutant, 'a haircut for that ITN reporter.'

The tailpiece was a technique which had to be handled with care, to ensure that it did not degenerate into that widespread sin of the broadcaster, facetiousness. It depended too on the earlier part of the bulletin being packed with hard news and strong film, to set this final shaft in perspective. Yet night after night for our first three or four years we were able to find an item or a quip which ended the day on a touch of humour. The tailpiece became an important element in establishing and sustaining our link with the public. By the time it died away – as such things will – that bond was strong enough to endure.

Our signature tune, 'Non Stop', also played an important part in establishing our individuality. It struck exactly the right note for those pioneering days, with its lack of pomp and pretension, with its implication that something exciting and yet significant was about to be reported. It was a musical statement of the proposition that news is too serious to be taken too seriously, expressing the jaunty confidence not only of a news medium, but of a country at last emerging from war and austerity.

'Non Stop' was not the work of a professional musician. It had been written by a Wimbledon solicitor, John Batt, based on a tone poem he had composed whilst still at school, in response to a challenge from his music master that dance music could never be as good as classical music. Needing money as a law student, Batt had hawked his compositions around the London music publishers, finally selling the copyright to Frances Day and Hunter for one shilling and half the royalties for ever. That half must have made a pleasant addition over the years to John Batt's other professional fees. 'Non Stop' is still used by ITN at weekends, even though with the coming of 'News at Ten' it was to be ousted from the main bulletins.

However bright and human we might be, I knew that in the long run we would be judged by one basic test – how clearly, rapidly and fairly we reported the news. We would be judged in the end as a news service, not just as a television programme. We worked hard to strengthen our professional under-pinning, working at the subbing and scriptwriting, at the copy tasting and at the selection of the stories for our scarce camera teams to cover. I knew that in due course some major crisis would break out which would put to the test the loyalty of our audience. There was always the danger that our viewers might then prove fair weather friends, finding us entertaining when the going was good, but turning back, if big and dangerous events loomed up, to the BBC which had served them so well during the war.

We were working to establish ITN's standing at a time when the Independent Television system was still regarded with suspicion and distaste by many opinion formers. The outcry against early programmes like 'People Are Funny' still echoed in the papers. However innocuous by later standards these programmes now seem, there was something not quite respectable about ITV in 1956. As Maurice Wiggin was to put it in the *Sunday Times*, 'Switching over from the BBC to ITV in those early days left one with the feeling that one was dropping in at a house of ill-fame on your way home from the vicarage.'[2] It was against this background that we had to assert not only our dash but our professionalism.

We had to set our own standards day by day. Few signposts had yet been established in this new pictorial journalism. One event which guided us resulted from a coincidence which, had it occurred in fiction, would have seemed impossible. When Arthur Miller married Marilyn Monroe, a woman reporter working for *Paris-Match* was killed in a car crash on her way to cover the wedding. A freelance cameraman filmed her body by the roadside. In the picture her face was clearly visible. The film was used in a weekend bulletin which I had not seen on rehearsal. Watching in my home I recognised the dead girl as Princess Mara Scherbatoff, a White Russian who had been our secretary in the *Daily Express* Paris office before the war. I had not seen her for some years, but even so the shock of the picture was considerable. I realised that to a relative or very close friend the impact would have been severe, quite unjustified by any legitimate news demands. We established then and there the ruling that in an accident the faces of the dead or maimed should not be shown – as later, in reporting funerals, we decided that close-up shots of grief were seldom if ever permissible.

Another story presented me for the first time with a problem which is with television to this day. How far is a story which is undoubtedly news invalidated by the fact that it is also propaganda – and intended as such? A freelance cameraman had spent some time behind the lines with the Algerian guerrilla forces, then in the early stages of their long and grisly struggle with the French. He had filmed the ambushing of a French paratroopers' jeep. The film showed the guerrillas lying in wait by a dusty road, opening fire on the jeep and gunning down in the open the one man who escaped the first burst of firing. It was an arresting sequence at a time when such scenes on film were rare. The cameraman made no secret, however, of the fact the ambush had been laid on especially for him to cover. This made me pause. We were only ten years away from a war which had cost millions of lives. British troops were still being killed and wounded daily in Cyprus and Malaysia. There was enough death in the world without it being especially organised for television.

The story also seemed to me journalistically invalid. Specially staged as it was, it was propaganda as much as it was news, propaganda which was claiming a place in the bulletins because of its dramatic impact. I resented having my hand forced in this way, resented material forcing its way into the bulletins because it was vivid picture. This was not the only film available of the Algerian war, though it was certainly the most dramatic. We were not suppressing the news if we did not show this particular sequence. For these double reasons, human and journalistic, I turned down the story.

Yet the stance I had adopted was soon to prove hard, if not impossible, to sustain in the future. The imperatives of the picture asserted themselves, by which the vividness and the violence of the action recorded became of interest in itself, and so became newsworthy, whatever its propaganda content. Indeed much news has, and always has had, inescapably, such a content. The answer lay not in keeping such material off the screen, but in keeping it within limits, and above all in setting it in perspective, and in identifying clearly those elements which were propaganda. Yet this Algerian ambush in the summer of 1956 had demonstrated the dangers as well as the advantages to society which the camera was bringing, and I do not regret halting to consider them before plunging down the road ahead.

14

Money and Time

In parallel with these editorial problems I had to grapple with the question of costs, made all the more urgent as by mid-summer 1956 the fortunes of the programme companies were at their lowest ebb. The first management document which awaited me on my desk when I took over as Editor and Chief Executive was the report of the Board sub-committee which had been set up to scrutinise ITN's operations, and whose appointment had precipitated Crawley's resignation. It did not make agreeable reading. Not only did it call for further stringent controls on day-to-day spending, it also proposed that six members of staff be dropped from the film operation, and two from the ranks of the engineers. The small editorial staff had already been effectively cut by one, since there was no plan to appoint a Deputy Editor in place of Richard Gould-Adams.

I needed only a few days in Television House to realise I must block this plan. The cuts in film staff would have left us with virtually no film at weekends, and the dismissals could have precipitated a bolt for the exit by other key staff, who would feel their jobs threatened too. I won some time by claiming that I could not give a worthwhile opinion on these proposed cuts until I knew more about how ITN worked. I also discovered that there were two senior posts, one in film and one in engineering, other than those recommended for the axe, which we could drop without damage, as earlier economies had left us with proportionately too many chiefs for our few indians. By dropping these, and by cutting our operational costs to the bone, we got through into the autumn. I had then to accept a budget for the second year of ITN's operations, which began in September 1956, at the same low level of £350,000 a year on which we had operated. (This was roughly the amount of ITN's costs for one week, twenty-five years later.) But I had kept the operational staff intact.

An even sharper crisis faced me in the summer over the length of the bulletins, that other issue which had precipitated Crawley's first resignation. In August Val Parnell, the vaudeville impresario who had become Managing Director of ATV when Norman Collins lost control of that company to the Prince Littler group, demanded a cut in the early evening bulletin. It was five minutes in length and Parnell, anxious to get a flying start with entertainment programming, wanted it reduced to three minutes. To keep within the required limit of twenty minutes of news a day, the late bulletin would have been extended to seventeen minutes. Though the cut by present-day standards seems very small, in those days of silent film stories it meant the loss of up to three film reports. It would have reduced the early bulletin to little more than radio headlines. I was determined that this would not happen, not least because to the staff it would have looked as if I had caved in to the pressures which Crawley had resisted.

I took my case to Sir Robert Fraser, assuming that the Authority would prevent what was an obvious breach of the spirit, if not the letter, of the Twenty Minute Rule. It was my first official contact with him since I had joined Independent Television. Fraser was the grandson of an Australian judge, and there was much that was judicial in his bearing. Tall, erect, with a somewhat flattened aquiline countenance, he combined a quietly appraising air with a kindly and always courteous manner. In pre-war years, after graduating from the London School of Economics, he had had political ambitions, and had nursed a constituency as a Labour candidate. But in the Ministry of Information during the war he had revealed a talent for administration, which had led him after the war into the ranks of the Civil Service, from which Sir Kenneth Clark had drawn him into the ITA.

Fraser quietly but firmly made clear to me that the Authority would not intervene in any argument about how the companies divided up the required daily ration of news, so long as it amounted to twenty minutes. So I had to fight my battle alone. Val Parnell, though he was not a Director of ITN, came to a special meeting to consider my objections. I argued that in Fleet Street journalists were accustomed to having to pay their way, to winning the circulation on which the commercial success of every newspaper depended. In television we were equally prepared to carry our share of winning the audience. ITN did not seek to ride on the back of any other programme. I looked for a metaphor in a widely advertised product of the day, and said, 'News is good programming in its own right, and should not treated as a Carter's Little Liver Pill to be forced on viewers to enable them to digest the entertainment programmes.'

Val Parnell leant his burly Irish frame back in surprise, studied me closely for a moment, and said, 'If the Editor is really prepared to take a commercial attitude towards his job, then that changes matters. In that event I'll go along with a five minute bulletin.'

I learnt one basic lesson that day – that we could look for no help from the Authority beyond the basic requirement for twenty minutes of news a day. I resolved then and there never to appeal again to the ITA for help against the companies, and I never did so, until eleven years later when the crunch came on the half-hour news. Yet there was a good side to the non-interventionism of the Authority. For never once in that eleven years did Fraser try to back-seat-drive my editing of the bulletins.

During the first eighteen months of my Editorship the Chairmanship of ITN was shared, in alternating periods of six months, by Captain Brownrigg and by Norman Collins. Brownrigg had been brought into television by Rediffusion, the radio relay company which formed half of Associated Rediffusion, the company which had won the plum London weekday contract. He had retired from the Navy, and was manager of the new town being constructed at Bracknell in Berkshire, when he attracted the attention of Rediffusion by calling a meeting of all those likely to dig up the roads of the new town – the gas, electricity, water, telephone and relay organisations – and by digging up the streets for them once and for all. Undismayed by his lack of knowledge of entertainment or journalism, Brownrigg set about as General Manager of A-R organising the company on the same lines as the Singapore dockyards. They proved sound lines, for though A-R tended to be a company of lavish spenders, they had a clear-cut organisation, with a distinct chain of command, and forthright relations with the unions.

Norman Collins was at this time the best-known figure in Independent Television. He had created it by resigning from the BBC in 1950, where he had been Controller of Television, and leading the fight for an alternative, commercially-financed system. His reputation as a best-selling novelist as well as a broadcaster gave respectability to a move which was assailed fiercely by the cultural and political establishment. Yet having been the prime maker of the ITV system, Collins had had control of his programme company, the Associated Broadcast Development Company, dashed from his grasp because he could not raise enough money to get under way. The gap was small – only £350,000 – but his failure to bridge it forced him to surrender control to the show business group of Parnell, Littler and Grade, who dominated what came to be called ATV. Though great wealth was to come to Norman Collins he was denied the chance to shape this new system on his own lines. Yet he carried this blow with dignity. With his large handsome countenance, his fine head of hair, his unfailing calm, he betrayed no outward sign of the disappointment which he must so deeply have felt.

My personal relations with Norman Collins were always easy, even though we differed sharply on many issues. Such differences lay behind, I suspect, a saying of Disraeli he once quoted to me: 'Every time I made an appointment I lost a friend and made a hundred enemies.' He had been one of Howard Thomas's allies in putting pressure on Crawley, and was a reluctant spender on ITN in its early years. But in a number of tight editorial corners he gave me firm backing.

One such occasion arose when we experimented with turning the late bulletin on Saturday nights into a short news magazine. It carried an item about stately homes being opened to the public, and said of one such home that it had the additional attraction of possessing the largest flock of black sheep in the country. The presenter, a freelance who was not one of our usual contributors, had devised a neat link into the next story. It was, 'And speaking of black sheep, the Duke of Windsor is due to visit London next week.' The Duke's solicitors were on to us within a matter of days. Norman Collins dealt with them himself, and extricated us without having to pay damages or make a public apology.

These developments with ITN took place against a background of financial crisis within the programme companies. By July their losses totalled £10 million. The summer of 1956 was the period when, as the ITA were later to assert, the system was on the point of collapse. It was the wettest summer since the war, and the black clouds which seemed permanently banked above Television House seemed only too apt an omen.

No sign of these strains showed in the mien of Captain Thomas Brownrigg, striding through the entrance hall in bowler hat, dark suit and stiff-collared shirt, wearing always the tie appropriate to the occasion – the A-R tie with its golden sunburst on Associated Rediffusion Board days; the ITN tie if the ITN Board were to meet; the *TV Times* tie if their affairs were on his agenda. His insistence on unquestioning obedience was put to the test when the companies networked their first venture at Shakespeare – a full-length production of *Hamlet*. It was an important occasion, for here on screen was an answer to criticisms that ITV was not concerned with culture. The programme came live from an ATV studio, for we were not yet into the videotape era. Captain Brownrigg, with long naval experience of planning for the unforeseen, suggested that the commercials which were due to follow the end of the play should all be run from a common source instead of from the companies' separate presentation studios, in case the play overran its allotted time. Val Parnell of ATV rejected the idea out of hand. He prided himself on being a professional, well able to ensure that a production finished on time. Brownrigg, who had played a leading role in planning the naval operations for D-Day, did not take such a rebuff lightly. He issued instructions to his presentation controller that, come what may, the commercials in the London area were to come on air at 10.30 p.m. sharp, the time the play was due to end.

As the clock in the presentation suite moved towards the half-hour, Neil Bramson, the Production Controller, could see on the monitors that the final scene of the play was still in progress. Hamlet and Laertes still had their rapiers out, and the clash of metal was still mingling with Shakespeare's words when, precisely at 10.30 p.m., this picture changed abruptly for the London viewers. It was replaced immediately by two oranges, their peel cut to represent faces, which broke into a jingle extolling the virtues of Sunkist oranges. Of the many endings which Shakespearian productions have experienced across the centuries few can have matched this. Within seconds every telephone in the control room was ringing. Bramson was dealing with one call when he heard his assistant taking another from Lew Grade. Even at a distance Lew Grade's voice could be heard crackling in the earpiece demanding, 'What happened? What happened?' The assistant had a quick answer to hand. 'What happened, Mr Grade, was that they all died.'

Within ITN the summer of 1956 was a time of combined pressure and exhilaration. We knew our very survival was at stake, but at least we had our hands free to fight for it. Our technical and financial resources might be limited, but our editorial initiative was unfettered. Every day new possibilities as well as new problems opened up, and we could tackle them unhampered by tradition. No hierarchy breathed down our necks, no higher command demanded explanations or laid down guidelines. The companies and the Authority had too many difficulties of their own to be greatly concerned about ITN. We sought no guidance from others. We could not afford to journey to the United States or Europe to study their output. We had no course but to go our own way, which we did with alacrity, as if not only independent television but television itself had just been invented.

And there was the nightly reward of seeing our product on the screen. I usually watched the main evening bulletin from the control room, my seat a canvas-backed chair on the grams dais – for we ran to no reserved space for visitors. This was the moment when there came together the results of the day's conferences and discussions, of the filming and interviewing and recording in the field, the processing and evaluating and editing in the cutting room, of stories pondered, stories cut, stories rewritten. All this now faced its unforgiving thirteen minutes, fifty-eight seconds on the air. I knew too that elsewhere in the building others were watching equally intently. In the newsroom the journalists would be gathered around the corner set; in the preview theatre the film editors would have switched off the film projector and have turned on the television monitor; from the processing plant the operatives (unless they had some last-minute film to put through the bath) would have come to the preview door, to watch the monitor from there. In the gleaming telecine room the white-coated operators would be ready to set their machines in motion; in the dubbing theatre, dark except for the lights above the reading desk, the 'voice' of the day and the scriptwriters would be ready for their turn; in the racks the engineers would be at their posts. For the moment we were no longer just in journalism. We were in show business, as dependent for the success of our product on its final presentation as is any playwright or any theatrical producer. This gave both an added tension and an added satisfaction to our work which newspaper journalism did not have. All of us in ITN, journalists as well as technicians, shared in the elation of a good bulletin, or the dismay if one went awry. If I had missed the transmission of a programme I could tell from the faces of the staff as they poured out of the lift afterwards whether it had been good, bad or indifferent.

It was an exacting way to end the day – but an exhilarating one. It left me – unless disaster struck – curiously refreshed, with fatigue and worry for the moment banished, to drive home through the darkened streets of North London, my batteries already partly recharged for another day on the morrow.

15

Suez Challenge

On 26th July, two days after the sound cameras had shown their paces at Longbridge, the biggest story of the decade – indeed of several decades – broke without warning. President Nasser of Egypt announced that he intended to nationalise the Suez Canal. We were plunged into a period of news unlike any which post-war Britain was to experience until the Falklands crisis, a period in which interest in the news was dramatically heightened by the possibility of war. For a news service barely a year old it was a formidable challenge.

During the fourteen days which followed Nasser's speech Suez was to provide the lead story for every one of our main bulletins, and for most of the early evening bulletins as well. For the first two of these days we had, however, no film coverage from Egypt. The Middle East was one of the areas which we relied upon CBS to cover, and forty-eight hours were to elapse before their pictures of Nasser making his speech at Alexandria could make the journey from Egypt to New York, and back again to London. All we could offer viewers the next day were shots of vessels passing through the Suez Canal, obtained from wartime film in the possession of the Central Office of Information, and a glimpse of Nasser speaking into a microphone, from the CBS library. Only late on the Saturday evening did we have the actual scenes of Nasser telling a wildly cheering crowd that Egypt 'would meet force with force'. It was to be another three days – five days after Nasser's speech – before any further film reached us from Egypt, when CBS came up with a brief sequence of Egyptian troops standing guard outside the seized offices of the Suez Canal Company.

The mind boggles at what would happen on such a story today. Within hours electronic news-gathering teams and film crews, commentators, reporters, producers and film editors, traffic managers and news organisers from all over the world would be descending in their hundreds upon Cairo and Ismailia, pouring out their pictures by satellite or by air freight, filming every inch of the Canal from Port

Said to Suez, interviewing every Egyptian spokesman in sight against a background of the waterway, flashing pictures of every public meeting and demonstration on to our screens within minutes of their happening. By today's standards our coverage was austere indeed. Yet at the time its impact was remarkable. For this was the first major crisis to hit Britain in the television age, the first which could be seen as well as heard. Any pictures were a bonus gladly received by the viewers, accepted as providing a further dimension to the coverage in the newspapers or on radio in a way which was new and almost magical.

We were helped too by the fact that the centre of the story moved quickly from Egypt to London, where the decisions lay as to what action Britain and the other countries of the West should take. This brought the story within range of our home-based cameras, the only ones we could afford to deploy. On Sunday 29th July French and American Ministers flew to London for the first of many meetings. Robin Day was newscasting that evening, and his opening story reflected his style, personalised and yet dramatised: 'At this moment, as I am talking to you, the Foreign Secretary, Mr Selwyn Lloyd, is talking to the French Foreign Minister, Monsieur Pineau, and Mr Murphy, the American Deputy Under Secretary of State, talking, of course, about what to do next about President Nasser.'

This is a good example of the approach we adopted to our audience at that time. We were conscious we were talking to individual viewers, many of them newcomers to the medium, and that our first task was to engage their interest. We were conscious too that news was something to be spoken, not announced, or proclaimed. It was a style which, as film became more abundant, was to become less intimate, as pictures rather than words provided the link between the viewer and the news. The Carlton House meeting had started too late for us to have film of it in the bulletin. So the task of creating the atmosphere of an important meeting in progress at that moment fell to the newscaster himself.

Three days later the crisis assumed a new and more formidable shape. All countries whose ships made considerable use of the Suez Canal were invited to a further conference in London. At the same time the Government announced that the Queen had signed a proclamation calling up a number of reservists. The RAF stated that leave had been curtailed at a number of bomber stations; the Navy were preparing tank landing craft for service (withdrawing for this purpose some TLCs from their new civilian role of transporting liquid milk from Ireland). For good measure the Foreign Office was advising British subjects in Egypt to leave as soon as possible.

These were all portents of war – as was to prove the case. That afternoon I had a call from the Prime Minister's official spokesman, William Clark. He had been a wartime information officer in the United States who had joined the *Observer* after the war, and had returned to officialdom to serve Sir Anthony Eden at No. 10. We were old friends and colleagues, and had gained our first television experience on the same programme, 'Press Conference'. We talked in his ground floor office overlooking Downing Street, where a small crowd of holiday sightseers strolled and stared from the far pavement.

William came straight to the point. The Government meant business. The partial mobilisation was not a bluff. Whatever happened in the weeks ahead, it was important to bear in mind that the Government was not going to let Nasser get away with seizing the Canal.

Clark made clear he had taken the decision to tell me this entirely on his own initiative. It was not a statement I could use, or attribute in any way to him. It was intended only as guidance in a situation which was likely to get confused in the weeks ahead. 'However different things may seem from time to time, as events unfold, I think you will find that this is what the policy turns out to be.'

Clark's information was of value to me in a flurry which blew up about our late bulletin that evening. I had had to take a telephone call during the rehearsal, and had failed to check part of the copy. I was taken by surprise, therefore, when the newscaster, Ludovic Kennedy, after film portraying the detailed measures for this partial mobilisation added the words, 'Whether all this means we are preparing to back our beliefs by force, or is a piece of gigantic bluff for the benefit of Colonel Nasser, your guess is as good as mine.'

This was not mere speculation. Kennedy had maintained the links he had made during his wartime service in the Royal Navy, and had good contacts with senior naval officers. They were aware of the difficulties of mounting an invasion of Egypt, and had good reason to believe that the Prime Minister could be bluffing.

I could not cite Clark as proof to the contrary. Nor was that the heart of the matter. What seemed to be posed here, illuminated by the glare of crisis, were the proper limits of newscasting. This was how the *Daily Telegraph* saw it the next day, when it rapped us over the knuckles in an editorial. 'No one is going to contend that this is a blunder of major importance, out of which Colonel Nasser is likely to make capital,' it argued. 'But it offends against a principle which newspaper experience at any rate has established as of permanent value, that of the separation of comment from news.' In fact that was not the issue. Kennedy's words were not so much comment, not a view on the rights and wrongs of the issue, as an interpretation. Our mistake was to have raised a major, basic question about the Government's strategy without exploring or examining it fully. We had in effect said, 'Eden may be bluffing,' without offering evidence for or against this vast proposition. Today a host of pundits and experts would be on the air in a host of programmes, analysing and probing the issue from every angle. But in August 1956, except for 'This Week' once a week, the ITN News was the only actuality programme on Independent Television. We had no scope in a fifteen minute bulletin for any analysis in depth that evening. It had been all we could do to pack in the day's news.

I was concerned that our estimate of Eden's intentions might serve to harden Nasser's attitude, and so make a settlement less likely, that the newsboys outside the Continental Hotel in Cairo the next morning might be proclaiming, 'British TV say Eden is bluffing.' But the Egyptian newspapers did not pick up the story, or if they did we never heard of it. We were able in the next day's bulletins to get back on course by underlining the statements of the British and French Governments that they meant business, and by stressing their words that they were 'prepared to use force if necessary to secure an international Canal authority'.

Yet if we did not mount studio discussions of the Government's policy, the issue did not go undebated on the air. For we carried at considerable length reports of the Parliamentary debates on the crisis. Indeed we reported these at greater length than was done by television of the Commons debates on the Falklands issue, devoting at times seven and eight minutes to Robin Day's account of the events in the House. Each night Day had to rush back by taxi from the Commons Press Gallery and deliver his report live into the bulletin. He spoke from notes, as there was no time to type out a script. Yet the outcome was a series of verbal sketches of which a veteran Gallery sketch-writer could have been proud, mingling description with an element of evaluation which was then rare, if not unknown, in political broadcast reporting.

Two days after the reservists had been called up we were into

August Bank Holiday, and our cameras caught the strange spectacle of one part of the nation spending its holiday watching the other part get ready for war. Seaside holiday-makers crowded quays to see equipment and troops being loaded onto the aircraft carrier HMS *Theseus* at Portsmouth. Holiday traffic was caught up on roads jammed by convoys of Army lorries. We filmed the wedding of a paratrooper due to leave within hours for the Middle East, and interviewed him and his bride just before they parted. It ran alongside film of the Battle of Flowers in Jersey, and of Derek Ibbotson running the mile in 3 minutes 59 seconds in drenching rain at the White City.

The contrast of that Bank Holiday was best caught by our Chief Cameraman Ronnie Read in a sequence showing HMS *Bulwark* moving down the Solent on her way to the Mediterranean. Sunshine broke through the storm clouds as holiday-makers watched from a hillside. No reporter's words could have better conveyed the emotions of the moment than did Read's pictures, as men in white shirts and grey flannel trousers, or wearing army surplus khaki shorts which were the accepted holiday garb of the time, and women in bright print dresses watched the great ship move steadily away, leaving a wide gleaming wake in the sunlight.

16

The Party Conferences

In the autumn of 1956 both major parties were for the first time prepared to allow television to cover their annual Conferences fully – a major advance in the televising of politics. For the two previous years the Conservatives had allowed the cameras to cover all their debates, but the most which the Labour Party under Clement Attlee had agreed to was coverage, as an experiment, of one half-day of their proceedings in 1955. With Hugh Gaitskell now installed as Labour Leader that was changed. He saw television as a valuable counter-balance to a predominately Conservative press, and readily agreed to allow full coverage of the Labour Conference.

During the previous two years the BBC had recruited outside

specialists like Robert McKenzie, William Clark and David Butler for their special Conference reports, and in 1955 Aidan Crawley had brought in Percy Cudlipp, the former Editor of the *Daily Herald*, to strengthen the ITN team. Though neither Robin Day nor George Ffitch had previously covered a Party Conference, I decided to gamble on them alone. If we were to build up a truly professional reporting team, we must give our own staff every bit of experience going.

On Monday 1st October the Labour Party Conference got under way in the ornate Tower Ballroom at Blackpool. All our coverage had to be on film, for unlike the BBC, the ITV system had as yet no down lines on which live pictures could have been carried to London. The first day was harassing, for the film had to be shipped by train from Blackpool, and rushed from Euston by dispatch rider. Coverage of the morning session did not reach us until six o'clock in the evening, and only the early part of the afternoon's proceedings got to us in time for the late bulletin. I was thankful for the experience I had gained at Lime Grove the year before in the selection of film excerpts, and thankful too for the swift competence of the ITN film editors with whom I worked in a tiny cutting room, half of it filled by the Steenbeck editing table. The last segment of the film was still 'green', its emulsion soft from the developing tank, when we dealt with it.

The result was encouraging. We had caught well both the atmosphere and the arguments of the main debate, on Suez, and of a debate on industrial policy which had brought a fine clash between Sam Watson, the Durham miners' leader who had taken over Ernest Bevin's mantle as leader of the right, and Frank Cousins, newly emerged as a left-winger. Robin Day rounded off the proceedings neatly with an interview with a cheerfully stubborn Irishman called O'Reilly, the one lone delegate who had opposed the official line on Suez. He wanted us to attack Egypt, whether or not the United Nations approved.

The next day the cameras caught the drama of the announcement of the voting for the National Executive, and we followed our report of the debates with contrasting interviews with Aneurin Bevan and George Brown. Once again the camera work from the hall was first class. Like cricket coverage, filming Party Conferences called for skill in anticipating the big moments – for speakers like Aneurin Bevan never dreamt of working from a script – together with swift reaction to interruptions or heckling. Some of the older speakers co-operated with the camera crews by using dodges that stemmed from the days of the cinema newsreel. Manny Shinwell, for instance, would pause and mop his forehead with his handkerchief as a sign that he was about to reach the key passage of his speech. But with speakers called to the rostrum from the floor that was not possible.

The third night disaster struck – or what seemed to me at the time to be disaster. The film editing shift had changed and a new team of editors worked with me on the story. On transmission the first half of the report was fine, but the second half, prepared against the clock, was, in the parlance of film editing, 'out of sync'. The movement of the lips of the speakers was manifestly not synchronised with the sound of their words.

I could envisage the scene in the hotel lounges at Blackpool, as the Conference delegates gathered to see how this new ITN service was making out in competition with the BBC, only to find that we had bungled it. I insisted then and there that the rosters be reshuffled, and that the other shift, who had made no such mistakes, come back to handle the final two nights of the Conference. Today such a demand would bring the whole network to a stop within five minutes. Then it was accepted readily enough. Even if the film editors disagreed with my method, they respected my aim, and contented themselves with putting up a notice in the preview theatre: 'We will all sync or swim together.' I ensured, however, that the offending shift were back on duty for the Conservative Conference the next week, on which they worked flawlessly.

A further technical hitch the next night arose from the practice of using cut-away shots to portray the reaction of the audience to the speakers. We did not have enough cameras to film simultaneously both the speaker on the rostrum and the audience in the hall. So we used a device long practised by the newsreels, under which a sound camera filmed and recorded the speaker, whilst another camera would film shots, termed cut-aways, of the audience in different moods – applauding enthusiastically, or lethargically, or listening in stony silence, or looking interested, or bored. The reporter would note on the film dope sheets which type of audience reaction would be appropriate, and the film editor would seek such a shot from amongst the cut-aways. There was an element of cheating in this, for the audience might have been reacting to a different speaker. But it was a legitimate element, provided we sought to convey accurately the audience's response.

But on this occasion the method came unstuck. Harold Wilson made a powerful speech from the platform. The editor, working as ever against the clock, put in a cut-away shot showing the audience clapping vigorously. It was, however, from another debate, and it showed, well to the fore amongst that audience, none other than Harold Wilson, applauding vigorously. What the viewers made of this I do not know. Perhaps they put it down to the marvels of this new medium.

The Tory Conference a week later at Llandudno proved even more of a logistical nightmare than had Blackpool. To get film of Sir Anthony Eden's main speech on Saturday afternoon back in time for use that evening we had to charter a light aircraft. Watching the coverage on the Steenbeck screen only twelve months after I had at Lime Grove viewed him speaking at Bournemouth, I was struck by the manifest strain in Sir Anthony's voice and manner. Even in the black and white negative the traits of a man feeling great tension were noticeable. To round off this Conference Robin Day sought out two women prominent in the Tory Party, so giving the public the first chance to study in close-up Lady Clarissa Eden and Lady Antonia Fraser.

This extensive political reporting was made the more palatable because there was plenty of other news with which to leaven the bulletins. Princess Margaret went off on her closely watched tour of East Africa. We had no money to cover such an extended journey, but we devised a scheme under which our cameraman shot en route some training film for an airline in return for a free passage. In covering this tour Ronnie Read demonstrated to the full his skill as a portraitist with a film camera. One shot, showing Princess Margaret in a balldress, and wearing a tiara, coming down a staircase for a ball in Nairobi, dazzlingly symbolised her return to the public stage. Another caught the almost imperceptible tightening of her expression as she came face-to-face, at a diamond mine in Tanganyika, with Peter Townsend's brother, who was an official in the Colonial service. But it was Read's filming of children along the Princess's route which gave these reports their remarkable quality. A childless man himself, he was a master of picking out in crowds the eager or drowsy, alert or solemn faces of children as they waved their flags or shouted their greetings.

Another story which enlivened that grim autumn concerned the hat-loving lady discus thrower. One outcome of the visit of Bulganin and Khrushchev to Britain in April had been an agreement to increase sporting and cultural links between the Soviet Union and Britain. A Russian athletics team came to compete with Britain at the White City, to be followed by the first post-war tour of the Bolshoi Ballet. This cosy rapport was disturbed when the Soviet Olympic champion lady discus thrower, Nina Ponomerova, was stopped as she left C & A Modes in Oxford Street, and later charged with stealing five hats to the total value of £1.12s.11d. When she failed to appear in court a warrant was issued for her arrest. The Russians called off the athletics match, declared Mrs Ponomerova had been a victim of a 'dirty provocation' and threatened to cancel the visit of the Bolshoi 'for fear they might be exposed to similar provocation'. In the end, however, the Bolshoi's visit took place. At a press conference soon after the arrival of the dancers their director, Mr Chulaki, was asked a somewhat double-edged question. Would the dancers be allowed to go shopping in London? He replied carefully, 'If they have the money, they will.'

This reply nearly landed us in a legal tangle that could have found its way into the textbooks. At the last moment, into the script of the story about this press conference, one line of comment found its way. To the report of Mr Chulaki's reply about shopping were added the words, 'Let's hope if they don't have the money, they won't.'

Those ten words would make a neat subject for study by students of law and journalism. They contained two libels, one contempt of court and the makings of a diplomatic incident. Set against the background of the yet uncompleted Nina Ponomerova trial, the words libelled her by implying that she had stolen the hats; they libelled the members of the Bolshoi by implying that they might steal rather than buy; they were in contempt of the court which had not yet completed the proceedings against Mrs Ponomerova; and they could well have led the Soviet authorities to take such offence that they might have cancelled the Ballet's tour. When I heard them on rehearsal I leapt from my seat at the back of the control room, heading for the studio. In the doorway I collided with the Chief Sub-Editor, also rushing towards the door. He sent me flying against the wall, nearly knocking me out, but did not stop. He leapt across the studio, seized the copy and struck out the final line. It stands there, hastily pencilled through, in the ITN archives to this day, an interesting reminder of one that did not get away.

17

Test by Battle

From mid-October onwards the Suez crisis entered its final dramatic stage. At Malta and at Cyprus, at Toulon and at Algiers the invasion forces were gathering. At the United Nations session in New York the Canal became the main issue, the debates well depicted by the United Nations' own television cameras.

On to this scene burst suddenly the upheavals in Eastern Europe which were to culminate in the Hungarian uprising. The first signs of trouble came from Poland, where mass meetings demanded the return to power of Gomulka, the leader ousted by Russia. We had no means of getting a film crew into Poland but the Polish authorities, intelligently alive to the value of publicity in the West, made available to us excellent 35mm coverage of the mass meetings and of their Party leaders. We backed this with an interview with John Strachey, the former Labour Minister, and former apologist for the Soviet Union. We had no reporter available to question him when he reached London Airport from Warsaw, but the cameraman, Cyril Page, put to him a series of questions telephoned through from Arthur Clifford. It was an action which cut across two of our agreements with the unions, but those were other days, and there were no repercussions.

Poland did not hold the public's attention for long. On Wednesday 24th October the uprising began in Budapest. This time we were determined to get our own cameraman on to the scene. I drew on my experience in the Spanish Civil War and in Finland in 1939. I learnt there that in wars and revolutions there is a period of some days when matters are flexible and uncertain, when one set of red tape has not yet been replaced by a new set, a period when journalists can roam about with surprising freedom. I had been able to report at first hand on the opening battles in the Arctic Circle in Finland by the simple expedient of getting on a train and going to the front, without any special pass.

To cover Budapest we chose Martin Gray, a big, quiet, resourceful former Movietone cameraman who had filmed in 1944 one of the war's most spectacular actions, the Allied bombing of the monastery at Monte Cassino. Like all our cameramen he carried his passport always with him, and in a matter of hours was on a plane to Vienna. There he hired a car and set out for the Hungarian frontier. Around the frontier post milled a crowd of reporters and cameramen held up because they had no visas for Hungary, and could get none. All Gray could do that first day was to film these frontier scenes, put his film on a plane from Vienna, and phone us through a report on events in Budapest as told him by a business man who had just got away from there. For Gray, too, there was no punctilio about demarcation lines. It was good, on-the-spot material, but it took second place in that night's main bulletin. We had an even stronger lead to hand, for an hour before we went on air news reached London that the Israelis had invaded Egypt.

That evening, Monday 29th October, the Guild of Television Producers was holding its second annual dinner and ball at the Savoy Hotel. It was not yet the television spectacular it has since become, but it was important for us because Christopher Chataway had won the award for the outstanding personality, largely because of his work for ITN, and ATV had won an award for 'Sunday Night at the London Palladium'. Hugh Gaitskell was to make the presentations. I was sitting near him at the central table when a waiter asked me to take a telephone call. It was from Arthur Clifford. 'The Israelis have invaded Egypt,' he said. I scribbled a note and placed it beside Gaitskell's plate. He at once hurried to the telephone in a nearby room, spent several minutes on it, returned to distribute the awards, and then drove back to the Commons.

We had got the news on to the screen within minutes of its reaching us from the agencies. Arthur Clifford had persuaded the Transmission Controller at Rediffusion to flash the information by a primitive but effective technique. A slide on which was written in crude lettering 'Israel has invaded Egypt' was put on the screen in the midst of 'Son of Fred', the witty, somewhat surrealist satirical comedy show of the time. It was a rough-and-ready method, but it worked.

The Israeli attack was part of the plan secretly agreed at Sèvres in France five days earlier. Under this Britain and France were due the next day to issue an ultimatum calling on Egypt and Israel to stop fighting, and to withdraw ten miles from the Canal. Its publication would mean that we were virtually at war. It seemed to me essential that we should have a series of news flashes between the 7 p.m.

bulletin and the late bulletin. So early that Tuesday afternoon I sought out Val Parnell to ask his backing for these.

I found Parnell in an angry mood. In the rush of the previous night's bulletin we had committed, it seemed, a heinous crime. We had reported that ATV had got an award for '*Saturday* Night at the London Palladium', when the show was, in fact, on *Sunday* nights. He met me with a blast of Irish indignation about the inability of a news service, which cost him far too much money anyway, to get even the simplest facts straight. I countered with my request for time for news flashes. He was genuinely surprised. 'Interrupt the programmes on the hour every hour through the evening? What on earth for?'

'Because we are about to go to war – and we may have to announce that this evening.'

'What do you mean?' It was clear he was no close student of events in the Middle East. 'The Israelis are already at war,' I stated. 'And we could be in it at any moment, too.'

'You really mean that?' Concern mixed with incredulity on his face.

'It's a virtual certainty,' I said.

Parnell rose from his chair, strode across the room and opened the door into an adjoining office. Cigar smoke billowed out through the doorway. 'Lew,' he called. 'Lew! Come out of there and get your bloody machine gun – and get it quick. You are at war. Do you know that, you're at war?' Through the tobacco smoke emerged Lew Grade, holding a cigar almost as big as a machine gun. He moved out quickly, his soft-jowled yet strong face radiating alarm, but not fear. He looked for the moment as if he expected to find Val Parnell's office full of Arab invaders.

'Geoffrey Cox says your Jewish pals are already at war, and that we might be in it at any time. And he wants a minute every hour on the hour tonight to tell us if we are. What do you say?'

'Give it to him,' replied Lew without hesitation. So I returned to the first floor with my news flash time secured. We were beginning to get what mattered even more than money in a crisis like this – time on the air.

We had, in fact, already hit upon an unexpected source of extra time for the main bulletins. Since we were the last programme of the night it was possible to secure an extension of several minutes to the late bulletin simply by ringing up the Transmission Controller at Rediffusion, who would then notify the other companies of the length of this over-run. These gave us one of the greatest boons a television newsman can have – a flexible length to his programme. It was a flexibility we were to utilise fully, until we were putting out bulletins nearly half an hour in length. In the pressures of that extraordinary autumn the half-hour news format was tried out some eleven years before it found a permanent form in 'News at Ten'.

Though we had no film of the Israeli invasion of Sinai – the Israeli censors saw to that – we were able to illustrate the story with earlier shots of Israeli troops on patrol in the desert, of Egyptian troops in their trenches, of air raid precautions in Tel Aviv, and of HMS *Theseus* sailing from Southampton with British reinforcements. From Hungary, too, we had Gray's film of the aftermath of fighting just inside the border, and more stories of the revolt from eye witnesses who had escaped to Austria. Contrasting with this were pictures of the previous night's Royal Film Performance, all the more vivid for being shot on 35mm cinematographic film, under an arrangement with the newsreels. It showed the Queen and Princess Margaret in full evening dress meeting, in the theatre foyer, Marilyn Monroe and Brigitte Bardot, Victor Mature and Michael Powell.

Martin Gray had meanwhile found an unguarded side road on the Austro-Hungarian border and together with John Davis of the *Daily Express* had driven the 200 miles to Budapest. He filmed there for a couple of hours, and then he and Davis started on the long haul back to Vienna, snatching a few hours of sleep there before setting off on the road again. This was to be the pattern of their days for the rest of the week.

Despite these pressures, Gray's coverage was admirably shot. Here for the first time were the students and workers of the new Militia, their shoulders draped with bandoleers, rifles and machine guns in hand, patrolling the streets of their liberated capital. Huge Soviet metal stars were hauled from the front of Communist headquarters; a statue of Stalin was toppled from its pedestal and smashed. One gripping sequence showed secret police of the old regime, curiously young, with lank, dishevelled hair, their faces white with terror, being escorted at rifle point from their headquarters. In another a frenzied crowd dug away at rubble barring the entrance to a building where other police agents were still holding out. Here indeed was television news fulfilling its role, catching a moment of history in the making.

This coverage from Budapest was all the more dramatic because the war in which Britain was herself engaged had, except for the continued bombing of Egyptian airfields, entered a curious limbo.

Time was needed to move the cumbersome invasion forces from Malta, Algiers and Cyprus towards Port Said and the neighbouring Port Fuad, time filled only by reports of the attacks on the airfields and by the fierce debates in Parliament and in the United Nations.

On Saturday evening, 3rd November, Sir Anthony Eden addressed the nation on television and radio, to prepare the public mind for the assault which was to be launched on to Egyptian soil in the small hours of Monday. Soon before he was due to speak I had a call from Hugh Gaitskell's office. He lived only a couple of blocks away from my home in Hampstead. He had no television set. Could he come round and listen to Eden on mine? He did so, and then and there sat down at my dining-room table and wrote his reply. Had he stuck to that first script, his broadcast the next night might have been better. As it was he was harried and buffeted by advisers throughout the day, and appeared tense and edgy when he spoke on both channels the next evening, Sunday 4th November.

We carried this reply of the Leader of the Opposition in a massive bulletin lasting twenty-six minutes. For on that Sunday the Suez story moved to our very doorstep, to the streets converging on Trafalgar Square, where the biggest demonstration since the war had been mounted by the Labour Movement against the forthcoming invasion. Even so that demonstration did not lead the news, nor did our reporting that a landing of British and French troops was imminent. What led that Sunday night programme – for 'bulletin' was no word for a report of that length – were the messages from Budapest that Hungary's brief freedom was in its death throes.

By Saturday 3rd November it was clear inside Budapest that the Russian forces gathered around the city were about to strike. Martin Gray realised that if he were caught in the city he would have no chance of getting his film back. So, together with Jeffery Blyth of the *Daily Mail*, he set out by car for the frontier early on the Sunday morning. On the road outside the city they suddenly saw, pounding towards them, a long column of Russian T 34 tanks, dark and powerful against the drab winter landscape. Through the windscreen, with the wipers clearing a cone of vision through the rain, Martin Gray filmed these tanks, so securing one of the classic film stories of the crushing of the Hungarian revolution.

Near the frontier the road was closed by a Russian patrol; when Gray moved his hand to his pocket to pull out his passport the guards misunderstood the gesture and fired a volley of warning shots through the car roof. They turned Gray and Blyth back to a small town inside the frontier. There they met Noel Barber of the *Daily Mail,* his head in bandages, both sides of it having been grazed by Russian machine gun fire in Budapest. Barber was confident that, as a wounded man, he would not be searched, so he took over Gray's film and safely brought it across the frontier to Vienna. There Gray, having made his way by sideroads into Austria, collected it. It reached us in time to show the next day – the fateful Monday of the landings at Port Said.

Gray's film remained the only coverage by a British cameraman out of Budapest during the Hungarian uprising, all other being the work of American network crews and of the UPI film agency.

But on that Sunday night we had to rely on words alone to tell the story of the fall of Budapest. 'First, today's grave news from Hungary,' was the way Robin Day began his report. 'The Russians attacked Budapest this morning, and claimed to have crushed the Hungarian revolt for freedom.'

The main picture story was, however, the mass demonstration which filled not only Trafalgar Square, but every street leading to it, and which was addressed by Aneurin Bevan and Michael Foot from the plinth of the Nelson statue – the first of a multitude of such demonstrations to be caught by television news cameras. This differed from later rallies in its spontaneity, in its absence of hectoring, slogan-shouting stewards, in its desire to impress the watching newspaper reporters by sheer weight of numbers, rather than to catch the eye of the cameras. It was the last of the pre-television era demonstrations, as well as the first of those for the small screen. The people who poured on to the streets that afternoon did not have foremost in their minds how the outcome would look on television, which many of them did not in any event yet watch. They came to express by their presence the belief that there should be some other way than war in which Britain could resolve the Suez question. And certainly they did not come with a view to stirring up violence in order to publicise their case.

Except for one scuffle in the late evening in Whitehall, which our cameras recorded, the day was peaceful.

18

War on the Screen

That long Sunday bulletin ushered in one of the most extraordinary weeks in British journalism. One great story pounded on the heels of another, all set against the highly emotive background of a country finding itself yet again at war.

The announcement that the attack had begun, with British and French paratroops dropping on to the Port Said airfield and around Port Fuad, came early the next morning. The first film we could expect would come from the cameramen who had been selected to cover the action on a pooled basis for BBC, ITN and the newsreels. One cameraman went in with the airborne troops and another with the main forces following up by sea. Censorship had been imposed and all coverage would have to come back through Cyprus to the War Office in London. It would be twenty-four hours before we could expect to have any film of the landings.

We had, however, good coverage from Cyprus of paratroops boarding planes, of their weapon canisters being loaded, and of the accompanying bombers being armed. Ludovic Kennedy skilfully wrote his story so that it could be underlaid by this film, conveying the atmosphere, if not the actuality of the event. And if film was scanty from Egypt, there was good material from the Israelis, at long last, of their advance into Sinai; there were Martin Gray's chilling shots of the Soviet tanks on the rainswept road to Budapest; and there was, to finish another long bulletin (it ran some twenty minutes), the first of what was to prove a heart-rending series of reports from the Austro-Hungarian border, as refugees began to stream across from reconquered Hungary. Among them were a group of bewildered children, some with labels tied to their clothes by parents who could not accompany them, giving their names, and their families' addresses.

This group came across at the frontier post, just before the Russians closed it. But others were to escape – and to be filmed escaping on subsequent days – at a point where the frontier was marked only by a narrow stream into which men, women and children slithered and floundered their way, clinging to a rope until the Austrian guards on the near bank could rescue them. To British people, many of whom had seen their own children labelled for evacuation in the early days of the war, and whose minds were filled with film shots of the long calvary of World War II refugees along European roads, these shots had a poignancy which most later coverage of refugees has not aroused. They were to provide a highly emotive final item in bulletin after bulletin for nights to come. One sequence in particular struck at the emotions. A Hungarian carrying a large, closely-wrapped parcel stepped into the icy river and, holding the parcel carefully above the water, moved with slow care to the Austrian bank. Once there, under the lens of the camera, he unwrapped the bundle carefully, even tenderly, to reveal inside it a baby, its eyes alert and eager, reflecting the joy and thankfulness on the man's face.

Ludovic Kennedy, who did much of the newscasting in these crucial days to enable Robin Day to report from Westminster, conveyed by his bearing and his tone the emotion these scenes stirred in him. I agreed one evening that he should read, over that night's film of the refugees, a letter he had received, postmarked Uxbridge. Its words were: 'Dear Mr Kennedy, I hope you will not mind this letter direct to you, but I have been wondering, after seeing last night's late news, if you could find out the name and address I could apply to to take one of those poor bewildered little children who crossed into Austria with labels attached to them. My husband and I adopted a little girl eight years ago, and I think if we could give some of the happiness to one of those little mites that our own little girl has brought to us then perhaps we may be helping a little bit towards the awful problem of those brave people.'

Presented with mawkishness or insincerity, this could have struck a false note, but done with the genuine feeling which manifestly animated Kennedy, it gave expression to the mood of the country, and did much to set on foot the schemes for Hungarian relief which were to follow.

Dramatic viewing though all this was, we knew that the real test would be our coverage of the landings at Port Said. I was confident that Cyril Page would serve us well. Very tall, in his early thirties, he had a boyish face and manner which belied his swashbuckling assertiveness in pursuit of news. He was the only ITN cameraman to have joined us from the BBC rather than the newsreels. For the

BBC's 'Television Newsreel' Page had covered much of the ugliest fighting in the Korean war, and when that quietened down he had devised a programme called 'Messages for Home', in which he filmed troops sending a message to their friends or families. He used as interviewer a young correspondent for the *Exchange Telegraph* called Alan Whicker, who in this way took his first steps into television.

With Page's assertiveness went considerable artistic skill. Even after he had joined ITN two examples of his work continued to appear on BBC screens – 'The Potter's Wheel' and 'The Swans', two of the short atmospheric pieces with which the Corporation marked the intermissions between programmes. Page had too one further quality invaluable for a cameraman – luck. That luck held when, among the score of cameramen waiting in Cyprus, he won the draw to go, as pool cameraman, with the invasion fleet. At that stage another future television star was written into the script. For the conducting officer in charge of the press was a young National Service officer, Second Lieutenant Michael Parkinson.

Page landed at dawn on Monday 5th November with the first wave of supporting infantry, on a beach alongside the airfield which the paratroops had captured shortly before. After filming the paras dug in around the airfield perimeter and advancing into Port Said, Page made it his task to liberate a large lemon-yellow Chrysler Bel Air convertible touring car, conveniently placed in a showroom window. With this he rapidly toured the town, filming the bomb damage, the bodies lying in the streets, the troops and tanks moving forward, and one particularly macabre scene of dead bodies being loaded into a Coca-Cola truck. But he knew that film, however good, had little meaning unless it gets back quickly to base. Soon after mid-day, therefore, he drove back to the airfield, found an officer about to fly to Larnaca and persuaded him to carry the film with him.

Under the pooling arrangements, the film should have gone through Army Headquarters in Cyprus, where all potential users would have been advised of its existence. At Larnaca, however, the officer saw a plane about to take off for London. He gave the film to the pilot, who delivered it to the War Office in Whitehall. The next day the War Office handed the film on to us without any reference to its having been shot for pool use. Along the way the dope sheets, the written report in which Page had recorded his coverage, had gone astray. Overnight, too, the cease fire had been declared, and the Services had abruptly lifted all censorship. In this sudden change the pooling arrangements were forgotten. When Page's film reached us in Kingsway we assumed in good faith that it was our own, and used it as such. The BBC, equally in the dark, made no effort to claim a copy. So chance, coupled with Page's swiftness and ingenuity, gave us a scoop on the biggest story of the year.

Except for the one particularly horrific shot of the mangled, fly-encrusted face of a dead civilian, all of it was material which manifestly could and should be shown. We cut it into a story seven minutes long – an epic in those days of scrappy film sequences. Most of the shots were self-explanatory, and we could interpret them without the dope sheets. One sequence, however, raised baffling questions. This showed a body, shrouded in a grey army blanket, being buried in a hastily dug grave in a public garden near the waterfront. The Army firing party which fired a salute over the grave left the obvious assumption that this was the burial of a British soldier.

It was emotive material, which brought home sharply the human cost of these operations. British casualties had been slight, but in at least a handful of the watching homes this body in its grey blanket shroud might well be that of a husband, son or brother. Yet we had no sure knowledge whose body it was.

I decided we should show it, with a brief commentary that neither posed nor answered the question of identity. 'The dead were buried where they fell,' were all the words needed. On the screen it formed a deeply moving conclusion to the report, evoking the realities of this struggle under the drab grey skies of an Egyptian November. It was only when the dope sheets finally escaped from the web of official red tape a week later that we learned that it had, in fact, been the funeral of an Egyptian. He was a lone sniper who had held out so bravely against the paratroops that they had accorded him this final tribute.

As I made these decisions, crouched over the cutting table with minutes ticking away towards transmission, I sensed how powerful was this new force of television in the coverage of war. It was the first time that it had fallen to an editor to make such rulings about scenes of battle on which our own troops were engaged. All previous film of action had been subject to censorship. The military authorities had decided what scenes should or should not be shown. Only the sudden accident of this two-day war, which was over before any film had come in from the front, had removed that censorship, and placed this unique responsibility on our shoulders.

Even though the fighting was over, I knew that these scenes would stir deep feelings, political as well as human. The pathetic, crumpled bodies in the streets, the shattered buildings, the burial of this unknown soldier displayed the cost of war, arousing emotions only partially off-set by the sense of strength and accomplishment conveyed by the British troops moving cautiously but steadily forward through the streets. This came through most vividly in a spectacular sequence of a Centurian tank racing towards a street corner and then swinging its gun in a ninety degree arc before moving on towards the Canal. The scenes of death and of damage would provide powerful arguments for those who opposed the action, and a stern glimpse of reality for those who supported it. In films of the Second World War few such casualties had been shown. In all the footage of D-Day, used over the years in countless documentaries, you will seldom see a British or American soldier fall as the troops storm ahead – and then only in a distant shot. Moreover, those scenes were at the time viewed only in the cinema, and some days later. These pictures were going into the homes of people throughout Britain almost as soon as the action had taken place. Yet I could see no other guide to their presentation than to present them in full, cut only for the purpose of clarity, except for the one peculiarly grisly shot whose loss detracted nothing from the impact of the whole. I was thankful that I had had to face these decisions only briefly. It was not an editorial task to be relished over a long period.

Excellent though Cyril Page's coverage of Port Said had been, it lacked the added dimension of natural sound. We had not been able to afford the extra fares necessary for a sound crew. But a chance to get a recordist on to the scene arose when the Central Office of Information asked us to film damage done by Allied bombers in Port Said. They wanted the material to answer allegations that there had been widespread and wanton destruction of civilian areas. We were not caught up here in making propaganda, as our task was a purely contractual one of filming the scenes and handing the material over to the COI. Once this was out of the way, we were able to use the sound crew for our own purposes. Robin Day eagerly took on the task of reporting with them from Port Said, thankful for a break after his long days and nights in the Press Gallery at Westminster.

The venture produced some noteworthy material, in particular of the moment when the Danish troops, as part of the United Nations force, took over from the British troops in their foremost positions along the road towards Cairo. In the sunshine of a bright Egyptian December morning the turning of the tide of British imperial power was recorded by this new and potent portrayer of history. Danish troops, tall, young, gangling conscripts, wearing the blue-painted helmets which were to become the hallmark of the United Nations, lined up on the roadside, with the waters of the Canal gleaming behind them. The curt commands of the young and very correct subaltern commanding the forward platoon of the Yorks and Lancs were clearly heard on the film, as were the click of rifle slings and the clatter of boots as the riflemen clambered out of their slit trenches, and lined up on the Canal bank ready to begin their march northwards, as they – and the British Empire – withdrew.

Robin Day made the most of this, his first foreign assignment. He interviewed General Stockwell, the ebullient and forthcoming commander of the Anglo-French force, against a background of the harbour of Port Said, where the masts of sunken blockships still showed above water. Twenty years later the General was to recall 'the young Robin Day, with his insistent questioning'.[1] Day discovered, too, that a neighbour of his, the Borough Engineer of Chelsea, had been recalled to the Royal Engineers to get the damaged sewage system of Port Said working again. Day began his report by popping up out of a sewer, lifting the manhole cover, and starting his commentary. He ended neatly, 'I return you now from the sewers of Port Said to the ITN studio in London' – a line which Ludovic Kennedy received with the words, 'I am not sure that I altogether like that.'

Day's task was eased by the fact that Cyril Page was now an established figure in Port Said. He had been accorded the accolade of a nickname, conferred by the Force Commander himself. To General Stockwell the sight of this figure in a well-tailored uniform driving up to his headquarters on the Port Said dockside in a lemon-yellow convertible on the first day of the invasion must have added a final surrealist touch to the already bizarre experience of the stop-go battle he had been called on to conduct. Told that this was the commercial television cameraman, the General burst out, 'Good God, don't tell me we've got Omo mixed up in this war as well.' Omo became Page's Army name from then on. This tribute to the effectiveness of one of the earliest detergent commercials endured. Fifteen years later the dignitaries waiting in the courtyard of Caernarvon Castle for the arrival of Prince Charles for his investiture as Prince of Wales were not a little surprised to see a figure in the full dress uniform of a Field Marshal rise from their midst and greet a passing television cameraman with a cry of, 'Omo, Omo, my dear fellow, how are you?'

We had been able to get on with the task of reporting the Suez invasion largely free of the pressures brought to bear by the Government on the BBC – and staunchly resisted by the BBC – at the height of the crisis when the Prime Minister tried to prevail upon the Corporation not to broadcast reports of the split in British public opinion over the Anglo-French armed intervention. Eden's concern was above all with radio, which was not only the dominant medium at home, but was the voice of Britain to foreign countries – and above all to the troops putting their lives at hazard. The Prime Minister did, however, make one important approach to Independent Television. He chose as his point of contact Sir Kenneth Clark, whom he knew well personally. As events moved towards their climax in late October Clark was called to Downing Street. 'I was on my way to give a lecture on Raphael,' Clark recalled later, 'when Eden asked me to see him at No. 10. He asked me, in the national interest, to slant the news about Suez. Even had we been inclined to do so – which I was not – I told him it could not be done. We were working under an Act of Parliament which called for impartiality. I left, and went on my way to give my lecture, and never heard another word about it.'[2]

Clark was accustomed to taking decisions on his own initiative. He had settled the matter on the spot, and that was that. Had there been a less independent-minded spokesman at Downing Street than Sir Kenneth's namesake, William Clark, this attitude of the Prime Minister's might well have also found expression at official level. But William Clark, with whom I maintained close contact throughout the crisis, saw his task primarily as ensuring that we were kept as fully informed as was practicable, believing that that was the best way to secure fair coverage. One or two minor complaints, chiefly about points of emphasis, were relayed by him to me, but we sorted them out quickly at the time. Only one complaint was of any substance, and it proved to arise from a BBC item wrongly attributed to ITN. I suspected that the origin of these protests was Lady Eden, who was an avid watcher of television – a rare activity in Whitehall in those days.

19

'News to Fit the Medium'

By mid-December, when the pressure at last eased off, and we were able to study the viewing figures, it was clear that we had held the audience throughout the Suez and Hungarian crises. In the areas where both ITV and the BBC could be seen, on average 55 per cent of the viewers had watched our main bulletins, even though BBC News had been on the air fifteen minutes ahead of us. We had laid the bogey that in a major crisis the audience might turn back to the BBC. We had scored with the critics, too. The *Sunday Times* noted that 'ITN did well to get back the first moving pictures from Port Said.'[1] Even the BBC's own journal, *The Listener*, was on our side. It praised the BBC's use of the radio telephone to bring in spoken reports from capitals around the world, but added, 'but it did not bring us pictures as graphic or as red hot topical as those of the Budapest funerals or the rebels digging up the street with their hands to get at secret police in their basement hiding place. These were ITA picture scoops.'[2] The *Sunday Times* also praised the BBC's radio network, but commented, 'ITN lacks these facilities, but they go some way to making up the leeway by the zest with which they go out after a telling interview. They don't lose a moment. Nobody is too high and mighty to be approached, and their interviewers are up to the job of asking the hard questions with dead pan tenacity – that difficult sort of objective neutrality which is yet not nerveless nor flaccid. It makes for lively bulletins.'[3]

The constant pressure of major news throughout the five months since Nasser had nationalised the Suez Canal had hardened and sharpened our bulletins into a form which was not only to endure for some years ahead within ITN, but which was to influence the format of BBC bulletins and to have repercussions on television news presentation in many other countries. Suez and Hungary were the crucible in which television news was to be shaped for a decade.

The central feature of our format was the use of the film camera to catch the sight, and if possible the sound of events as they happened. These weeks in which great news stories had come racing towards us like ocean breakers had reinforced the primacy of the camera as the key reporting instrument for television. One basic rule had emerged to guide television News Editors – to thrust the cameras as quickly as possible into the heart of the news. 'Get there fustest with the mostest men' had been the maxim of the Confederate cavalry leader, General Jeb Stuart. 'Get there fastest with the mostest cameras' was an equally good maxim for this new journalism. Gray and Page had set a tradition which was to endure, so much so that when two decades later Turkish paratroops dropped into Northern Cyprus they found an ITN crew awaiting them at their landing point.

Suez and Hungary had also shown that the technique of newscasting, as distinct from newsreading, could measure up to news of serious import. Its more personalised style had not cost us authority or impact. It had indeed strengthened our contact with the audience. John Beavan, the London Editor of the *Manchester Guardian,* had noted this. Reviewing the week's television for the *Spectator,* he wrote, 'The last item was another moving newsreel from the Hungarian frontier. At the end of it Ludovic Kennedy spoke one simple sentence about this concluding the news for the night. Kennedy did not conceal, as a BBC announcer would instinctively have done, that the film had affected him as deeply as it had us. Here I think is the real difference between the BBC and ITV News. The BBC announcer is a real purveyor of information. The ITV newscaster shares the news with the viewers.'[4]

We had increased our newscaster team by two new men. Huw Thomas, a young Welsh barrister, dark and handsome, proved to have an almost three-dimensional quality for projecting himself on television. Even when nervous – and he suffered acutely from nerves in his early broadcasting days – he seemed to come out of the screen, right into one's living room, radiating warmth and sincerity. Antony Brown, who worked for us on a freelance basis, was a quieter man, less assertive in personality, but an admirably clear presenter of news, an excellent counterpart to the more forceful figures of Day and Kennedy. Brown's quiet manner was deceptive, for he was a playwright of quality, and in later years was to prove an excellent anchor man for investigative programmes on Tyne Tees Television.

This widened newscasting team proved able to sustain the note of relaxed professionalism, of combining authority with ease of manner, which Christopher Chataway had struck so early in ITN's development. An important element in its appeal in those days of clearer class distinction was that we spoke to our audience in a tone and in a manner which, if not class-less, was not noticeably upper class, was not the voice of the officers addressing the Other Ranks, of Them talking to Us. Robin Day had no trace of the strangled vowels or manifest condescension which marked the speech of so many men in public life at that time. Ludovic Kennedy was an Old Etonian, but so confidently and unselfconsciously so that he made class seem irrelevant. Huw Thomas's voice retained just enough of his Welsh origins as to be hard to place in the English class spectrum. He had grown up as a Welsh speaker. When I once showed some impatience with his tendency to stress unduly 'the' and 'a' (a widespread broadcasting fault to this day) he protested, 'But it's not my native language.' George Ffitch had come from an East London grammar school. Reginald Bosanquet had had some years at school in Canada to offset his Wykehamist background. All in all ITN presented on the screen little of the formal, middle-to-upper class, Oxford-accented man who in those days embodied the Establishment. By accident as much as by design ITN sounded and looked something new in broadcasting. We appeared as a group of outsiders who had got inside, and who were now telling those still outside what was going on, a group with whom the general public could readily feel in touch.

One invaluable by-product of the Suez-Hungary months was the added vitality and zest which became apparent in every part of the bulletins, as our confidence grew and as it became plain that the public liked and the professionals respected what we had to offer. As so often happens in journalism, the excitement of covering a big story spilt over into other parts of the enterprise, so that the whole product improved. This showed itself not only in the interviewing and the writing, but in flashes of humour, all the more valuable when the news was grim. In mid-October, just as Suez moved towards its climax, we had filmed a hat show. Those were the days when most women wore hats – as indeed did most men until a bare-headed young President of the United States changed things – and the seasonal hat shows were part of the news. Into the predictable script – 'Anne, in a neat black straw model for street wear' – came the surprising words, 'This is Marie, Flaxman 2237 . . . Oh, sorry, I don't think that was meant to be read.' Carefully rehearsed, skilfully read, this apparent slip was all the more effective for also being manifestly contrived.

Five months of almost continual pressure of major news was fatiguing as well as fulfilling for our small editorial staff. Just how hard-pressed they were was borne in on me one afternoon in mid-October. Arthur Clifford, his face unusually worried, told me he had an excellent story on offer, but no one to cover it. A male boa constrictor had escaped from a pet shop in South London and lodged itself in a drain. To lure it out a keeper from the London Zoo was on his way to the scene with a female boa constrictor. We had a camera crew en route, but no reporter. The only one who might have been available was Bosanquet, and he was enjoying a rare day off duty, which he refused to interrupt.

Would I ring Reggie and ask him to do this job? I realised that Clifford would not have put this request to me unless he were really up against it. He was the last man to ask anyone to share the burdens of his job. So I rang Reggie. He made a very reasonable case against breaking into his free day. He had worked seventeen days on the trot – and 'on the trot' with Arthur Clifford needed to be taken literally. He wanted to take his daughter out for a rare treat. We did not pay overtime for such work – all we offered was the distant promise of time off in lieu.

But I shared Arthur's desire to secure this lighter story to balance the gloom and doom which filled the bulletins, and I urged Reggie to make this one further effort. With a sigh he agreed. I nodded to Clifford that all was well. 'Before you hang up, let me have one word with him,' was Arthur's reaction. When he took over the phone, he was warm in his thanks, and then said, 'And I want you to wear an old sports jacket. Why? Because I want a shot of you with the bloody snake around your neck.'

It was in this period too that Lynne Reid Banks established herself as television's first woman reporter. Barbara Mandell continued to do some work in front of the cameras, but we needed her even more behind the scenes as a scriptwriter. Lynne had originally been engaged to cover the arts and show business, but our shortage of staff meant that she carried her share of work of all kinds. With her wide-set eyes, good-humoured mouth and sharp intelligence, she soon became an important element in our screen persona, coached, encouraged, chided and praised by Arthur Clifford, for whom she would have tackled any task on earth. She had got an early scoop from the Soviet Deputy Premier, Malenkov, by the simple process of pushing through the crowd outside the House of Commons and thrusting a microphone under his nose. Finding this charming girl in front of him, Malenkov made a quick politician's speech, which his interpreter translated, and Lynne Reid Banks had an interview without asking a single question.

The range and style of her work can be seen from an article she wrote at the beginning of 1957:

> 'Thanks to the Bolshoi,' she wrote, 'ballet really hit the headlines in 1956. I spent days in and around Covent Garden interviewing gallery queues, officials and commissionaires.
>
> 'At last the corps de ballet arrived, hundreds of them, shabby, weary and uncomprehending. In the crimson and gilt foyer of the Opera House, Margot Fonteyn greeted Ulanova, and what a contrast they made. Dame Margot, sparkling like a handful of jewels, all diamonds and jet and scarlet silk; Ulanova, unmade-up, her pale gentle eyes circled with tiredness, incongruous amid the plush and crystal in her putty-coloured mac and clumsy shoes.
>
> 'On the first night when all the glitter and glamour had been swallowed up in the dark breathless auditorium, my secret hope was fulfilled. I was told I might stand at the back of the circle. I watched Ulanova, incredibly transformed from a colourless middle-aged woman into a soaring goddess.'

Of another evening's work she wrote:

> 'As I was leaving the office, we learnt that a jet plane had crashed in a Kent village. I drove most of the way, the "meat waggon", as we called the lighting truck, skidding and jolting through the dark. I hated the journey, and feared what we'd find at the end of it.
>
> 'We arrived at last. The plane had crashed into a store after tearing the tops off some little houses, and they were all still burning. The street was a morass of mud and glass, snaked with firemen's hoses: through the streaming rain and hot flying cinders, the blaze lit up the sky and silhouetted hurrying, shouting figures.
>
> 'We found a fireman, who had stopped work long enough to have his cut face dressed, to tell us what he had seen and done. Two hours later the film was on the ITN screens.'[5]

When the newspapers came to assess television at the year's end, they reinforced the approval we had won over Suez and Hungary. 'Consistently the news had led not only its BBC rivals, but most of the programmes around it,' wrote Bernard Levin of the *Manchester*

Guardian.[6] The *Spectator* declared, 'ITN . . . have for the first time presented news to fit the medium, rather than ignoring the camera while reading the news. The considerable improvement in the BBC's standards is largely due to ITN's splendid pioneering work.'[7] They made pleasant reading within an organisation not yet two years old.

20

Truly Live Television

The New Year was barely under way when another big story hit us. Sir Anthony Eden's strength gave out, and on 9th January he resigned the Premiership. It gave us our first chance to use an Outside Broadcast unit on a continuing story. A-R stationed one in Downing Street – we of course had none of our own – and John Hartley reported from there at intervals. Maurice Wiggin in the *Sunday Times* found this to his taste: 'Mr Macmillan didn't actually appear in Downing Street, but it is fun to have a look with the crowd. You get a sense of the stir of history; half baked, second hand, superficial, still it's better than none. The man with the mike picked on an individual with a deer-stalker. He was not as hot on the trail as Holmes. At 7.30 he was still waiting to learn who was going to be PM when the ITN man told him. "Oh dear," he said. "Bristol University won't like that at all."'[1]

This gave us good material for the bulletins. But we needed to amplify it with comment and discussion. I cleared with Rediffusion that we could over-run – and indeed we were to extend that bulletin to a record length of thirty-five minutes – and set to work to gather in some commentators. My efforts were to land me, and ITN, in some strange goings-on both on and off the screen.

Randolph Churchill was one obvious choice. He knew Macmillan well, and had been the only journalist, apart from Guy Eden of the *Daily Sketch,* to forecast his appointment. Randolph could wreck any discussion in which he took part, yet he could also make it by the excitement and unpredictability he exuded. I had known him since wartime days in the Middle East, and was on the list of people he greeted with bantering abuse. I rang him in Suffolk. 'I don't like your bloody programme,' was his reply. 'But since no one else has asked me to appear, I'll come.'

Though it was still early afternoon, there was a hint in Randolph's voice that the champagne was already flowing in East Bergholt to celebrate this famous victory. I decided I had better flank him with some others who knew the new Premier. So we enlisted General Gale, who had served with Macmillan in North Africa, and Lord Bessborough, another of Macmillan's wartime aides, and who was now a director of ATV. One other administrative detail was quickly arranged. By chance Randolph Churchill's former secretary, Mary Lennon, was now secretary to Norman Dickson, our General Manager. Randolph had asked that she be available to type any last-minute notes for him. She agreed to stay until 10 p.m., when her last train went.

By ten o'clock, however, Randolph had not arrived. Calls from East Bergholt had indicated that he was running late and, unless I misunderstood the hints, running a shade under the weather. When he finally arrived – as the bulletin rehearsal was under way – it was clear that this was the case. He was furious to find that he was not to be alone on the programme, and doubly furious to find on the premises Tom Driberg, who had come in to record a comment in his role as Chairman of the Labour Party. Randolph seized from me the whisky bottle which I was hastily trying to get back into the cupboard unnoticed, poured himself half a tumbler of neat spirit, and drank it on the spot. Still rumbling with anger, he took his place in the small, crowded, hot studio just before the opening titles came up on the screen.

When the bulletin ended, and cameras swung to Randolph to begin the discussion, his face was not only gleaming with perspiration, but his eyes rolled as he sought to focus on the camera lens. The last item in the bulletin had been Tom Driberg's comment. It did not much matter, Driberg suggested, who led the Tory Party, as, since Suez, the moral leadership of the country rested with the Labour Party. Randolph's first words were directed to this.

'Who,' he declared, in magnificently rounded tones, as if addressing a public meeting, 'who is Mr Driberg to start talking about moral' – and he gave the word massive emphasis – 'about moral leadership?'

Robin Day then asked each of the panel in turn for their estimation of Harold Macmillan as a man. Lord Bessborough praised Macmillan the statesman; General Gale, Macmillan the frontline soldier. 'The men loved him. He had the common touch,' Gale concluded.

'The common touch!' Randolph broke in. 'That's the kind of bloody fool thing a General like you would say. He had the uncommon touch,' and with a superbly histrionic gesture he underlined with his voice the prefix 'un', sweeping his hand up from near the floor to high above his head. 'The uncommon touch – and that is what we need.'

Robin sought to restore the situation by asking Randolph Churchill what he thought would be the chief change we would see at Downing Street now that Mr Macmillan had replaced Sir Anthony Eden. The reply was swift. 'The country will no longer be run by a woman.'

Robin moved with comparable swiftness. 'Mr Churchill,' he said, 'I think we can leave Lady Eden out of this.' In all his long career of broadcasting, I doubt if Robin Day has ever done a better job than in that retort. In ten brief words he knocked on the head the thought, which must have occurred to most viewers, that Randolph Churchill was implying that Eden was either effeminate, or as weak as a woman was then assumed to be. That was not Randolph Churchill's intention. His reply was meant to signal his belief that Lady Eden's Churchillian blood – she was Sir Winston's niece – had led her to play too large a role behind the scenes at Downing Street. Randolph went on to widen the target of his criticism. 'At last we will be governed by a grown-up, instead of all the babies who have inflicted themselves on us in the past.'

After ten minutes Robin brought the discussion to an end. He had carried ITN's reputation in his hands throughout that perilous discussion, and had never let it slip for an instant. The General and the Earl did not linger afterwards, but Randolph, Robin and the production team gathered in my room to demolish the rest of the whisky. Randolph was still in fighting mood. When Norman Dickson told him, 'Mary was sorry not to be able to stay, but she had to leave at ten to get her train,' Randolph countered thickly, 'Mary, Mary, who the hell is Mary?'

'Mary Lennon, your former secretary, now mine,' Norman explained.

'Good God!' exploded Randolph. 'Are you one of those bloody people who call their secretaries by their Christian names? You mean Miss Lennon.'

Norman Dickson was a big man, who had played rugger for Watsonians, and he was not going to take this. He hit Randolph hard, not on his face, but on the chest. He fell back on the couch, shook himself, and came out, fists up. Robert Verrall and I moved in, peace was restored, and the whisky bottle circulated again. Randolph got immersed in an argument with Robin Day about Anthony Eden, and it was nearly midnight before we shepherded him downstairs and into a waiting cab. He collapsed on the back seat and uttered one word which might well have formed the final line of a chapter from an Evelyn Waugh novel. 'White's,' he said. And the cab driver, well versed in London's clubland, drove off without a moment's hesitation.

I drove home through the deserted streets of North London with plenty to occupy my mind. Had we, in this one dramatic but shambolic discussion, undone much of the good of the past year? Were we going to be assailed by the papers for having treated a major event in the nation's life as a fit topic for a bear garden? Were the phones going to be busy as infuriated political dignitaries got on to their friends in the programme companies and the ITA? Could I indeed hold my job if such a storm blew up? Those were the days when editors were fired with a rapidity and a capriciousness confined in later years to football managers. I consoled myself with the thought that if this did mean the end of the chapter for me, we had got one or two good things down on its pages.

When I got into the office the next morning my worst fears seemed about to be realised. Sir Robert Fraser, my worried secretary told me, had already rung twice. Would I ring him right back? I took a deep breath, and did so. 'Ah, Geoffrey,' his quiet voice began. 'Are you aware that you broke the Act last night – and broke it seriously?'

Phrases from Section 3 leapt in my mind. 'Offensive to public feeling'; lack of 'necessary balance' – no doubt we were guilty of them all. Which one did they plan to hit me with?

'Yes,' Fraser continued. 'You were seriously in breach of the Act by putting a director of a programme company on the air to speak on a matter of public policy. Lord Bessborough is a director of ATV, and you had no right to put him on the air.'

Relief flooded through me. If that was all that was worrying the Authority, then we were in the clear. I munched an appropriate portion of humble pie, and put down the phone. A moment later Arthur Clifford was in the room, carrying in triumph the early edition of the *Evening Standard*. Peter Ustinov had given us a rave review. 'Intensely amusing, unpredictable, alive, even if it did reveal more about Mr Churchill than about Mr Macmillan . . .' read the assessment.

'Randolph, flushed perhaps with triumph after his brilliant scoop for the *Evening Standard* yesterday, banged his spoon on the arm of his high chair, and poured abuse on little brother Driberg, as he told the watching world that he wanted to be governed by a grown-up after all the babies who had in the past inflicted themselves on his patience.' When at the weekend the *Observer* declared that ITN had 'established their usual lead over the BBC's News Department in handling the picking of the new Premier', and the *Sunday Times* declared bluntly that 'ITN beat the BBC on the big story', I knew we had skirted one more precipice safely.

21

'Roving Report'

In March 1957 we secured for the first time a chance to produce a weekly news in depth programme to flank the daily news bulletins. Whether the organisation which provided the daily news should also produce current affairs and news in depth programmes had by then become a lively issue in broadcasting, and has remained one ever since. In journalistic terms the issue did not arise. In newspapers the news pages and the feature pages have always come under the ultimate control of one individual, the Editor. In American broadcasting no such division has arisen. The News Departments of all three United States networks control current affairs and documentaries as well as daily news. In Britain the split first occurred because, in the Twenties, the newspapers had been able to prevent the BBC from gathering its own news. This left the Talks Department as the one BBC body free to deal with current affairs, which it gathered under its hand. Within television this artificial separation was intensified by a clash of personalities. Under the cautious leadership of

Tahu Hole, BBC News moved slowly into television, leaving the way open for the more dashing Grace Wyndham Goldie, as head of Television Talks, to seize much of the no-man's-land which exists between what is clearly news and what is clearly current affairs. In particular she appropriated for 'Panorama' and 'Tonight' the task of probing news in depth which in radio had been done by the News Division in 'Radio Newsreel'.

When competition got under way in 1955, this division of functions was carried over into Independent Television, where it fitted only too well the structual division between the companies and ITN. Crawley had hoped, and had indeed been led to believe, that ITN would be charged not only with covering the daily news, but with interpreting it in a weekly news programme on the lines of his highly-successful 'Viewfinder' programme. So sure was he that this would come about that one of the arguments he advanced to me for my joining ITN as a newscaster in 1955 was that he and I could alternate in presenting this weekly news programme. But in that first traumatic autumn the task of producing a weekly news programme went to Associated Rediffusion, who brought into being 'This Week'. Sir Robert Fraser supported this allocation of functions. 'Documentaries and news features are the consciences of the programme companies,' he told me at a later stage. 'If these were taken away from the companies, and given to ITN, the companies would be only entertainment-makers, entirely given over to the show-biz mind.'[1]

During my first eighteen months in Kingsway I was too busy grappling with the task of turning news into television to have any territorial ambitions in current affairs. When, however, early in 1957 Rediffusion asked us to provide them with a weekly programme on foreign affairs, I accepted at once. The chance came our way because the Postmaster General had agreed that the Toddlers' Truce should end, so allowing the broadcaster to put out programmes between 6 p.m. and 7 p.m., the hour which had been kept bare on television to enable children to be put to bed, or perhaps even to read a book. This ruling was made abruptly, and both the BBC and ITV had to do some rapid planning. The BBC decided to let Donald Baverstock try his hand at a nightly news magazine, and so 'Tonight' came into existence. Within ITV the time was shared out amongst the programme companies, and A-R decided to sub-contract part of theirs to ITN.

Associated Rediffusion envisaged an interpretative programme, with a studio discussion, and perhaps one film item, and had pitched the fee accordingly at the low figure of £600. I decided to give them literally more than they had bargained for. This was an opportunity to treat foreign affairs in a truly television way – and in the way for which ITN had proved itself excellently fitted – by sending a camera crew and a reporter to where the news was. An immediate story cried out for this treatment. The new Prime Minister, Harold Macmillan, was about to leave for Bermuda to meet President Eisenhower for the first Anglo-American top-level talks since the Suez débâcle. If we could get Robin Day and a camera crew into America, to test American feeling towards Britain at this juncture, we would be doing our proper job. Other organisations could look after studio discussions. Our place was out in the field, amidst the news.

To do this, not just once, but for the full thirteen weeks for which we were contracted, called for a producer, and for money – much more than £600 a week. A good producer was available. Michael Barsley, who had been the first head of 'Panorama', had recently parted company with the BBC. He had a daring, if at times zany mind which attracted me. We had him on the job within a couple of days. The money was more difficult. Norman Dickson squeezed another £200 a week out of A-R's Programme Controller, John McMillan, but that was the limit. It was clearly a moment to try John Cotter's contacts again. An airline, which shall remain for ever nameless, gave us a free return passage to New York for Robin Day, if we allowed their aircraft to be seen on the film. CBS organised a camera crew for us at a specially cheap rate. Robin, knowing Washington and New York well from his days there with the British Information Service, worked fast. When Hubert Humphrey, a member of the Senate Foreign Relations Committee, could not spare us time for a formal interview, Robin talked to him on the little underground train which connects the Senate offices with the Capitol, adding in the process a far more interesting background than the normal static office scene. In New York Day met Mike Wallace, then famed as the rudest interviewer on American television, and out-interviewed him, opening with the question, 'Is it true that you earn £150,000 a year for hitting below the belt?' In Central Park he posed a dazzling blonde against a background of skyscrapers for an interview, and disclosed that she was not only the CBS weather forecaster, but was also a Mormon missionary. In Grand Central Station and at the top of the Empire State Building he applied our technique of street interviews to test the American reaction to Suez and to Britain. Within three days he was back in London with the film.

When Michael Barsley and I viewed it, I disliked only one sequence. In it two middle class American matrons showed themselves blissfully unaware of any Bermuda Conference, or of Suez, or of anyone called Harold Macmillan. This seemed to me trivial and irrelevant, and I ruled that we should drop it. Michael Barsley skilfully ensured that, for technical reasons, it became impossible for him to execute my ruling – my first experience of a long-established BBC technique for outwitting the man above you. When I saw the item on the screen I saw that Barsley had, in fact, been right, but I stressed that one such manœuvre was enough. Barsley countered by sending me Bernard Levin's review of the programme. 'The two charming ladies,' Levin wrote, 'scarcely seemed to know what or where the United States was, let alone what this nice young Englishman with the American spectacles was wanting. Now as a contribution to a discussion on American views or world affairs, the two ladies were absolutely null; but as television they were memorable. Some genius (Mr Day? Mr Barsley? Mr Cox?) insisted they stay in.'[2] I recognised I had not only hired a skilled producer, but a skilled publicist.

We called the programme 'Roving Report'. After we had put out that first edition John McMillan telephoned me. 'That was very good,' he said. 'But how are you going to keep it up?'

How indeed? We had spent on that first edition, even with our free air travel, some £1800, the fees for nearly three programmes. But there could be no retreat to a studio discussion. We had to bluff, wangle or force a way forward. We did so by stretching to the full the requirement of the Television Act that all advertising must be clearly labelled as such, and set apart from programmes. We interpreted this as allowing us to take free air travel, free sea travel, and any other facility we could get in return for showing discreetly (we hoped) the aircraft or ship in our film. We stretched the definition of foreign affairs (for we were strictly warned off covering home events, which were the preserve of 'This Week') to cover home-based foreign stories, such as American air bases in Britain, or the revived idea of a Channel tunnel. Rediffusion also allowed us to count a special programme on the Budget as a 'Roving Report'.

It had more than its share of problems. Rediffusion had stationed an OB camera at the door of Television House to enable Robin Day to interview passers-by on the Budget. But when we came on the air just after 6 p.m. the street was empty. It was a cold, wet night, and the few people who came into view were in no mood to stop and be interviewed. So a barrister who had come along to see this strange new world into which his friend Robin Day had strayed found himself being interviewed at length. Day then turned to the only other figure in sight, an ever-cheerful newspaper seller with a pitch outside Television House. He proved to be a television natural, who responded by tearing the Budget to bits with copious use of Cockney slang.

With that hurdle surmounted, Day moved towards the doorway and the lift, ready to mount to the eighth floor and take the chair in a studio discussion. To give him time to get there, we had organised an item from Birmingham. But there was a muddle about lines to the Midlands, and the Birmingham report was lost. The only course was for the newscaster, Huw Thomas, to chair the discussion until Day arrived. But Thomas, busy with a complicated bulletin, did not know the names of all the panel. Earpieces for newscasters had not then been invented. The only way a message could be got to Thomas was for the Floor Manager to creep across the floor, out of camera range, and slip a note on to his desk. There was however a complication about this, for the Floor Manager, Diana Edwards-Jones, had just come back from a skiing holiday with one leg in plaster. The astonished panel – but not the viewers – saw her suddenly sink to the floor, drag herself across the studio, and push a note on to Huw Thomas's desk. Throughout all this Frank Cousins, the one member of the panel Thomas recognised, sustained a denunciation of the Budget without any hint of what was going on at his feet. A couple of minutes later a breathless Robin Day was on hand to take over.

Our most useful device for stretching the funds allocated to 'Roving Report' was to have long-term implications for programme-making. We found that if we combined making a travelogue with making a news report when we went overseas, we could get two programmes for the travel costs of one. When Bosanquet went to Kenya, for instance, he combined his news report on Kenya's moves towards independence with extra programmes on the game parks and on the Masai tribe. 'Travelogue' was at that time a dirty word among documentary makers, largely because it was associated with the uncritical, saccharine, publicity-drenched cinema travel films of Edward G. Fitzgerald ('And so we say farewell to sunny Hawaii . . .' or Naples, or Morocco, or Singapore). The oncoming generation of documentary producers wanted none of this. They wanted to exploit the newly-opened seams of social and economic investigation. I did not share this scorn for travel films, particularly at a moment when package holidays were getting under way, and when people sought information about places they might visit. So I set 'Roving Report' the subsidiary goal of making the travelogue respectable. By candid, mature commentaries, by trying to convey the whole scene, and not just the picture postcard aspects of it, we gradually did this. When in time the Alan Whickers, the Trevor Philpots and Fyfe Robertsons moved into this field, 'Roving Report' had ensured that the rehabilitation of the travelogue was well under way.

Barsley brought to the programme not only an unquenchable, quirky zest, but a capacity to write clear, stylish, often witty English, which gave the commentaries distinction and sophistication. With his broad forehead, large glasses, and wide gourmet's mouth, he had an air half clerical, half worldly. One could envisage him as an energetic lay brother in a medieval monastery, keeping the accounts and chivying the tenants, and trading theological arguments with the brothers at the same time as ensuring that they had good food and very good wine. He did not always share my views on impartiality, which led us into occasional passages at arms. After one or two programmes which had led to argument, he produced at Christmas time a travel programme on the Holy Land. When it was over I rang through to the control room, offered my congratulations and a comment that at least that was one programme where no problems of impartiality arose. The reply was quickly forthcoming: 'I would not be too sure. We've just had a call from a man called Pontius Pilate who says he demands a right of reply.'

'Roving Report' was to remain, except for one break of three months, an integral part of ITN's output for the next seven years, after which it was to merge into 'ITN Reports', before being absorbed into 'News at Ten'. Even that did not bring its life to an end. ITN's international newsfilm subsidiary UPITN took over the title in 1967 and has continued to make the programme for sales overseas. For many television stations, particularly those in smaller countries which can afford to make few documentaries themselves, it is an important element in their schedules – a development which was certainly unforeseen when on that morning in March 1957 Robin Day hurried off to Heathrow to take a plane to New York.

22

The Nasser Interview

'Roving Report' gave ITN not only an important new programme, but also enabled us to undertake wider and deeper coverage of foreign affairs for the bulletins. This was shown most vividly in June 1957, when we secured the first interview with President Nasser which he had given to any British or American journalist since the Suez fighting had ended six months earlier. It was a scoop which not only filled the headlines of the British press, but which carried ITN's name around the world.

It was not an easy interview to arrange. Though no state of war existed between Britain and Egypt – indeed none had ever been declared – all diplomatic relations between the two countries had been broken off. To a large part of the British public Nasser was seen as a dangerous if somewhat contemptible enemy, a man whose actions Sir Anthony Eden had likened to those of Hitler. British lives had been lost in opposing him, British prestige badly damaged in our efforts to oust him. At this moment two British businessmen, Mr Stanley and Mr Pittuck, were on trial for their lives in Cairo, accused of acting as spies. To bring Nasser on to the British screen could seem like treating with an enemy.

Against this was the fact that six months had elapsed since Suez, during which tempers had cooled. I sensed that despite all that Eden and others had said, Nasser had never quite rated a place in the popular demonology of the country's enemies. Egypt was known at first hand to hundreds of thousands of wartime troops and post-war National Servicemen. It did not seem truly a foreign country, more a colony which had broken away. There would be a genuine public interest in seeing and assessing this man who had so recently been portrayed as Public Enemy No. 1. If we were busy proclaiming the virtues of television as a means of truly understanding those in power, Nasser was surely a proper subject for interview.

All of this was true provided the interview was forthright, and done on our terms. If we merely appeared as giving Nasser a chance to use the screen for propaganda, we would be excoriated by a large section of the public – not least by the large section of the working class whose reaction to Suez had been instinctively patriotic. On the other hand, if we antagonised Nasser by clumsy or discourteous questioning, we could further damage relations with Egypt, and be blamed for doing so.

I was confident Robin Day could walk the narrow path between these two dangers, provided we secured from the outset the agreement of President Nasser that he would be interviewed on the same basis as we had established with British politicians, with no areas of questioning excluded. We must be free to ask all the questions which were uppermost in the minds of the British public. On that basis, I gave approval for the project.

We got in touch with Nasser's office through the Indian High Commission in London. Within a few days an answer came back from Cairo. President Nasser would be prepared to be interviewed on the terms we had set out. If we sent our reporter and camera team to Amsterdam, visas would be issued there, and they could travel by KLM to Cairo. Within a few days the project was under way.

All now depended upon the way the interview was conducted. No one could share with Robin the responsibility which would settle on his shoulders when he found himself face to face with Nasser, under the eyes and ears of the cameras, and, ultimately, of the world. But we could help him prepare. George Ffitch and I took it in turns to sit in as Nasser, answering questions which Robin put to us, trying to parry his supplementary questions, working over the facts of Egypt's situation, and above all her relations with Britain, with Israel and the Soviet Union. Few interviews can have been so thoroughly prepared.

I had decided early in the project not to inform the Foreign Office of what we were up to. They could not help; they might well seek to hinder. At best, prior knowledge would be an embarrassment to them. It was only, however, when Robin and the crew – Cyril Page as cameraman, Ronnie Hubbard as recordist – were in Amsterdam waiting to take off, that I realised that I had not told the ITA either. I rang Sir Robert Fraser. As always, where matters of journalistic judgement were concerned, he reacted with the cool head of an old Fleet Street hand. He saw no reason to intervene. It was justifiable journalistic enterprise. But he urged me, once the crew were under way, to advise the Foreign Office. I did so. They were magisterially aloof.

A couple of hours before the team were due to leave Amsterdam, the Chief Sub came hurrying into my room, his face grave. He put on my desk a slip of agency copy from Cairo. The trial of the two Britons had come to its conclusion more rapidly than had been expected. Both Stanley and Pittuck had been found guilty of espionage, and sentenced to death. The sentence had been passed to President Nasser for his confirmation.

It posed a hideous new complication. If the sentence was confirmed – and Israelis similarly convicted of spying had been executed – we could, by interviewing Nasser, be seen as shaking hands with a murderer, for this is certainly how the British public would have reacted. Yet if I cancelled the interview at this late stage, that might well fuel Nasser's anger, and influence him to go ahead with the hanging. I decided the second was the greater danger, and sent a message to Amsterdam for the team to go ahead. But the shock of this turn of events was like a blow in the stomach. I gave up all attempts to work and tried to assuage my anxiety by playing a round of golf with John Cotter at Highgate.

That anxiety persisted throughout the next forty-eight hours. All that we had built up in ITN since 1955 seemed at stake. We had no means of contact with Cairo, no knowledge indeed whether the interview was already under way, whether we were suddenly going to learn that we had interviewed a man who had just sent two Britons to their death. Then, at eight in the morning, my telephone rang at home. The Duty Sub at ITN read me a Reuter cable from Cairo stating that Nasser had commuted the death sentence to a term of imprisonment. We could breathe again.

Nasser kept Robin Day and the crew waiting for a week in the Semiramis Hotel in Cairo before they were summoned to his villa near the pyramids in Giza. During this time Egyptian officials tried to persuade Robin Day not to raise some of the most sensitive issues, and in particular to keep away from Egypt's relations with Israel. To strengthen his hand, should such pressure arise, I had given him in writing authority to pull out of the interview if there was any last-minute attempt to limit his right of questioning. The basis of the interview was still uncertain when the camera team set up their equipment in the garden. Robin Day has given his own account of what followed:

> 'The Egyptian President came walking out into the sunshine with one of his little children . . . I strolled with him in his garden, and explained that I felt it essential to raise certain points in the interview. Before I could go into details he brushed the matter aside, and said he didn't mind what I asked. It was a moment of great relief after the long week of waiting in Cairo, a week of wondering when the interview would be fixed, whether it would ever be fixed at all, and whether I would be prevented, when the time came, from asking vital questions.'[1]

The interview, eighteen minutes in length, arrived back in London in time to be shown on the evening of Monday 1st July. We ran a brief segment of it in the bulletins, followed by the full interview at five minutes past eleven – the best time the programme companies were prepared to allocate. Every paper the next morning carried copious reports. James Cameron, in the *News Chronicle,* saw this as much more than just another journalistic scoop:

> 'Sitting in the garden of his Cairo home,' he wrote, 'President Nasser leaned forward last night into British television screens.
>
> 'And he asked that we reunite in friendly relations. He did thus something that has never been done before in the history of international diplomacy.
>
> 'For the first time on record a national leader, submitting a major point of national policy, by-passed all protocol and sent his message directly into the homes of another state – at a time when the two were not in diplomatic relations.
>
> 'Only on Israel was his composure disturbed. When Day asked him, "Is it right that you now accept the permanent existence of Israel as an independent sovereign state?" Nasser replied, "Well, you know, you are jumping to conclusions." "No," said Day. "I am asking a question." '

The news agencies sought the full text, and circulated much of it around the world. The *Daily Telegraph,* in an editorial entitled 'Foes in the Flesh', approved of both the Nasser interview and of an earlier CBS interview with Khrushchev which we had shown, asking only if it might not have been highly valuable if, during Suez, Robin Day could have grilled Dulles in this way, and if Eden could have spoken to the people in the United States. When *Time* magazine devoted nearly a full column to the story, beginning with the words, 'Sitting before the cameras of Britain's Independent Television News – as Russia's Khrushchev did for CBS in the US – Nasser sent an amiable grimace into several million British living rooms,' we were entitled to claim that ITN had arrived on the world stage. To add to our pleasure the Britons accused of spying were reprieved. On the morning of our interview they were released from prison. Not only had we done them no harm; we might well have helped to secure this release.

It was therefore in a mood of some euphoria that I went off the next night to the party which Elizabeth Taylor and Eddie Fisher were giving in the Battersea Pleasure Gardens to mark the opening of *Around the World in Eighty Days*. It was a soakingly wet night, so wet that the guests were issued with plastic macs, a garb under which even the most glittering celebrities found it hard to maintain their glamour. Yet that made little difference to my sense of well being. I savoured our success all the more because I was well aware that in journalism such moments are transient, that your latest scoop has got at most only a month or two's life in it.

23

The Road to Rochdale

The Suez crisis had one immediate effect on the broadcasting of politics. It brought to an end the Fourteen Day Rule, under which broadcasters were forbidden to discuss any issue which was to be debated in Parliament in the coming fortnight, or to invite any MP to discuss on the air any Bill before the House. The Rule represented Parliament's last effort to keep some grip on the choice of subjects to be broadcast, as distinct from insisting that public issues should be treated impartially. It had come into being after the war, and had at first rested on a gentleman's agreement between the BBC and the political parties. With the coming of ITV it was, however, made into a formal Rule, promulgated by the Postmaster General, Dr Charles Hill, in July 1955.

This re-affirmation owed much to the attitude of Sir Winston

Churchill. He was concerned about protecting the House of Commons against the rise of a rival forum, the television studio. With remarkable prescience he sensed the power of this apparatus which could carry pictures in the corner of every sitting room in the land. He believed that democracy could be endangered if access to it was controlled by people chosen not by public vote but by producers not directly answerable to the electorate. 'It would be a shocking thing,' he said in the Commons debate on the Rule in July 1955, 'to have the debates of Parliament forestalled on this new robot organisation of television and BBC broadcasting.' The rights of Members of Parliament must be protected 'against the mass and against the machine'.

The Suez crisis was too big to be contained within such rules. Every interview we did at London Airport, every report on public reaction, even every street interview was a breach of the Fourteen Day Rule. When the Rule came before the Commons for renewal early in December, Eden yielded to the logic of the situation and abandoned it.

In the aftermath of Suez another more fundamental inhibition on political broadcasting also began to be undermined. This was the taboo on the coverage, during Parliamentary elections, of the arguments of the candidates and of the parties. Ever since 1945 the BBC had confined its coverage of the arguments put forward at elections to a summary of the manifesto of each party, and to the formal party political broadcasts, carefully allocated by agreement amongst those parties with a substantial number of candidates in the field. Apart from these, the only election news was on the movements of Party leaders and candidates and non-contentious information about the number of contestants and the arrangements for polling. Anything which could influence the way people voted was rigorously excluded. This had been sensible enough in the conditions of 1945, when the General Election was conducted whilst we were still at war with Japan, and when opening the air waves to controversy could have had repercussions far beyond our borders. It persisted, however, throughout the General Elections of 1950, 1951 and 1955, surviving even such a manifest absurdity as the banning from BBC news bulletins in 1950 of any reference to a proposal made by Sir Winston Churchill in an election speech at Edinburgh for a Big Three conference on the future of the atom bomb. This decision was described by a leading historian as 'neutrality carried to the lengths of castration'.[1]

One reason why this ban was continued into the Fifties lay in the

Representation of the People Act of 1949. This had set in train a long overdue redrawing of constituency boundaries. It had also cleared up an obscurity about election expenses. There had for many years been legal limits on the amount of money which a candidate might spend in pursuing his campaign. But the growth of the newspapers, with their widespread coverage of elections, had produced a grey area. Was newspaper support for a candidate, or news about him and his activities, to be reckoned as a contribution to his expenses? The 1949 Act ruled clearly that it was not. In clearing up one obscurity, the Act produced another. For it remained silent on whether broadcast coverage was equally exempt – a point which at the time passed unnoticed not only in Parliament, but in the press. Yet the Act as it stood could be taken by any rigidly-minded lawyer – or broadcasting executive – as implying that any reporting of elections on radio or television was an election expense. If this were so, any broadcaster who covered the arguments of an election campaign risked a fine, or even a year in prison.

Independent Television had not been on the air at the time of the General Election in April 1955, and none of the by-elections during 1955 and the early months of 1956 had been of sufficient interest for us to consider reporting their campaigns. Soon after Suez, however, a key by-election was called at Melton in Leicestershire. Not only did it provide the first gauge of public opinion since Suez, but it was in the seat vacated by Sir Anthony Nutting, who had resigned both from the Foreign Office and from Parliament as a protest against Eden's policy. It was clearly a story we should cover.

In planning its coverage I did not take up time seeking a legal ruling on the Representation of the People Act. That did not seem to me the heart of the matter. More important than such legal niceties was the attitude of the main political parties. The experience of four post-war general elections seemed to have confirmed in the minds of politicians the view that broadcasting was too powerful, and too potentially dangerous a force to be set loose at election times, except within the confines of party political broadcasts. So long as this attitude prevailed at Westminster, no progress could be made with the reporting of elections on television, because for that to be done we needed the co-operation of candidates and of Party leaders to bring across the sight and sound of the election debate – and an election is nothing if not a debate. Yet the politicians, if they chose, could effectively veto such coverage simply by refusing to take part in it. Refusal by any one candidate could, moreover, throw our coverage out of balance, and so bring us up against another Act of Parliament whose requirements were clear beyond doubt, the Television Act, with its insistence on impartiality in politics. We had to achieve, therefore, not so much a change in the Representation of the People Act as a change in attitude of the politicians. The first step towards this was to demonstrate that television could cover elections fairly.

Robin Day suggested a way of doing this by stages. We could cover the Melton campaign as if it were just another news story, but hold back the presentation of our report until the late bulletin on polling day. This would give our report immediacy, but would mean that it would not have gone out before the polls closed at 9 p.m., and therefore could not be held to have influenced the result. We would mount, as it were, a dry run of an election report, and broadcast it at a time outside the constraints of the Act.

So Robin Day went off with a camera team into the mists of Leicestershire, to work out a pattern for constituency coverage of elections. A month later George Ffitch repeated the same process in the drab, bomb-damaged streets of South Lewisham, followed by another report set against the hillsides of Carmarthenshire. In these reports we evolved a pattern in which we showed scenes of the constituency to establish its nature; we interviewed voters about the issues; and in particular we interviewed the candidates, securing from them a statement of their policies, so bringing the election argument for the first time clearly to the screen.

The next step was to apply these techniques to reporting an election whilst it was still in progress, by putting out the report some days before the polls closed. Early in 1958 an opportunity offered itself in a by-election at Rochdale. It had caught public attention because Ludovic Kennedy had announced that he was resigning from ITN to fight as the Liberal candidate – the first time that a television personality had turned politician. We were preparing our coverage when a new factor intervened. Granada, within whose transmission area Rochdale lay, invited the three candidates to appear in a series of programmes which they intended to mount. The Labour and Liberal candidates accepted, but the Tories held back whilst they took advice as to whether such appearances would breach the Representation of the People Act. I decided to meet this problem by not carrying the actual voices of the candidates, but by setting out the main points of their election addresses over film of them canvassing. This we blended with film of the constituency, and with interviews with electors about the issues. We got on with this report whilst the lawyers argued. So in our main bulletin on 31st January 1958 the first election report containing the arguments of the contenders in a Parliamentary election, whilst the election was still in progress, appeared on the British screen. *The Times* noted the fact the next day in a paragraph austerely headed 'Interviews by ITN'. The *Manchester Guardian,* under a headline 'Fair Shares at Rochdale', underlined the fact that this was the first ever broadcast of an election campaign:

> 'Whatever the complications to be sorted out by parties, Government and lawyers, the Rochdale by-election went on the screen last night, and ITN gave a substantial slice of politics and opinions in that most independent and "awkward" of Northern towns.
>
> 'The Gothic gloom, the murky sky, the solemn, unshaken face of Rochdale were fairly shared among all three claimants. This was the opening, while George Ffitch, the reporter, stood there amid the mist summarising the parties' claims, fairly, always fairly . . . Then to the man and woman in the street. Here Rochdale showed a confident and canny face: nothing was given away easily. There was the bus conductor who, when asked about international affairs, said, "Well, the atom bomb seems to have something in it." . . . To sum up, ITN's sally into by-election reporting – the first time it has ever been done – could do no harm, and might do much good, if only in making politics a little more real and down-to-earth for people far outside the range of Rochdale.'

Over the weekend the Conservatives decided that it would be proper for their candidate to be heard as well as seen on television, and five days later the first of two Granada election programmes were broadcast. In one the candidates were questioned, each in turn, by a panel of three newspaper editors. In the other each candidate made a statement about his policy, after lots had been drawn to determine the order of speaking. This was accompanied by film of the constituency and interviews with electors along the lines we had already made familiar. These two programmes carried the broadcasting of elections an important stage further. In them for the first time the voices of the candidates were heard arguing their own policies. After Rochdale the right of television and radio to report elections was never in any doubt.

The accuracy of our diagnosis that the key to establishing the right of the broadcasters to cover Parliamentary elections lay less in arguments about the law, and more in convincing the political parties that we could do so fairly (which the early dry-run reports had demonstrated) was emphasised some five and a half years later, when we went ahead with the coverage of a by-election in defiance of one of the candidates. This occurred in the by-election in Perthshire in which Sir Alec Douglas-Home sought a Commons seat after resigning his peerage on being made Prime Minister. There were seven candidates in the field. One of them, the Liberal candidate, refused to allow his meetings to be filmed, and refused to co-operate in any way with the television coverage. He was a local man, Alister Duncan Miller, who had nursed the constituency assiduously over the years. He held that television, with its power to present candidates and issues swiftly to the public, conferred an unfair advantage on newcomers who were contesting the seat without having put in any such ground work. Nothing we said could persuade him to take part in the programme which we had planned.

This was the obstacle we had feared back in 1957 and 1958, but by 1963 the climate of opinion had changed. The televising of politics was by then a commonplace, accepted as a normal part of the political process. We decided therefore to challenge Mr Miller's stance, and prepared a report which included film and interviews with each of the other six candidates including the Prime Minister. We filled the gap left by Mr Miller's refusal by showing a still picture of him, and reading a summary of his policy over it. The Liberal Party protested, but not too much, and accepted the clear victory which Sir Alec Douglas-Home subsequently won. The ITA had supported us in our action, though they banned a later Granada programme which, because the Liberals had refused to co-operate, was about to be presented with the Liberal case going unstated. It was a further small victory for the televising of politics, but it was to prove short-lived. The Representation of the People Act was in due course amended so as to authorise the broadcasting of elections, but also to make it necessary, before any one candidate can appear in a programme about a constituency, for all to be willing to appear.

A fortnight after the Rochdale by-election political broadcasting took another big step forward when for the first time a Prime Minister was interviewed at length on the air. Mr Harold Macmillan, perhaps to offset the defeat his Party had suffered at Rochdale, agreed to be interviewed on the BBC's 'Press Conference' and, three days later, by Robin Day on a new programme we put out early on Sunday evenings called 'Tell the People'.

No previous Prime Minister had been prepared to submit to interrogation outside the House of Commons. Neither Sir Winston Churchill nor Mr Attlee would have contemplated giving an interview on radio, let alone on television, a medium which Churchill regarded as an unworthy upstart. Had he been younger, no doubt he would have mastered it, as he mastered radio. But the added visual dimension was not something which he welcomed. When in 1948 it was suggested that he and Mr Attlee should each make a television broadcast, Churchill spurned the proposal in these words: 'When I was very young, if one said something in one's constituency which might have led to trouble if it was spread abroad, nothing happened. Now one has to weigh every word, knowing all the time that people will be listening all over the country. It would be intolerable if one had to consider also how one would appear, what one would look like all over the land.' He never gave a Party Political Broadcast on television, nor appeared in any television programe – other than when filmed for the news as he went about his business – except to make a brief, moving and unscripted statement to the cameras after watching a BBC programme in which many of his friends paid tribute to him on his eightieth birthday in November 1954.

It was left to Sir Anthony Eden to be the first Prime Minister to grapple with television. Though Eden had used the technique of the direct talk on television as a means of addressing the country on three occasions – once during the visit of Bulganin and Khrushchev, and twice during Suez – he had confined any interviews to brief occasions at London Airport. Harold Macmillan had followed the same pattern. It was in one of these short airport interviews that he had dismissed the resignation of his three Treasury Ministers as 'a little local difficulty'. His readiness to be interviewed at length in February 1958 represented therefore a distinct change of policy towards this new medium.

The Prime Minister's appearance before a team of three journalists on 20th February had made little impact. *The Times* described the BBC inquisitors as 'a restrained group' and the Prime Minister seemed equally restrained in his replies. That was certainly not the case in 'Tell the People'. Mr Macmillan was in good form from the moment when, in black coat and striped trousers, and wearing a red and blue Guards Brigade tie, he walked into ITN. He noted appreciatively that the producer of the day, Robert Verrall, was (by virtue of his wartime service as Sergeant R. Verrall, Welsh Guards) wearing the same tie, and settled himself into a chair beside Robin Day. To facilitate the changeover with the newscaster, whose bulletin would finish in the same studio only a couple of minutes before the interview was due to begin, Day was due to occupy the newscaster's chair, which had a higher back and was altogether grander than that provided for the visitor. Mr Macmillan commented drily on these seating arrangements. Robin Day at once offered to change chairs. 'Not at all, not at all,' insisted the Prime Minister. 'I know my place.'

The interview filled the front pages of the morning papers the next day, chiefly because Robin Day had raised the most sensitive political issue of the moment, the question of whether the Prime Minister had any intention of moving the Foreign Secretary, Mr Selwyn Lloyd, from his post. Though this was being widely canvassed in the papers, the 'Press Conference' panel had not raised it. The Prime Minister took it in his stride, dismissing the idea as being 'not in accordance with my idea of loyalty'. The papers found Mr Macmillan as showing himself 'firm and confident in the face of vigorous cross-questioning, certainly the most vigorous cross-examination a Prime Minister has been subjected to in public.'[2] Mr Macmillan was later to say that it was in this interview that he first felt he had mastered television. Certainly from then on he was readily willing to appear before the cameras, to face up to, in both senses of the word, television as part of the democratic process.

24

New Faces – and New Methods

After the Rochdale by-election Ludovic Kennedy did not return to ITN, but went off to BBC's 'Panorama'. The loss of his stylish authority was a blow, and a warning that the daily bulletins and an under-financed 'Roving Report' offered dangerously little scope to men of talent. But we had a strong replacement to hand. I had invited Ian Trethowan, who had succeeded me as Political Correspondent of the *News Chronicle,* to become a newscaster. He accepted without delay, demonstrating two of the qualities which were to carry him in time to the Director-Generalship of the BBC – decisiveness and a readiness to accept responsibility.

Like many journalists trained to express themselves through their pens rather than their voices, Trethowan was at first somewhat stiff and restrained on the screen. But his natural style gradually asserted itself, until it provided what his former paper, the *Yorkshire Post,* saw as a good counterpart to Robin Day's approach:

> 'Mr Day, his head set deep in his powerful, forward-thrusting shoulders, his chin jutting like a cliff over his polka dotted bow-tie, the bridge of his nose puckered in a frown, is the searching, pointed questioner who seems to drive his man back in his chair.
>
> 'Mr Trethowan sits erect, but not severely, his handsome head set well above his shoulders. He has a remarkably young face, lean but not hungry, with an appealing ghost of a smile which draws the answering smile. He makes a man feel his equal, on occasion charming him to the edge of his chair, eager to tell all.'[1]

In these two men the newscaster system reached a major peak. They embodied the aim which both Crawley and I had sought, to have the daily news presented by authoritative journalists, one trained in newspapers, the other developed in the more rapid forcing house of television itself, who were concerned above all to present and analyse the news, not to add their opinions to it. They were both men of strong opinions, but they accepted fully, as one of the disciplines of their profession, that they should keep these out of the news they presented, that their task was to tell people what had happened, not to tell them what they should feel or think about it.

They were flanked by Huw Thomas and Antony Brown and, on a freelance basis, by Brian Connell. With his beard – a rarity in those days, and to this day a rarity among regular television screen personalities – his touch of Edwardian flamboyance, his beautifully clear diction and his self-confidence, Connell rapidly established himself as a screen figure, recognised by strangers in the street, greeted by every newspaper seller within a mile radius of Kingsway, a favourite subject for cheerful wisecracks from the Covent Garden porters as he walked through the market on his way to ITN.

Connell was an able reporter in the field as well as in the studio, and in the spring of 1958 he carried the use of the sound camera a stage further as a reporting instrument in his coverage of the return of General de Gaulle from his self-imposed political exile in the village of Colombey-les-Deux-Églises. The value of the 16mm camera had been greatly increased by the introduction of magnetic strip recording, under which the sound was recorded on a thin band of magnetic tape running along the edge of the film. This provided a much better quality of sound than had been possible by optical recording, and simplified the editing of the film. Connell used the cameras to turn two news occasions into two television occasions, drawing the viewer into the story by participating in it himself. At the press conference in Paris at which de Gaulle announced his intention to be a candidate for the Presidency in May 1958, Connell stationed himself at one side of the ornate chamber in a position where the camera could depict the General, huge and erect behind the conference table, or pull back to show Connell at one side of the room. Crouching low and speaking low, Connell translated into the microphone, sentence by sentence, the General's speech as he delivered it, giving the story virtually the force of a live outside broadcast. It underlined too our role as a news-gathering organisation. Here was a big occasion – and here was ITN in the thick of it.

Ten days later Connell repeated the process. In the Place de la République a huge demonstration of left-wing parties and trade unionists formed up to oppose de Gaulle and the Army in Algeria. The marchers, twenty abreast, filled the wide boulevard as far as the eye could see. The camera recorded this in long shot, and then moved in towards the politicians and trade union leaders who formed the front row of the marchers. It picked out in their midst the bearded figure of Connell. Microphone in hand, he walked with the leaders, interviewing them as they moved forward, and adding his own commentary as the march advanced. Once again we were giving the news, and giving it from the centre.

Foreign news became dramatic film news again two months later when US Marines moved into the Lebanon to counter a revolutionary crisis in Iraq. The Marines came ashore from their landing craft in classic D-Day style on beaches to the south of Beirut. The Beirut dentist who was also our enterprising local cameraman drove fast to the scene, and arrived in time to film the landings head-on. He caught the moment as the landing craft edged in, dropped their ramps and allowed the Marines, rifles and light machine guns in hand, to pour out through the shallow water and storm ashore, moving towards the camera with their faces set and ready for battle. But there was no battle. The landings not only took place unopposed, but on a holiday beach at the height of the tourist season. Bathers grabbed their towels and watched with astonishment as the Marines moved up the beach, fanned out into the sandhills, and began to dig slit trenches. It was an extraordinary comic opera mixture of the banal and the dramatic. Children, lollipops in hand, stood in wide-eyed groups around troops preparing positions and setting up their machine guns. The inevitable Middle Eastern touts, including even a carpet-seller, were soon on the scene, offering their wares to exasperated and embarrassed Marine officers. The story was rounded off by shots of a powerful column of tanks and armoured troop carriers rolling on towards Beirut, headed by the American Ambassador in a long black Packard with a fluttering Stars and Stripes flag, whilst in the background the mountains of the Lebanon rose against a clear Mediterranean sky.

The Middle East crisis of the summer of 1958 marked a watershed in television journalism. During it, according to a Gallup survey, the public for the first time turned to television as their main source of news. Until then radio and the newspapers had vied for first place. Now research showed that during those tense days it was to television news that the people had turned night after night to learn what was happening. This development may have been accelerated by a recent decision of the BBC Radio to move their main evening news from nine o'clock, the hour hallowed by wartime practice. But it owed most to the growth in the ownership of television sets. Combined television and sound licences now outstripped those for radio alone. Increasingly when people said, 'I heard on the news last night . . .' they were referring to television news. Indeed they now frequently used the words, 'I saw it on the news.'

We now had to be comprehensive as well as vivid, to face every evening the test of having covered all the main news – and covered it in picture. Fortunately the means for doing this had improved steadily throughout the past two years. All over the world cameramen had equipped themselves with the light 16mm cameras suited to television work. The product of their labours could also reach us more quickly. In July 1958 the first Comet airline service had started across the Atlantic, ushering in the age of jet air travel. This speeded up the transit of film, and enabled camera crews to be more rapidly deployed to the scene of the news. To this we added, in the autumn of 1958, the use of the Eurovision network, not only to transmit news, but to allow it to be viewed live.

Plans for a week's trial exchange of daily news between five European countries, including Britain, had been laid for October 1958. Each day at midday the newsrooms of the five were interlocked through the Eurovision control centre at Brussels and each made available its best stories free to the others. Just as this was getting under way, news came from Rome on 6th October that Pope Pius XII had died at his summer home at Castel Gondolfo, in the Alban Hills south of Rome. When his body was carried by road to Rome, RAI, the Italian broadcasting service, stationed their outside broadcast cameras at points along the route, providing coverage which was a blend of Italian showmanship and Roman Catholic ceremonial that was spectacular and yet intensely and sincerely moving. This was the first time since the Coronation in 1953 that Eurovision had been used to cover hard news.

I had travelled this route as an Eighth Army liaison officer on the morning Rome fell on 4th June 1944, making my way alongside the unshaven, dust-grimed American infantry moving forward in single file, as the Sherman tanks nosed forward to reconnoitre each street crossing. Now the cameras were bringing the sight of the Papal cortège, with its long line of dark shining vehicles, moving through lines of darkly-clad onlookers, as sharply as if I were there again. As never before, the force of this new medium was carried in on me. Today we take such live coverage as commonplace, and would be indignant if we could not see every moment of a World Cup football match, or every second of an Olympic final, as it takes place. But that afternoon it was a magical new experience.

Yet of the RAI coverage that October ITV viewers saw only excerpts in the news bulletins, taken either from these OBs (as outside broadcasts were called) or from the Eurovision news exchange. The network was not yet interested in news at length. Of the many hours of pageantry which was also news, as one Pope was honoured in death, and another selected, only some fifteen minutes in all reached our screens, in two- or three-minute excerpts in the bulletins.

The European newsrooms continued to exchange their daily news film intermittently throughout 1959. In May 1961 the exchange was put on a regular basis, with a daily closed circuit transmission at 17.00 hours Central European Time, on which each European station offered its best news stories. In 1968 this was supplemented by a further exchange two hours later in the evening, and in March 1974 by a third exchange at noon. These developments owed much to the enterprise of the RAI cameramen in the sunlight of that Roman autumn.

When Fidel Castro finally won power in Cuba in January 1959 we were presented with a new editorial problem. For the first time we had on film the scene of an execution, of the deliberate taking of human life. A former police chief of the Batista regime had been sentenced to death. The CBS cameraman had shown him, in trousers and white shirt, hands bound, being taken in an open truck to a field. There he was tied to a post and blindfolded. Half-a-dozen troops lined up a few yards away, an officer's voice rang out and they fired. The policeman's body gave one sudden lunge, and then slumped in its bonds. The officer walked across, held a revolver to the lolling head and fired one final shot.

The moment of death, the sudden transformation of this living, if pinioned and helpless human being, into a sack-like object, was all the more hideous because one knew, up to the second, that it was coming. It conveyed a sense of drama, but also of shame, of the stirring of the basest of human instincts, the making of a spectacle of a fellow human being deprived of life. I decided that we would show all the sequences except the actual moment of death, when the bullets thudded into the tethered body. We had done away with public executions in Britain nearly two centuries previously. I saw no reason to restore them to the public gaze – and to the gaze in the sitting room, rather than at Tyburn or New Palace Yard.

It is a ruling which was to prevail in ITN when other such film reached us from other revolutions and other wars. I saw no reason to change it, even when other producers across the years have thought differently. Indeed one ITV current affairs programme a few weeks later showed the full Cuban execution sequence; another a year or so later equally gave every moment of the shooting, in a public execution in a street in Saigon, of a group of black marketeers. In the wider context of a current affairs programme these sequences had somewhat less shock effect than when packed into the confines of a news bulletin, where they were viewed alongside other very different news items. Even so, I held to my view that they had no place on the television screen.

25

News Is Costly

Expansion of film coverage posed for ITN serious problems of finance. Film is expensive; foreign film is even more expensive; and foreign film shot with a reporter's commentary, on a sound camera, is very expensive. When we sent Martin Gray to Budapest in 1956 we had to meet the cost only of his one air fare, with perhaps some extra payment for excess baggage for his camera gear. When a sound crew went abroad, however, we had to pay for four places on the aircraft – one for the cameraman, one for the recordist, one for the reporter, and the equivalent of a fourth for the gear. Their hotel bills, their local travel, their entertaining and general expenditure all mounted sharply; the modest sums allocated for film coverage in our budgets had proved no longer adequate. By the summer of 1958 the cost of the news service, which had been the cause of Aidan Crawley's resignation in 1956, had once again become a central issue for the ITN Board.

Six companies were now represented on the ITN Board. To the original four network companies had been added the first two regional companies, Scottish Television, which came on the air in August 1957, and TWW – Television Wales and the West – which began transmission in January 1958. Each of the newcomers appointed one Director. This brought on to the Board the Managing Director of Scottish Television, James Coltart, who was to play an important role in ITN's development when the struggle for 'News at Ten' got under way. Coltart was a small, lively, friendly Scot who combined firmness with sympathy, counting the pennies but also appreciating and encouraging creativity.

When from 1957 onwards money became at first plentiful and then abundant within the ITV system, I did not at first seek any large increases in the annual budget which fixed the total sum the companies were prepared to pay for the ITN service over the next twelve months. I took pride in our not only having done well, but in having done so at a low cost. The fact that we ran a tight ship seemed one reason for our success, for it meant that we had to think a way out of our problems, rather than buy our way out of them.

But as more film became available from around the world, and as the cost of bringing it in over Eurovision, and over the coaxial cable from the burgeoning ITV newsrooms increased, we began to need not only more money, but much more money. Getting this did not prove easy, despite the wealth of the companies (in 1959 Rediffusion declared a profit of £7 millions, and ATV was soon paying profits of 100 per cent). The companies were not readily convinced that we needed these increases. Since ITN was the only programme company operating in the field of national and international news, they had no touchstone by which to judge our claims. News had proved itself one of the most expensive of television programmes, with a cost-per-minute matched only by opera. The ITN subscription loomed large as an item in programme company budgets. Yet it was an item out of their day-to-day control. Within their own organisations the Managing Directors – many of whom sat on the ITN Board – could restrain or condone any sudden rise in programme costs. Within ITN they could exercise effective control only when the ITN Budget for the year was drawn up. In the interests of the efficient operation of this high-spending subsidiary, as well as in the interests of keeping their own costs down, it was understandable that they should take a very hard look at the Budget we brought forward each summer.

Tests for settling that level were not easy to establish. Normal commercial criteria did not apply. We were not a profit-making company, so the yardstick of our annual profits was removed. There was no way of determining how far we contributed to pulling in advertising revenue. We could not expand our output to generate more funds, because the companies who owned us were also our competitors for air time, who wanted every spare moment for their own programmes. In the end decisions about what the ITN service was worth came back to subjective decisions about the quality of the news which the system required. Here too there were snags. However keen individual directors might be on providing a service of the highest quality, it was not necessarily in their company's interest – at any rate in the short run – for that quality to be achieved at a high cost. Any 'brownie points', to use a phrase from a later period, which ITN might score with the Authority would not be placed to the credit of any individual company, to be chalked up against the day when contracts were renewed or cancelled. Indeed praise for ITN might have the opposite effect, by highlighting shortcomings in the companies' own programmes, as was to be demonstrated when the Pilkington Committee singled out ITN alone within ITV for approval. It is reasonable to believe that most companies would have been happy to have had a good, serviceable news service from ITN, something which attracted no blame but which equally did not win too large a share of the limelight, a service as reliable as, but no more noteworthy than the weather forecasts. Instead they had been presented with an excellent service, and it is little wonder that when the bills for that excellence came in not all were eager to meet them. Captain Brownrigg was quite forthright on this point. When I argued that we would have to have much more money for film if we were to prevent the BBC News from overtaking us, he retorted that he saw no need for Independent Television to have a better news service than the BBC – or even one as good. 'What we want from ITN is that it holds the audience, and does its job as economically as possible. It is hammocked between two strong programmes, so that it will not lose its audience, even if its quality were to slip a bit. I see no reason why we should pour out money just to be better that the BBC at something which ought, in any case, to be the BBC's prime responsibility.'

Brownrigg's attitude may have been influenced by that distrust of journalists which many in the Armed Services share. This certainly seemed to be the case when Brownrigg found himself face to face, at an ITN salaries sub-committee, with Arthur Christiansen, who sat for a short while on the ITN Board as an ATV director. Christiansen had only recently parted company with Lord Beaverbrook after his many years as Editor of the *Daily Express,* and in the sub-committee he supported readily my claim that we should raise the minimum rate for sub-editors to £1500 a year. Captain Brownrigg would have none of this: '£1500 a year is more than a navigating officer in the Royal Navy gets. Sub-editing does not demand anything like the same skills. It calls only for a knowledge of basic English and for common sense. Any good navigating officer could learn to do it in a month.'

This was too much for Christiansen, who had elevated sub-editing to an art. He leant across the table and snorted, 'And any good sub could learn to steer your bloody ships in a month.' We got our £1500.

All in all, prising money out of the companies for the news service called for a high level of salesmanship when each ITN Budget was drawn up. I was not a salesman: I was an editor, and it took me some time to learn the art of selling my product in this forum where selling was part of life. It took me time, too, to appreciate the rate of technological change in television, and to make provision for the upsurge in costs this could bring.

The outcome of these pressures was that during the lush years for the programme companies ITN continued on a relatively austere diet. Though we steadily secured additional funds we never had, until after the Pilkington Report, any margin by which we could experiment readily, or gather in reserves of talent, or gamble on ways of exploiting the strengths of this new journalism. This provided a valuable discipline, not least on myself, in exercising great care in selecting those who joined our ranks, and in pruning out those whose work was not first class. It forced us to remain economical and prudent in our operations. But it also put us under considerable strain, forcing me ever to be on the alert for economies, to be ever demanding that everyone gave always of their best.

I took this attitude all the more rigorously because, once each annual Budget had been adopted, I was determined to keep within it. For that was the key to editorial freedom – and editorial freedom was ITN's most precious possession. If we started straying over the limits of the Budget the companies would devise ways of controlling more closely the way we spent the money voted to us. From that it would be only a step to their exercising control, albeit indirectly, over editorial decisions. It became one of the ironies of life in Kingsway that the years of Independent Television's greatest riches were for ITN years of constant financial strain, reflected often in tense and captious

Board meetings. Yet because of the editorial freedom I retained they were also years in which we managed to keep ITN in the forefront of the development of television news.

26

Covering a General Election

In the autumn of 1959 broadcasters for the first time embarked on untrammelled coverage of a British General Election. The precedent set at Rochdale had thrust aside the inhibitions which had limited radio and television coverage in the past.

The BBC's self-imposed ban during previous Elections had left us with no guidelines by which we could steer. We had learnt much from covering by-elections. But reporting a contest within a single constituency was much more manageable than one spread over 630 constituencies. Power was at stake in a General Election in a way which was not the case in a by-election, however significant its result might be. Our coverage would be watched with very sharp eyes by the politicians whose fates we could influence, and by the press which until now had held a monopoly of the reporting of election campaigns. If we got it wrong we would not halt the televising of politics: that had now a momentum of its own. But we could damage the reputation of ITN, and of Independent Television as a whole. Though the system was too firmly established now for the Labour Party, if they won the Election, to carry out their threat to abolish ITV, it could be burdened with new controls if it was decided that we had been unfair. Amongst the Tories there were still the old opponents of commercial broadcasting to be reckoned with, together with some new ones suspicious of this new power in the land. And there was always the risk that, however fairly we might cover the Election, the loser might seek to blame television, would emerge crying 'Foul' against the cameras.

Yet we moved towards the Election with reasonable confidence. Ffitch, Bosanquet and Connell had all had experience of covering by-elections on television, and Trethowan and I had our newspaper experience of the past three General Elections to draw on. This confidence held even though in May 1959 Robin Day announced that he would not be with us during the Election. He had accepted an invitation to contest Hereford as a Liberal candidate. Under rules which the Board had adopted when Ludovic Kennedy had announced his sudden entry into politics this meant that Day would have to give up newscasting immediately, in order to ensure not only that we were impartial, but were seen to be impartial. We paid him a retainer, and I helped him get a contract to write a weekly column for the *News Chronicle,* which he did with pungency and humour.

Election Day was set for 8th October 1959. The newspapers were quickly on to us to ask about the principles which would govern our coverage. I replied that we would cover the Election – as we covered any story – on the basis of its news value. This is a good broad journalistic term which covers a multitude of interpretations. I had no doubt in my own mind what those news values were, in the context of a General Election. They meant ensuring that the share of time devoted to the sayings and doings of each political party should be roughly in proportion to the number of candidates it had in the field, and that within individual constituencies the amount of time devoted to each candidate should be equal. A General Election is a contest confined within certain rules, which in turn impose their own rules upon any broadcaster working under an obligation of impartiality. The only test we could apply to ensure – and to be seen to be ensuring – impartiality was that of time, of minutes and seconds allocated to parties and to candidates. Our by-election coverage had made plain that an election is above all an argument, a clash of conflicting claims and conflicting statements by different politicians and different parties. What criterion, other than the stop-watch, could be used to decide the news values of these arguments, the relative space which should be accorded to them? What might seem to a person of Conservative inclination to be a statement of great interest and importance might seem an irrelevance, or a downright falsehood, to a Labour opponent – and so on, to and fro across the whole political spectrum. No News Editor aiming to present a fair picture could do other than fall back on the clock to guide him. The sharing of time would not have to be exact within any bulletin or any one electoral report. Different issues would arise on different days, different leaders would be playing varying roles from day to day, and these differences would have to be reflected in each day's coverage. But over the period of the campaign as a whole, the amount of time devoted to the various parties must be broadly in line with the part they were playing in the Election – which in turn meant the number of candidates they put into the field.

We had learnt from our by-election coverage one further important lesson. The principle of fair shares must apply to the facilities used to cover a story as well as to minutes on the screen. The technical equipment employed to turn political argument into television could affect the impact of those arguments. This was most noticeable in coverage of a speech. If we used the sound camera, so enabling the candidate to state the argument of his policy in his own voice, the outcome was more authentic, and the impact undoubtedly greater, than if his words were relayed by the neutral voice of a commentator. This impact was liable to be all the greater if the politician was speaking in the emotionally-charged atmosphere of a Party Meeting, with the applause of the faithful to reinforce his message. Similarly Election news reinforced even by silent film would have greater force than news relayed only by the newscaster. We would therefore have to allocate our cameras, and in particular our sound cameras, with care. We were, in fact, applying in television terms the principle which the farsighted John Reith had laid down in 1923, that 'if on any controversial matter the opposing views are stated with equal emphasis and lucidity, there can at least be no charge of bias.'[1]

To secure that equal emphasis and lucidity I defined, therefore, the basis of our coverage of the Election as one of 'news values plus parity of technical resources'.

We secured from the network a slot of ten minutes every weekday evening of the campaign. Trethowan and Connell presented it, and I edited it myself. It was a task which brought back the intensive daily rhythm I had known during Suez, with days that stretched from a morning planning conference until the night's 'Election Report' had finished its run at 11 p.m. Once again exhilaration was to outweigh exhaustion. For we were not just making television. We were forging a new way in which Parliamentary democracy could operate, finding methods by which this formidable new technology could fit into the complex organic structure of the British political system. Though this further, deeper goal was very much in my mind, I took care not to proclaim it. Good journalists armour their sensitivities with scepticism, and I knew that even those who thought as I did – and there were plenty in ITN who did – would not thank me if I put such thoughts into words. Better to base our approach on the hardened newsman's attitude that we were out to dominate the story and outpace the opposition.

On the opening night of the campaign both the Conservative and Labour Leaders planned important platform speeches, Macmillan in Manchester, Gaitskell in Bristol. The Prime Minister's speech presented no difficulty. The Free Trade Hall where his meeting was being held was close to the Granada studios. We could cover the speech with a sound camera and have the film processed and cut in Manchester in time for it to be piped down to London. But with Gaitskell the task was more thorny. Sound coverage was possible only if we could rush the film to Cardiff, to the TWW studios. As for the Liberals, their Leader, Jo Grimond, was well out of range in the Orkneys, and so would have to wait a day or two before we could give his meetings sound coverage.

Harold Macmillan's speech went according to plan, and well before the time of our 'Election Report' we had a neat segment of it cut and waiting in Granada's telecine. But Hugh Gaitskell's speech ran late. Though the cameraman drove madly with film of it from Bristol to Cardiff it was still in the processing plant by the time we went on the air. All we could offer was silent coverage of the Labour Leader arriving at Bristol.

The contrast was marked. Harold Macmillan was seen and heard, vigorous, confident and witty, against a background of cheering supporters. A silent, overcoated Hugh Gaitskell hurried along a station platform, to be greeted by a handful of supporters. From the studio in London George Ffitch gave a summary of Gaitskell's speech. This was clear, but manifestly at one remove from the real thing. Logistics were obviously going to be as important as editorial assessments in securing 'equal emphasis and lucidity'. As soon as I got to my desk the next morning Transport House were on the phone seeking explanations, and demanding that we redress the balance.

We were able to reassure them that justice would be done that evening. Gaitskell was due to speak at Battersea, on our very doorstep. To make sure that no hitch would occur, we had put two cameras in the hall. Macmillan was campaigning in the remote mountains of Wales and could not be covered on sound anyway. Still suspicious that we might have been playing in with the Tories (whom the Labour Party saw as the friends of commercial television),

Morgan Phillips, the Party Secretary, agreed to wait this extra day before making any formal complaint. 'But you had better get it right this time,' he told me, 'or I will throw the book at you.'

I was not worried. Special lights had been installed to supplement the hall lighting. Every possible precaution had been taken. If ever we had mounted a belt and braces operation, this was one. To make doubly sure George Ffitch went off with the camera crews to Battersea Town Hall. Gaitskell was due to speak at the reasonably early hour of eight o'clock, ample time for us to get the film back and have it ready for the 'Election Special'. I was in the preview theatre, watching film of Harold Macmillan starting off on his Prime Ministerial progress, when the phone rang. It was George Ffitch. 'I don't know whether to laugh or cry when I tell you this,' he said. 'But when Gaitskell came on to the platform, and we switched the lights on, the load proved too much for the electricity system. We blew all the lights in the hall. Not only is there no film, there's no meeting either.'

Hugh Gaitskell was a big-minded man. Instead of bursting out in wrath he continued the meeting by candlelight. 'So it was you, was it?' was his only comment to George Ffitch at the end of the evening. 'I thought it was either the Empire Loyalists or the Communists.'

Even Morgan Phillips, though the humour of it escaped him, had to admit that we could plead *force majeure*. He accepted my assurance that a close-range speech by Gaitskell the next evening, at Harlow New Town, would give us a further chance to get matters back into balance. We very nearly failed to do so. The dispatch rider, bringing back the film from Harlow, skidded on an icy road and was hurled into a ditch. The film broke from its container and was ruined. This time I knew no amount of explanations or apologies could meet the situation. Whatever the reasons behind the screen, we were not giving the public a fair picture of the election. I rang Waldo McGuire, the Head of News at the BBC. In my days as a radio news analyst we had often found ourselves at adjoining desks in the Egton House newsroom, as he finished his night shift as Chief Sub and I came in in the grey light of dawn to dissect the day's news for Australia and New Zealand. Could I borrow a cut of their coverage of Gaitskell?

I could, and did, and the crisis was over. We were able to make a speedy repayment. A day later it was McGuire on the line to me. Their film of Jo Grimond, flown down by air from the Orkneys, had been late. In an effort to speed up the processing the temperature in the developer had been raised – but raised too high. The emulsion had been boiled off. The *aficionados* of political coverage might have detected a marked similarity on those two evenings between the BBC's film reports and those of ITN. But no one in our respective hierarchies seemed to notice, and Waldo and I saw no need to draw their attention to the fact.

The relatively primitive technical conditions of the time helped to set in train another characteristic of televised Elections – the dominance of the Election campaign by the Party Leaders. Because sound film cameras were relatively scarce, television news editors were bound to give priority to coverage of the main speech of the day by the Leaders of the Conservative and Labour Parties, and reasonable prominence to a speech by the Liberal Leader. The outcome was that the Leaders were, night after night, heard as well as seen on the screen, whereas lesser but still prominent figures might appear only in silent film sequences. Harold Macmillan's genial confidence, Hugh Gaitskell's searing earnestness, soon established themselves on the screen. The Liberals, with their Leader far away most of the time in the mists of the Orkneys and Shetland, had often to be represented by Liberal speakers closer at hand. As a result the Liberal Chief Whip, Frank Byers, shared star billing with Jo Grimond. One back bencher whose speeches we covered on three occasions was Sir Winston Churchill. I was determined that in this, the last General Election in which he was likely to take part, his words should be recorded by this new medium.

By the time we had reached the last few days of the campaign I knew that, providing nothing went wrong in the final straight – and nothing did – we had met successfully the challenge of covering for the first time a General Election on television – and indeed of covering it for the first time in any form of broadcasting in Britain. The coverage logs which I had carefully compiled morning after morning showed that the two main parties were within a minute or two of each other in their total screen time. The Liberal's proportion had been equally fair, though we had had to scour the country in the second week to find suitable Liberal meetings to keep the records in trim. The minor parties had had a reasonable share of our scanty time. We had brought through the main arguments, shown the main personalities, reflected something of the cut and thrust of electioneering. None of the fears of unfairness or of partiality which had inhibited coverage during the four other post-war Elections had proved valid. From now on General Elections would be reported by television and by radio as a matter of course.

Our Results programme on Election Night was out-pointed by that of the BBC. They had Richard Dimbleby, then at the peak of his fame, as their main presenter, and Grace Wyndham Goldie as producer, with not only her natural flair, but the experience of three previous Election Nights to draw on – for there had been no inhibition on reporting the results, as distinct from the campaigning, in earlier Elections. Nevertheless we were in the battle right through the night. Our dual presentation team of Trethowan and Connell – foreshadowing the 'News at Ten' pattern – were clear and authoritative. We could claim, too, to have been first with the moment of highest drama. For it was on ITN that Hugh Gaitskell conceded defeat only four hours after the polls had closed. This was the first occasion on which a British Party Leader had conceded defeat on Election Night, and certainly the first on which he had done so on television. Gaitskell had spent the evening at Leeds Town Hall, where the votes in his constituency, South Leeds, and those in neighbouring constituencies were being counted. Towards 1 a.m., in a small, temporary studio inside the hall, he was interviewed for us by Neville Clarke. Opening his hands, then pressing his fingertips together, he said, 'It is obvious there will be a Conservative Government.' Television, by capturing and presenting this moment, had shown its power not only as a new form of journalism, but as an essential part of the democratic process.

27

News Specials

Shortly before the 1959 Election the programme companies had taken a decision which was to hamper seriously the development of television news. They cut the main evening bulletin back by nearly a third, to a length of ten minutes, as the price of promoting it to the peak hour of 9.25 p.m. This change was all the more painful because since early in 1958 we had been excellently placed at 10 p.m. The move to a better hour was not made to accord to the news pride of place. It was made because to the schedulers the main evening news was (and remains) a nuisance, a chunk of programming which breaks the evening into two less manageable halves.

This cut meant that just when news on film became more plentiful we had less space in which to show it. There was a further, equally damaging effect. A truncated bulletin left little time for newscasters and interviewers to exercise their skills (the studio interview was the first element to go by the board), which made it increasingly difficult to attract to ITN the men and women of talent who had been the secret of our success. The first sign of this was the decision of Robin Day not to return to us after the Election. Instead he followed Chataway and Kennedy to 'Panorama'.

At any time Day's going would have been a loss. The *Spectator* noted perceptively that no one had done more than Robin Day 'to create the persona of Independent Television News, to show that it is possible to be forthright without being prejudiced, fair without being mealy-mouthed. When ITN first began, Chataway made the more immediate impact, but it was Day who developed and perfected the technique of newscasting in a way which made the BBC's television news-readers by contrast dull and not infrequently embarrassing to watch'.[1] His going was the more noticeable because some months earlier I had had to withdraw Ian Trethowan from the screen in order that he could become Deputy Editor. Though I had gained invaluable experience by acting as my own Deputy during my first eighteen months with ITN, it was not a process which could continue. The first arrangements I made to provide myself with a Deputy had not worked out, and I had therefore asked Ian Trethowan to take on the task. He discharged it admirably, but the gap left by his departure from the screen was considerable, a gap now widened by Robin Day's going.

I recruited two very able news presenters in David Lutyens, the Science Editor of Penguin Books, and Tim Brinton, who had been a radio newsreader in Hong Kong. But their background was not journalistic. I decided therefore to give Reginald Bosanquet, who had appeared intermittently as a relief newscaster over the past two years, a chance as a front-line newscaster. It was a decision which was strongly attacked by some of the programme companies, who thought him too young, and who disliked the way in which, when he was tired, his enunciation could at times become slurred. This was due to a childhood injury, which caused the muscles on one side of his face to slacken when he was weary. I held my ground against the doubters, and Reginald Bosanquet soon acquired an ardent public following.

By now we were, in any event, no longer as dependent upon any one personality as we had been when Christopher Chataway had resigned. For by now ITN had developed its own personality, clearly if subconsciously sensed by the viewers. The individual newscaster contributed greatly to this, but other elements brought their own distinction – the quality of the film, the clarity of the writing, the selection and treatment of stories. One important new component which had been added since 1956 was the stronger presence on the screen of the reporters, who now frequently introduced their reports into camera from locations in the field, instead of appearing only as interviewers, seldom filmed except in profile or from over the shoulder.

We needed this strength and experience because by now the BBC competition had markedly intensified. Towards the end of 1956 the Corporation had followed our lead, and had named its newsreaders. BBC News had invested in better film-processing equipment, which improved greatly the quality of its pictures, and had been abundantly equipped with sound cameras. The success of 'Tonight', which came on the air in February 1957, not only raised morale within the BBC, but provided an alternative home for men and women of talent who might otherwise have come to ITN. In 1958 an even more fundamental change took place, when Hugh Carleton Greene moved over from Bush House to become Head of News and Current Affairs, and the formidable figure of Tahu Hole relinquished the grip he had held on BBC News for the past decade. Greene saw his first task, as he later declared, as being 'to restore freedom to the News Division . . .'[2] The requirement that television news should follow the same sequence of stories as the nine o'clock radio news – a requirement which had been less and less observed – was dropped. A four-man team of regular newsreaders – Robert Dougall, Richard Baker, Kenneth Kendall and Michael Aspel – replaced the former changing rota of several readers. BBC News became skilled at packing the shortened bulletins – for the BBC cut its main news back to twelve minutes when it too was placed in prime time – with fast-moving film stories. We moved into an era of intense nightly competition, each side developing new techniques, and each swiftly adopting those of its rival.

The pattern of short, film-packed mid-evening bulletins was to last in British television for the next seven years. The bulletins were gradually lengthened, until on the BBC the main bulletin lasted fifteen minutes and on ITN thirteen minutes. In the summer of 1962 our main ITN news was put at 9 p.m., that hour sanctified for news in the great days of radio. The move owed less to a feeling in the programme companies that this was the right time for news than to a hard scheduling battle in which they were engaged with the revivified BBC, who had brought their own main news forward to 9.15 p.m. But whatever the reasons, the change brought us to the peak of the evening in a most gratifying manner.

Despite the ingenuity of producers, these shortened bulletins could not, however, cope effectively with big news occasions. This led to the development in the early Sixties of the technique of the *ad hoc* special news programme. In this a big story was treated not just as news but as programme material. If it was urgent or dramatic enough time would be cleared, even in peak hours. For instance when Dr Verwoerd, the South African Prime Minister, was stabbed to death in the Parliament building in Cape Town, we were given the half hour from 9.30 to 10 p.m. for a news special. On the opening day of the Cuban missile crisis in October 1962 both ITV and the BBC filled the hour between 9 p.m. and 10 p.m. with film reports and studio discussions, in the course of which the American reconnaissance photographs, with their vivid evidence of missile sites being cleared in the Cuban countryside, were shown to the British public for the first time.

Several factors stimulated the growth of the special news programme. Videotaping had come into widespread use by 1960, enabling us to summarise and store the day's news more effectively than was possible with the slower, drabber technique of telerecording. European broadcasters, stimulated by the RAI coverage of the funeral of the Pope in 1958, vied with one another to offer live coverage of events. Highly televisual figures bestrode the world's stage – the new, young President John F. Kennedy of the United States and his beautiful, enigmatic wife; the ebullient, unpredictable Nikita Khrushchev; President de Gaulle, towering behind his ornate desk in the Élysée Palace as he made brilliant use of television to sustain his public support; Pope John XXIII, who was to make equally skilful use of television to make the Papacy more human and yet more powerful. New links with the broadcasting services behind the Iron Curtain through Intervision enabled us to meet the avid, if brief curiosity in the West for the great Soviet annual occasions such as the May Day and 7th November parades in Red Square.

In February 1962 the scope for special programmes was dramatically extended when Colonel John Glenn made the first American space flight around the world. Though Major Gagarin had done the same for the Russians ten months earlier, the Soviet authorities released no film of either the blast-off of their rocket or of the recovery of the astronaut. No such inhibitions affected the authorities at what was then Cape Canaveral. On to our screens poured, as the United States space programme got under way, coverage of the astronauts reaching the launching site and mounting to the capsule in their gleaming space suits; of the tense moments to the countdown; of the flaring and billowing as the great engines ignited; and of the rocket making its steady way into the sky. Even in the monochrome coverage of 1962 this was compulsive viewing. When in due course colour was added, and pictures from space itself, and of the brightly-coloured recovery parachutes opening above the cobalt blue of the Pacific Ocean, culminating in 1969 with the first pictures of man's landing on the moon, we had a series of programmes ideally suited to this new visual medium. Despite the many dramas which have unfolded since, there have been few periods when visual news was available in greater abundance than in the Sixties, when the daily fighting in Vietnam competed with these space spectaculars.

Within Independent Television special news programmes had begun in the autumn of 1960, when Khrushchev visited the United Nations Assembly in New York, where he was expected to announce a new blockade of Berlin. He did no such thing, but his unique mixture of clowning and menace provided some memorable pictures. The UN cameras did not, alas, catch the moment when he took off his shoe and hammered it in protest on his desk in the Assembly. But it did record the scene when he stood up, shouting an angry objection to a statement by Harold Macmillan, only to be met by a roar of laughter from the other delegates when the Prime Minister, with exaggerated courtesy, asked, 'Could we have that translated please?' But the event which established firmly the news special in our techniques was Hugh Gaitskell's speech at the Labour Party Conference at Scarborough in 1960, when he defied the ban-the-bomb majority with his declaration that he and his supporters would 'fight, fight and fight again to save the Party we love'. Granada put OB cameras into the hall, and recorded the whole morning session, from which an hour and a half special, with commentary by Ian Trethowan, was prepared. It caught the atmosphere in a way the film cameras, with their more limited duration, could not have done. Gaitskell's speech was not great oratory. He was too tense for that, his voice and manner too strained. But it was great television, winning for Hugh Gaitskell overnight respect and support far beyond the confines of the Labour movement.

In March 1962 we had OB cameras inside the hall during the count in the by-election at Orpington, as part of the first special coverage of a by-election. A month later the programme companies made available two and a half hours of time in the afternoon to enable us to present for the first time a special report on the Budget. David Hennessy, later as Lord Windlesham to be the Managing Director of ATV, was then a producer on Rediffusion. Using Rediffusion's OB cameras he mounted for us a programme which brought the scenes from immediately outside Parliament, even if we could not get into the chamber itself. It was a day of clear April sunshine, outlining the stonework on the Palace of Westminster and the hands of the clock on the Big Ben tower. From the Commons we provided a running commentary of the Chancellor's speech and of the tax changes – 'running' in more senses than one, for it involved a series of reporters sprinting from the Press Gallery to give their news into camera, or to phone it over to the special newsroom we had constructed in Studio 9 in the basement of Television House.

In June we covered another by-election, this time in Middlesbrough. We had George Brown on the panel of commentators in our studio. Owing to a misunderstanding, he was unaware that our programme was being seen only in the North East, the rest of the ITV network having at the last minute decided to carry a boxing match instead. When George Brown learnt this after the show, his fury erupted in a bellow of anger that literally shook the window panes in my room. No apologies would satisfy him, and he stormed out with a final taunt at the sandwiches we were offering our guests: 'At the BBC I would at least have had a buffet supper as well as a proper audience.'

Two and a half years later, when he became Minister of Economic Affairs in the 1964 Labour Government, I thought it time to mend bridges. I wrote him a letter of congratulation on his appointment, and of thanks for his co-operation with our reporting teams during the Election campaign, in which his whistle-stop tours had provided a stream of very viewable stories. I got a letter back thanking me for my good wishes and, in turn, for the fair treatment we had accorded him during the Election. He had signed this, but added a PS in his own hand: 'Dear Geoffrey,' it ran, 'This is what my staff drafted for me. I thought you gave me a lousy deal. Yours, George.' I knew then the bridge was firmly mended.

The most durable form of special programme came, however, in the autumn of 1962, when for the first time continuous live direct coverage of the Party Conferences was mounted. Granada, in whose transmission area the Tory and Liberal Conferences were due to be held, took the initiative, and Southern Television followed suit with coverage of the Labour Party at Brighton. The pattern established then has been followed to this day, with the programme companies providing the OB coverage from the hall, and ITN providing the main commentary with, in 1962, Ian Trethowan and George Ffitch identifying the speakers and explaining the procedures.

All three Conferences were dominated that year by debates on the Common Market. At Brighton this brought a clash between Hugh Gaitskell, who was strongly anti-Market, and his normal ally, George Brown, who was strongly pro. They continued the argument late into the night after the debate, when they joined us for a drink in the ITN office we had set up on the edge of the hall. Gaitskell that evening was at his best, combining intellect not only with passion – as he did in public – but also with an easy humour which rarely came through on the platform or in the Commons. George Brown too was in good form, demonstrating what Crossman was later to say of him: 'When George is good, he is very, very good. When he is bad . . .' It was well after one in the morning when I walked back with Hugh and Dora Gaitskell to the Metropole Hotel along the deserted sea front, the last time I saw him before his death four months later.

28

Time Is Short

Special news programmes, valuable though they were when big news broke, did not meet, however, the need for more time to cope with the flow of less spectacular but nevertheless important news. Not only was more news in pictures available from around the world, but more news was being deliberately cast in visual form. In 1958 the Campaign for Nuclear Disarmament had, by accident or design, devised in the Aldermaston March the first demonstration specially tailored for television. Mounted at Easter when other news was thin, and providing a viewable mix of action and human interest material, the March was able to claim for the next six or seven years a regular place in the bulletins. By 1961 the Committee of 100 were offering even more vivid fare, with sit-down demonstrations in Whitehall and outside bomber bases. Every Saturday bulletin – a day shrewdly chosen because on it news was apt to be scanty – soon seemed to have its shots of the frail, white-haired figure of Earl Russell, or the short-haired, shouting figure of Miss Pat Arrowsmith being carried away by burly policemen.

This lesson was not lost on others wishing to carry their case to the public. In industrial disputes the unions had at first seen television mainly as a way of arguing their case, through their union officials, in interviews. But in 1961 one of the least militant of unions, the nurses, secured wide screen coverage by marching to Parliament. From then on the mass demonstration became a major form of union pressure. Smaller groups followed suit – mothers seeking a pedestrian crossing at an accident black spot, conservationists wanting to block or divert one of the motorways which were beginning to spread across the countryside. The habit spread, as other less reputable elements found they could, by violence or even by unruliness, win a place on the screen which they would otherwise not have merited. Seaside fighting between Mods and Rockers became part of the Bank Holiday scene. By the mid-Sixties the normal, staid ending to football matches had been replaced by the spectacle of crowds erupting across the pitch, waving their scarves to Mum at home. And in 1958 we had within our camera sights the first flaring of the new phenomenon of racial violence, as street fighting broke out in Nottingham and Notting Hill.

All these events called not only for film coverage, but, equally importantly, for probing and explanation, for not all demonstrations were what they seemed. This underlined the need for longer news bulletins. This led me to formulate the idea of the two-tiered bulletin, with one segment in mid-evening time in which the most urgent news could be presented, and a second segment set around 11 p.m. in which that news could be amplified and explained. I put this idea to the ITN Board in April 1960, who told me to put it up again later when broadcasting hours had been extended, and to the Committee under Sir Harry Pilkington, who were then in the midst of investigating British broadcasting. For good measure I argued to the Pilkington Committee that ITN should produce a weekly news in depth programme, like 'This Week' or 'Panorama', and a morning news at breakfast time.

At the same time I set about adapting 'Roving Report' to a harder news role, lessening the travelogue and featurish elements in it. Michael Barsley had by 1961 earned a break from the treadmill of producing a twenty-minute feature programme, week in and week out with only a tiny staff to support him. I regretted the loss of his intelligent light-heartedness, his eye for the quirks of human nature, and above all his well-written scripts. But I had to put the needs of hard news first.

For this new-style 'Roving Report' I recruited and trained for television a number of experienced Fleet Street reporters, mostly on a freelance basis – John Ardagh of *The Times*; David Holden of the *Sunday Times*; Brian Widlake of the *Financial Times*; John Thompson of the *Observer*, later to be Director of Radio for the IBA; and Keith Kyle of the *Observer*. It proved a good training ground for producers, too. Derek Cooper gained his first television experience with us. Adrian Cowell developed, particularly in a series of 'Roving Report' from New Guinea, that skill in portraying primitive peoples which, in larger documentaries for larger companies, was to win him many awards.

The next Editor of ITN was amongst these recruits. He joined us partly by accident. I had known and respected Nigel Ryan's work as Reuter's correspondent in the Congo, and when Robin Day introduced him to me in a London restaurant I invited him to take a test the next day as a newscaster. He arrived nearly an hour late, flushed and out of breath, muttering apologies about London traffic. It was some years later that I learnt the real reason. Ryan had misheard my name in the restaurant, and assumed that Day was introducing him to Paul Fox, then Day's editor on 'Panorama'. He had duly reported to a surprised secretary in Paul Fox's office in Lime Grove, only to be told that Mr Fox had been in New York for the past week. Only then did the truth strike Ryan. He dashed out to find a taxi and travel across town to Kingsway.

Newscasting did not prove to be Ryan's role, but reporting with the camera did. In his first job for 'Roving Report' he produced a scoop –

the first interview Jomo Kenyatta gave after his release from prison. Kenyatta's image had been that of an unwavering leader of the tribe which had provided the ferocious Mau Mau. Now, carrying an umbrella and a briefcase, he strolled into camera range and sat down to argue that it was pure imagination to think that there would be unrest if he were allowed to bid for the Premiership of an independent Kenya. A few weeks later when Ryan reported on Yugoslavia, he spoke. not only to the official leadership, but sought out and inteviewed Milovan Djilas, Tito's wartime lieutenant, just released from Tito's jail. In Algiers a bomb explosion occurred when the camera crew were out on another story. Ryan got hold of their spare camera and covered the scene himself – and argued them into keeping their mouths shut about what could have precipitated an inter-union row.

It was to 'Roving Report' that Nelson Mandela, the black South African leader, gave his last interview before being incarcerated on the island prison off Cape Town. It was in 'Roving Report' that the first survey from within Castro's Cuba reached the British screen, and the first of the many programmes on the building of the Berlin Wall in 1961. Yet the programme was still strictly confined to foreign news, home news in depth being the preserve of 'This Week' and of the new weekly programme 'World in Action' which Granada launched in 1963 and which, under the aggressive and imaginative leadership of Tim Hewat, soon secured a firm place in the schedules, even if, as Hewat was later to claim, he constantly broke the Act regulating broadcasting.[1] Nor did 'Roving Report' meet the need for a programme of immediate daily news analysis, a need made all the more urgent as more and more news took a visual form which could mislead unless it was put into perspective.

In the autumn of 1961 a chance to mount such a programme of analysis came our way, even if it was a programme seen only in the London area. Our staunch ally in Rediffusion, John McMillan, commissioned from us a late night ten-minute programme of London news, to which we gave the title of 'Dateline London'. But this did not sit easily at a late hour, and after three months McMillan suggested we should turn it into a nightly scrutiny of the main story of the day. I grasped at this chance to put into practice what I termed the Oyster Opening Theory about the presentation of the background to the news. A Maori fisherman at Stewart Island, at the very south of New Zealand, had once told me that when you lift an oyster out of the sea, there is a split second when the two sides of its shell are very slightly ajar. Thrust the blade of a knife into the crack in that moment and you can open the oyster without difficulty. Leave it till later, and you need much pressure to open it up. The public mind, it seems to me, is like an oyster. Under the pressure of dramatic news – a riot, an uprising, a crash, an earthquake – it is wide open for additional information. If you put that background information quickly before people whilst their interest is aroused, they will take it in with avidity. But if you delay, other events or other interests will have forced public attention back into its shell, and your chances of catching their interest will be much less. A nightly programme which gave us this chance to move swiftly could be the knife blade with which we could open up the news immediately for analysis and interpretation.

We made the change in the function of 'Dateline London' early in December 1961. The new formula quickly proved its worth, as a means not only of analysing news but also of reporting it in depth. We found a good producer for it in Brian Wenham, who had joined us as a young scriptwriter from ATV, and who was to develop on 'Dateline' the skills which were to carry him in time to the leadership of BBC 2. Both 'Dateline' and 'Roving Report' endured – though 'Roving Report' changed its name from 1964 onwards – until they became part of 'News at Ten' because they met the fundamental need for television news to analyse as well as to report. Fifteen years had yet to elapse before Peter Jay and John Birt were to be acclaimed for declaring that television news needs instant analysis if it is to overcome what they termed television's 'bias against understanding'. Though we had not defined the problem in such vivid terms we had grappled with it in practice, as the scripts of 'Dateline' in the ITN archives demonstrate.

29

Satellite Era

The techniques of this new journalism were revolutionised by one huge technological development in the summer of 1962, the satellite transmission of television pictures. The development of rockets to carry man into space (and to allow nuclear warheads to be delivered over long distances) brought as a by-product the capacity to put a communications satellite into orbit. The first satellite, code-named Telstar, was launched from Cape Canaveral on 10th July 1962. The Post Office engineers agreed, with some reluctance, to let us broadcast live the first pictures the satellite was due to send back. We placed an OB camera in position at the GPO tracking station at Goonhilly Down in Cornwall, and Ian Trethowan stood by ready to comment.

Telstar passed across the surface of the globe at an angle which permitted messages to be sent up to it, and relayed down from it, for only twenty minutes at a time, and then only at certain periods of the day. The first such pass – we were soon learning a new jargon – would come at 3 a.m. on 11th July. All we could show the viewers in our main bulletin and in 'Dateline' on 10th July were the preparations at Goonhilly, at the French tracking station in Normandy, and at the American transmitting and tracking station at Andover in Maine.

At midnight the network went off the air. But at ITN we were as busy as if this was a peak hour, as we stood by ready to record on videotape the first transmission. As the clock moved towards 3 a.m. the control room was crowded. Diana Edwards-Jones, now an experienced director, was in charge. On our monitors we could see Ian Trethowan at Goonhilly, backed by the ranks of Post Office monitors in the tracking station's control room. The monitor linking the satellite with Goonhilly showed only a blank, flickering screen. Diana had an open line to the CBS control room in New York, whose engineers were talking to the engineers at the station in Andover, Maine, from which signals would go to the satellite. More new jargon reached our ears. 'Are you talking to the bird yet?' queried the CBS engineer. 'Any moment now,' came back the laconic reply from Andover.

Suddenly the blank monitor screen at Goonhilly began to quiver, and break up. Through the crackle of static, the shaking, wavering lines of the screen gradually formed into the face of a man. 'We have a picture – a man in picture,' came Trethowan's voice, triumphantly. And there, clumsy, incomplete, but recognisable, was indeed the face of a NASA official in New York. A new era in communication was, for better or for worse, upon us.

The next evening, when Telstar came within range once again, we were able to transmit direct to the viewers a series of items from America. President Kennedy presided at a news conference; a game of baseball at Yankee Stadium unfolded its complex ritual; the contestants for Miss Florida paraded in the sunshine. A formal two-way programme, with Richard Dimbleby as anchor man on the European side, was broadcast ten days later, and carried on both ITV and BBC, as well as by all other Eurovision stations. Bison charged over hillsides in Montana; the huge sculptured faces of Lincoln and Washington showed from their South Dakota mountainside. Europeans sat in cafés and sailed on lakes. When it was all over, the wonder of Telstar had become a commonplace. The critics were soon busy expressing doubts as to whether the programme-makers would live up to these new gifts the technicians had brought them and posing the question, 'What are satellites to be used for, anyway?'

On the answer to that question I had no doubt. Their main use must be for news. Immediacy was the quality which above all satellites added to inter-continental broadcasting, and immediacy was an integral part of news. I was therefore delighted when the programme companies decided that when both broadcasting channels were to be given access to Telstar, for ten minutes apiece, ITN should use the time allocated to Independent Television. I did not regularly keep a diary, but on this occasion I jotted down some notes of the next three days' events:

> 'Friday 27th July 10 a.m. Meeting at the GPO of the ITV-BBC Consortium for Telstar programming, with the officials of the Post Office who control the Goonhilly Down transmitter. Formal, high-ceilinged conference room is hung with portraits of earlier Postmasters-General. Reversal of roles since our previous planning meetings here. Then it was the GPO engineers who, under their studied calm, showed hints of strain. But since last week's successful programme exchanges, they are easy and relaxed. The tension is on our faces now – the programme planners.
>
> 'The quiet-voiced official confirms that the American Telephone and Telegraph Company are offering the United Kingdom twenty minutes of time on Pass No. 187 on Monday evening, between 8.20 and 8.40, to be divided between the BBC and ITV. This suits the BBC well for "Panorama", and they accept with alacrity. ITV has no magazine programme that night, so I make a quick bid for ten minutes for ITN News. Bid accepted. My mind is only half on the rest of the conference, as I tot up the problems involved. We have no correspondent in New York, no staff on the ground there, and

only a weekend in which to organise the programme – and no city is so dead at a weekend as New York. But we can rely on our good colleagues of CBS for help with studios, film, links.

'At last conference ends. Sprint down four floors of handsome GPO staircase, grab taxi back to Kingsway. Brian Connell is in the corridor as I come in. I borrow the new jargon. "It's all systems go. You're on 4 p.m. plane for New York." He and Robert Tyrell as producer are in the States by that evening.

'Norman Clark, our Foreign Editor, calls CBS, secures a promise of a studio and other assistance. But what are the news prospects for Monday? Lousy. Not a decent story stirring anywhere. Not even a flood? There's always a flood or a fire somewhere in the States. Not even a flood. There was one in Texas, but it has gone down. Hold on, there is one strong story. An Arizona court is due to rule on the thalidomide baby case. But it probably won't rule until after our transmission time.

'6 p.m. With planning for the day's normal ITN bulletins finished, Telstar looms up again, challenging our wits. We must get some Americans talking into camera. We must let Telstar do its other big job, letting the ordinary people of one nation see and meet the ordinary people of another. But this is a news programme. How are we to draw ordinary people into it? I move around the office questioning harassed executives for ideas as they get on with the nightly rush to get the 9 p.m. bulletin on to the air. Out of it all comes one plan. We must book an OB unit for Monday and use it to go out into the New York streets. We can surely find some news story which we can follow up with live interviews.

'8 p.m. John McMillan is on the phone from New York. Rediffusion have a "This Week" unit there with Desmond Wilcox as reporter. John offers us their help. Grasp it thankfully. Wilcox is just the reinforcement we need. Discuss with John placing of OB. He suggests Coney Island, or the amusement park "Freedom Land". Not too keen on either. Too much like the Seattle World Fair, the one dud item in the special Telstar programme from America earlier this week.

'9 p.m. McMillan on the phone again. Jones Beach. The middle class summer playground near New York. Atlantic rollers, Americans holiday-making. Sounds ideal. Ask CBS to fix it. Desmond Wilcox and unit hurrying from Washington to New York.

'1 p.m. Saturday. Call Connell and Tyrell. Catch them at

breakfast time. Shouts of "Put the orange juice on the table" in the background as we talk. Situation pretty grisly. Jones Beach no good. Will be deserted Monday afternoon. So will Coney Island. Opt for Central Park. Skyscrapers in the background will give us an opening title. Tyrell breaks in with suggestion that we track down an agency which specialises in American holidays for Britons, and get them to divert a bus-load of British tourists towards our cameras at transmission time, which would guarantee us people for Wilcox to talk to. Are there ordinary British tourists in New York? I thought only the rich can afford it. It seems there are cut-price tours. Ask them if they really can do it on fifteen dollars a day. That should be of interest to ordinary viewers. We settle on Central Park, plus American passers-by (we hope) plus British tourists. Connell breaks in with good news that Charles Collingwood has agreed to flank him in the CBS studio on Monday, giving us a two-man newscast, which will look different to ordinary bulletins. We have the bones of a programme. All we need now is some news to put the flesh on it.'

My diary notes ended there, as I became absorbed in the task of ensuring that we had enough news to justify all this high-cost technology. We were scheduled to come on air in Britain at 8.26 p.m. – which was 3.26 p.m. in New York, very early in the day for there to be any flow of hard news, particularly on film. At the UN the Security Council was discussing the Congo, which might provide at least one hard news item. In Albany, Georgia, the Reverend Martin Luther King was leading a protest about segregation in schooling. CBS would get him interviewed on the spot for us. But the only story which would grip the minds of most viewers was in a courtroom in Arizona. The thalidomide story was then new, and tragically fresh. A young American mother, Mrs Sheree Finkine, already the mother of four healthy children, had been treated with the drug whilst awaiting the birth of her fifth baby. She had applied to a court for the right to have an abortion. The hearing was set for this Monday, the day of our transmission. This should provide us with enough news to give force to the programme.

But we had reckoned without the weather. At six o'clock our time – lunch-time in New York – an anxious Robert Tyrell was on the phone from his hotel room overlooking Central Park. A sea mist had rolled in, covering the whole city. Visibility was down to a few hundred yards. He had rushed out to the OB site in Central Park. Not a single skyscraper, not a trace of the New York skyline could be seen – only forlorn, dripping trees.

Sea mists are a rarity in the New York summer. For one to plague us now was cruel. Yet it was out of the question to change to an inside site. Could CBS perhaps rig up another camera at their studios, to give us the alternative skyline shot we needed for the opening title, to establish we were in New York? No, that was out of the question. I assumed a confidence I did not feel. 'I know these New York mists well,' I assured Tyrell. 'They roll away by mid-afternoon without fail.' I checked hastily with the CBS correspondent in London. He whistled his sympathy. 'That's bad. Once those summer mists settle, they just don't move.'

The gods seemed to be against us. And not only the gods. For I learned that Captain Brownrigg had ruled that this first ever use of a satellite for ordinary programming should not be seen live in the London area. Viewers, he declared, were entitled to have the news at the hour they expected it – which was nine o'clock. Satellite or no satellite. Rediffusion was not going to break that pattern by putting the news out at 8.26 – for I had planned to follow these opening ten minutes from America with the rest of the news from London. We could record the transmission and put it out at the usual time. My plea that this would blunt the impact of the occasion, particularly to the critics, was met with a curt 'No'. I went up to the control room with the feeling that for once our luck was indeed out.

But the reverse was to be the case. As the clock ticked down towards the time of transmission a light wind sprang up in Manhattan and a triumphant Tyrell assured us he had a usable picture. We were due to follow 'Panorama', and as their pictures came through I saw, to my relief, that they had opted for a magazine format, instead of going for hard news. Richard Dimbleby came on screen interviewing a policeman in Rockefeller Plaza; James Mossman talked to customers at a drugstore food and drink counter, explaining that a hamburger cost three shillings. We had the news field to ourselves.

Diana Edwards-Jones and the CBS director in New York were talking to each other as calmly as if they were in adjoining studios in Kingsway. The figures on the time-elapsed clock on the control room wall flipped down towards 20.26. Then suddenly there were the towers of Manhattan on the skyline, a bit hazy, but unmistakable, and Central New York was in our midst – and in the midst of a multitude of British sitting rooms. A moment later and the familiar ITN News caption was superimposed, with an added line to it – 'From New York' – and the sound of 'Non Stop' was played on the disc which Tyrell had taken with him. Then, a few minutes before our transmission, Mrs Finkine came out of the courtroom and, on the verge of tears, told the waiting CBS reporter that the Court had refused to allow her to have an abortion. (She got one a month later in Sweden.) It was a strong human story, which would have crossed any national boundary. Told on the steps of this sunlit Arizona court house, and almost instantaneously heard and seen on the other side of the Atlantic, it was doubly poignant. The United Nations debate flared into argument in front of the cameras; Martin Luther King denounced the school authorities with vigour. Desmond Wilcox drew out his British visitors wittily as well as determinedly. Connell and Collingwood were authoritative, confident and highly professional. The picture quality throughout was excellent. Our ten minutes of satellite time flashed by. We came back to London to bring in three more stories, to round off the bulletin.

It was a good programme by any standards, matching the occasion. Even when it was repeated, as recorded, on the London air twenty-five minutes later, it had remarkable impact. Our colleagues recognised this, for six months later it was to win us a special award from the Guild of Television Producers.

Telstar fairly quickly wore itself out, to be replaced by Telstar II. But before it finally disintegrated Telstar was to help transmit from America film of the biggest news story since Suez and Hungary – the Cuban missile crisis of the autumn of 1962, when we moved to the very threshold of nuclear war. Though it was available for only brief periods of the day and night, it brought to us the scenes of confrontation between Adlai Stevenson and the Soviet leaders in the UN Security Council, and the ominous shots, filmed from American reconnaissance planes, of the long canvas-enshrouded shapes of the rockets on the decks of the Soviet cargo vessels heading for Cuba. It also enabled for the first time filmed reports from our own correspondents in New York and Florida to be brought immediately to the screen, so hastening the day when British television news would have to have a full corps of its own reporters to cover all the main stories, instead of relying to the degree we did then on agency reporters; a development which was to make inevitable the introduction of the half-hour news.

30

Rebuilding

These opening years of the changing Sixties were years of change within ITN itself. As television expanded, some of our senior staff were drawn away. James Bredin went to ATV, and later became Managing Director of Border TV. Arthur Clifford, too, was naturally keen for a command of his own, and in the autumn of 1961 he left ITN to become Head of News and Current Affairs for Anglia Television. This left a gaping hole on the Input Desk, so long dominated by Clifford's imagination and leadership.

After months of searching, I found in Donald Horobin of the *Birmingham Gazette* a News Editor as formidable and as daring as Clifford, if different in approach. At first sight Horobin did not look the News Editor. His neat suit, careful hair-style and precise, quiet manner were more those of a solicitor than of the popular concept of a short-sleeved, noisy extrovert with a green eye-shade. But I remembered that J. B. Wilson, the great News Editor of the *Daily Express,* had looked like a particularly ascetic bishop, so I offered Horobin the post, even though he had had no experience of broadcasting. From the first day he sat at the News Desk, I never had to worry whether stories were being followed up, ideas mulled over, or reporters pushed or inspired to their utmost.

At the same time we were hit by further losses of talent in front of the cameras. 'This Week' decided to build up an anchor man to match Dimbleby on 'Panorama', and offered the role to Brian Connell. Soon they drew George Ffitch away to be their political specialist, a member of a reporting team which included Paul Johnson and Bryan Magee, and which was to make 'This Week' a superb analytical programme. I scoured Fleet Street and the magazine world for replacements, testing day after day any possible screen figure I could persuade to come into the studio. But the main body of potential broadcasting talent in written journalism had now been drained away to the BBC and the programme companies.

To maintain the essential factor of authority, Ian Trethowan went back on the screen as Political Correspondent, and Denis Thomas, who had written so perceptively about television news and about ITN both in *Truth* and in the *Daily Mail*, joined us as Deputy Editor. It was to produce a structure which lasted only two years, for Thomas was first and foremost a writer, and though he proved to be a very good executive, he longed always to get his head back over a typewriter. But by the time he left us in 1963 David Nicholas, who had joined us as a sub-editor from the *Telegraph* in 1960, and who had swiftly shown himself to have a gift for television, was ready to take over as Deputy.

The Company was also strengthened by the appointment in the autumn of 1960 of William Hodgson as General Manager. Norman Dickson, who had done a sterling job in getting the Company under way, had left to become head of the BBC's newsfilm subsidiary, Visnews. The post of General Manager was a key one, for he was my Deputy for the other half of my task, that of managing, as distinct from editing. A very tall, lean, quiet man, Hodgson had been a Fleet Air Arm pilot in the war, with a repertoire of the hair-raising experiences which were the lot of that branch of the Services. A Londoner, with a grammar school education, he had become a feature film editor, and worked with Jean Renoir. He moved into management, becoming Assistant Manager of the Press Association.

He was to prove an ideal colleague, clear-headed, methodical, forthright, never dodging that most unpalatable – and most frequently avoided – of an executive's duties, that of drawing harsh facts to the notice of his superiors, and cornering them until they make a decision.

We were able in 1960 to expand our premises and enlarge our studio. ATV, awash now with money, built its own offices at Marble Arch, and moved out of Television House. This enabled us to move the editorial and administrative areas of ITN from the first to the seventh floor, bringing them at last alongside the technical areas. We were able, too, to enlarge and re-equip the studio, though we could do nothing about raising the ceiling, which continued to limit the lighting of our programmes and which made the studio dangerously hot if we were on the air for long periods.

Another pioneer left us at this time. Lynne Reid Banks, in such brief time off as she had in these hectic years, had written *The L-Shaped Room*. A best-seller which was to be made into an award-winning film, it made her independent of Editors and News Editors, and she went off to live her own life in a kibbutz in Israel, even though she was not herself Jewish. We found an impressive replacement in Elizabeth Kenrick, a graduate of New Hall at Cambridge, who joined us as a trainee and rapidly came through as a highly effective screen figure. Had she not left television in 1966 to marry, and become the mother of four children, she would have raced Anna Ford and Angela Rippon to fame.

One of our other pioneers, Diana Edwards-Jones, took over James Bredin's place as a Studio Director, a job to which she was to bring a power of swift decision, a deft sense of artistry, and a grasp of some of the more pungent words in the English vocabulary. With Diana in the director's chair, the control room bench was at times completely feminine, with Jo Hodgson as Chief Sub, and with other women doing the tasks of Production Assistant, Vision Mixer and Grams Operator.

Towards the end of 1961, after testing, it seemed, half of Britain, we at last found in Andrew Gardner, who had just come back to Britain after some years in Rhodesia, a further newscaster who could bring an added air of authority to the bulletins. Very tall, erect, with a quiet dignity, confident yet friendly, Gardner not only quickly demonstrated a high skill at presenting news with clarity and understanding. He also proved to be one of the few newcomers to television who possessed the instinctive contact with the British public which was Richard Dimbleby's great gift. It lay, I believe, in a respect for the ideals which animated a large part of our audience, the ideals of people struggling to raise families decently, to pay the rent and the hire purchase payments, or to meet the mortgage payments, to improve their gardens or their allotments, to save up for a car and a holiday – or a better car and a better holiday. He was free of the disdain for suburbia and would-be suburbia which animated so many who had been drawn into television in the post *Look Back in Anger* decade.

A year later Peter Snow joined us. Though he came almost directly from Oxford, he quickly proved able to assume the responsibilities of newscasting, the more so since he was keen to combine studio work with reporting in the field. When in due course Huw Thomas and Tim Brinton moved away to wider pastures, I had in Andrew Gardner and Peter Snow a new team ideally suited to the short bulletins of the time, embodying splendidly the sense of a young, strong, highly professional news service.

They were important on-screen reinforcements because Ian Trethowan had begun to feel the gravitational pull of the BBC. They had established a specialised political programme, 'Gallery', suited to his talents, and beyond that the wide prairies of BBC 2 were opening up. Trethowan stayed until the Pilkington inquiry into broadcasting was completed and then, in the autumn of 1962, told me that as soon as we could find a new Political Correspondent he wanted to follow Chataway, Kennedy and Day along the path to Lime Grove.

Fortune favoured us in a search for his successor. The BBC had recently rested 'Panorama'. In its place they had invited each of the intellectual weeklies, with professional guidance from the BBC, to put on a current affairs programme for one week. When it came to *The Economist*'s turn, one of their Assistant Editors had done an effective into-camera report on the economics of grouse shooting. In another item on the Gorbals area of Glasgow, he had used one phrase which stayed in my memory: 'Other cities allowed older housing to decay into slums; Glasgow built slums from the start.' I had noted his name – Alastair Burnet. I dug it out from my files and asked Ian to speak to him. The balance of influence within the media in those days made it unlikely that anyone would give up the prestigious job of Assistant Editor of *The Economist* to take his chance on the air, but Burnet proved interested, and took a screen test. There was a restraint and reserve in his manner before the camera which worried me, but I decided that if he was prepared to take the risk, so was I, and I offered him the post of Political Correspondent. In the many gambles I took over the years on screen figures, I never made a wiser choice. Though I did not know it then, I had brought on to the screen the best into-camera news and current affairs broadcaster Britain has produced, the one man who has given newscasting in Britain the enduring stature conferred on it in America by Walter Cronkite.

Reconstructing the Company twice in this way, within the four years since Robin Day had left, had been a searing experience. The task of constantly searching for new talent, constantly testing and assessing new figures was enormously consuming of time and energy. I never had ambitions to act the impresario, though in time my track record as a finder and developer of talent gave me confidence and made the task more enjoyable as well as laborious. Yet it was a heavy burden to add to the daily editing of the news. Somehow or other I had to staunch this constant haemorrhage of talent. We had now a range of good new men and women. These I was determined to keep. The only way to do that was, I knew, to win for ITN and for them wider scope on the air.

31

Newsyear '63

The flood of news in 1963, that *annus mirabilis* or, if you choose, *annus terribilis* for news, swamped the bulletins and made special programmes almost a regular part of the schedules. The year opened with Britain snowed up in the worst winter for years, and saw soon the death of Hugh Gaitskell and Britain's exclusion from the Common Market. Racial strife mounted in America, and guerrilla strife in Vietnam. Pope John XXIII died, and his successor was crowned. President Kennedy visited Berlin, to proclaim '*Ich bin ein Berliner*', and County Wexford to visit the village from which his forefathers had emigrated to the USA. Harold Macmillan resigned, and the 14th Earl of Home became Prime Minister. And winding through all these major events, like a stained thread in a carpet, was the squalid tale of the Profumo affair.

The Profumo affair posed for television a peculiarly difficult problem. It was a scandal reflected not just in gossip or allegations, but in the sworn evidence in the two trials of Dr Stephen Ward, in the privileged statements of a full-scale debate in the Commons, and in the findings of the judicial inquiry conducted by Lord Denning into the security aspects which arose because Christine Keeler had numbered among her friends the Soviet Naval Attaché as well as the British Minister for War. Material from these sources was unmistakably news, and as a result it involved television, essentially a family medium, in handling material which told of sex orgies and of two-way mirrors, of perversions and practices which until then were to be found only in the pages of Kraft-Ebbing or Havelock Ellis, or in pornography smuggled in from the Continent. We were not yet into the era of pornography on open sale in Soho, let alone soft porn on the shelves of the corner newsagents. I thought hard about whether we should suppress or at least bowdlerise the evidence which emerged. But to do so would have been to distort and indeed falsify the news.

Squalid conduct was the basis of the story, and it could not be reported with any meaning or any truth if that squalor was hidden. We deliberately bowdlerised our reports for the early evening bulletins, when children were likely to be viewing. But for the main bulletin our reports were frank, though shorter than the copious details offered by the press.

Court cases about scandal in high places were not new. In 1918 the Billing libel action, in which allegations were made (which proved bogus) that German spies had compiled a black book of the sexual weaknesses and perversions of British political leaders, had filled many newspaper columns. But its details were not spoken aloud in sitting rooms where families were gathered, and given added importance by the very fact that they had been broadcast. Long-established taboos, both of language and of subject, were swept aside during the Stephen Ward trials. The scandal which had started with the Profumo affair was the booster rocket of the permissive age. When in August that year it was joined by the robbery of the century, the sense of a society in disarray was further intensified. For it was on 8th August 1963 that the Glasgow to London mail train was ambushed in Buckinghamshire, and the Great Train Robbery passed into the mythology of British crime.

The final manifestation of the Profumo affair came in September when, at the extraordinary hour of midnight, we mounted a special programme to summarise and discuss the Denning Report – a programme which even at that hour commanded a substantial audience. From the window of my office I could see the queue outside the Stationery Office in Kingsway, stretching out of sight round the corner, as people waited for the Report to come on sale at midnight. Denning put paid to any question of security risks, and to virtually all the other rumours as well. Mandy Rice-Davies, the other girl in the case, provided her own pictorial postscript to the affair by being filmed, a copy of the Report in hand, as she wiggled her way in tight-fitting jeans across the muddy farmyard of a farmhouse in Warwickshire in which she had sought refuge.

October 1963 saw the arrival on the screen of that other phenomenon of the Sixties, the Beatles. That month they made their first appearance on the stage in London, in 'Sunday Night at the London Palladium'. After the show our cameras recorded a group of frenzied, shrieking girls chasing the four as they ran through the darkened street to their car. How far we had filmed a genuine manifestation of teenage feeling, or how far a carefully contrived publicity stunt, was never clearly established, but certainly from then on Beatlemania was a part of British life and of British news bulletins.

We were to see a lot of the Beatles in the months ahead, for from time to time they appeared in Rediffusion's pop programme 'Ready, Steady, Go'. This was mounted in the same basement studios in Kingsway from which we had presented the Elections, and the Beatles' presence there put Television House into a state of siege. Police cordons guarded all doors of the building, and traffic in Kingsway was brought to a standstill. Our camera cars could not come and go, and even motor cycle dispatch riders had difficulty in battling their way into the building any evening that RSG was on the air. The floor of the basement studio was crammed with rapt-faced boys and girls in their early teens, jiving intently but silently (the least noise during the broadcast meant that most terrible of fates, instant expulsion from the studio), the girls wearing exaggerated make-up that looked as if it had been hastily applied as they rushed here from school. A smell of sweat, chewing gum and popcorn hung in the hot, brightly-lit air, as the music, muted though it was by later disco levels, reverberated in the packed studio. The Swinging Sixties were under way on our doorstep, encouraged, enlarged, and no doubt to a degree created by this new medium which reflected these trends immediately into a multitude of homes.

32

Death in Dallas

Massive though the news stories of the first three-quarters of 1963 had been, they were all to be over-shadowed by the story which broke in Dallas on Friday 22nd November. At the time that the John F. Kennedy motorcade was approaching the Dallas Book Depository, many of the chief figures in British television were gathering at the Dorchester Hotel for the annual awards ceremony of the Guild of Television Producers and Directors. I was having a pre-dinner drink there when word reached me that Kennedy had been shot at, and wounded. In my dinner jacket I ran along Park Lane to my parked car and drove back to Kingsway as fast as the Friday evening traffic would permit. I knew that ahead lay not only a long night, but a long week.

One concern was uppermost in my mind – that the federal structure of ITV, with thirteen companies all broadcasting from different points, could lead to delay in putting out a news flash, particularly if the President had died of his wounds. The BBC was a unitary system, with most of its programmes going out from London, able to break into transmissions immediately. But Independent Television had to wheel all its stations into line before they could take a news flash from ITN. Though there was an interlocking telephone system, with red telephones which rang simultaneously in all control rooms, the process of arranging a news flash could be as cumbersome as changing the course of a convoy at sea by use of a semaphore.

I reached my office and turned on the set in the corner in time to see 'Emergency Ward 10', the medical soap opera of the day, faded out by Rediffusion and replaced by Sir John Barbirolli conducting the Hallé Orchestra. We had given the official announcement of the President's death a few minutes earlier, within two minutes of its appearance on the Reuter tape. The BBC had been ahead of us with the first news flash of his death, which they had got from a source not available to ITN, their monitoring service at Caversham, which listened to all the main foreign broadcasts around the clock. Caversham had picked up an unofficial report of the President's death, put out by the Voice of America, the official United States overseas radio service. This report was based on statements made by a priest who had just left the hospital in Dallas, and anticipated by several minutes the official statement from the White House. The BBC were at the time transmitting the 'Tonight' programme live, which enabled them to put out the Voice of America report without delay – though they took the considerable risk of hardening it up from being an unofficial report into a categorical statement that the President was dead. Granada, who had managed to get a line through from Manchester to New York – all lines through London were jammed – phoned through the same unofficial report to us after it had been broadcast in America on NBC Radio. But there was no way in which we could get it on to the air through the cumbersome ITV system in time to match the BBC's centralised operation, which had the additional good fortune of having an easily interrupted magazine programme on the air in which to flash the news.

The Hallé Orchestra continued with its programme of classical music until nine o'clock, when we put out an extended news bulletin, followed by a filmed profile of President Kennedy which we held ready against such an eventuality. This was to be the start of three days and nights of extraordinary news pressure, during which ITN was to fill six hours of air time, and the current affairs programmes many other hours as well. From breakfast time onwards the next morning we were on the air with special bulletins, in which we were able to show the first film, transmitted by Telstar, from Dallas. Throughout the weekend people turned to television as never before, seeking not only information, but needing to share the widespread and deep emotions the event had stirred. This was particularly so in the United States. As Theodore H. White was to write, 'The full acceptance of television as the nation's supreme forum was earned only by its performance over the assassination weekend . . . Sitting with friends in [Averell] Harriman's parlor and watching the tube was to be in touch with reality, to be part of the national grief.'[1]

Film of the moment of the shooting did not reach the screen for a day or two, when United Press International circulated the only film record of it, made on 8mm colour film by an amateur cameraman. But the other scenes had been widely caught by the cameras – the ambulance racing to the hospital; the anxious, tearful faces in the sunlit hospital corridors; the square and the Book Depository; the arrest of Lee Harvey Oswald; the swearing in of the new President by a Texas woman judge in the cabin of the Presidential Aircraft, Air Force One; Jacqueline Kennedy emerging from the plane with her suit still marked with dark bloodstains. Then on the Sunday evening London time came the extraordinary moment when the American television cameras caught, live, the actual shooting by Jack Ruby of Oswald as he was being escorted down the stairway in the police headquarters.

Though we did not yet have colour on British television, the poignancy of the later ceremonies was almost unbearably sharp. In the Rotunda of the Capitol the cameras caught the moment as Jacqueline Kennedy, erect and set-faced in her widow's black, led forward her six-year-old daughter, Caroline, to touch the Stars and Stripes which draped the President's coffin. Other cameras followed the funeral procession on its slow measured way past the Lincoln

Memorial across the Potomac, and up through the trees of Arlington Military Cemetry. The burial was at an hour when Telstar was in a position to carry these scenes to Europe, so that many millions on this side of the Atlantic watched and shared those moments with the American public. It was fitting that television should have marked in this way the passing of John F. Kennedy, for he was the first new leader of the television age. He was little known outside the United States until he reached the White House; yet within three years he aroused deep personal affection amongst millions. His hatless, striding figure and his ready – but not too ready – smile, depicted alongside veteran leaders like de Gaulle and Macmillan, or warily studying an ebullient Khrushchev alongside him on a Vienna sofa, or talking to Irish families amid the mud of Wexford, or with his voice ringing out in confidence and hope against a background of the Berlin Wall, had been portrayed by the cameras to a multitude of people and had given the sense that they knew him personally. He had come to embody for them hope, and it was the death of that hope which made these days and these scenes of his funeral so deeply moving.

33

Television Election

The General Election of October 1964 was the first truly 'television' election, the first in which television coverage was of supreme importance to the candidates and the parties. In 1959 our role had been new. We were still regarded as an interesting extra to the established means of election communication, rather than as the central forum. During that election the way the parties used television for their Party Political Broadcasts attracted as much attention as the way the broadcasters reported and analysed the contest. But by 1964 television had assumed a much greater significance. The ITV system had spread over most of the country. Some 90 per cent of homes now had television, as against 70 per cent in 1959.

Our coverage of the campaign followed the same pattern as five years earlier, though we had double the amount of time – twenty minutes a night – for our special 'Election Reports'. We relied mainly on our film cameras for coverage of meetings, but on eight occasions also made use of OB units. These added so much vivid authenticity that it seemed obvious that at least one major meeting of each of the main parties should have been broadcast in full, instead of the brief excerpts which were all that found their way into our reports. These excerpts no doubt gave the heart of the matter, but in cutting out the heart we killed the sense of occasion. Recordings of full meetings could have been shown late in the evening, but to do so would require the broadcasters to surrender large amounts of time, and for the parties to surrender some of the time they use for their own party political broadcasts. This has never come about. We have been broadcasting the annual Party Conferences live since 1962, but television has never yet broadcast in full an election meeting during a General Election campaign. It has so far been denied the chance to play its full part in this, the most important stage of the democratic process.

The prominence of television in the 1964 campaign led to much discussion about the telegenic strengths and weaknesses of the Party Leaders. 'Image' had become a cult word among Party managers. Harold Wilson, the first British politician to come through to Party leadership in the television age, set about mastering the techniques of the medium, and gave every sign of enjoying their use. He swiftly learnt to tailor the key point of a speech to a passage of some two or three minutes in length, providing an ideal cut for a busy film editor. In handling hecklers, he soon realised that the microphone seldom picked up their words. He would therefore repeat what they said, so winning marks for fairness – and at the same time giving himself time in which to think out a riposte.

Television has undoubtedly magnified the histrionic element in politics, but it did not invent it. Churchill's cigars and hats were used as deliberate props in the role which he set himself to play. That the role and the man were one and the same did not disguise the fact that he, consciously or subconsciously, projected a picture of himself. This was clearly to be seen at Westminster in the years of his final Premiership, in the early Fifties. As the time for questions to the Prime Minister approached, Winston Churchill could be seen waiting in the shadows of the lobby behind the Speaker's Chair – a stumpy, pale, loose-jowelled figure, shoulders bent under the burdens of age and responsibility. Then, as the House neared on the Order Paper the questions to the Prime Minister, he would suddenly draw himself upright, square his shoulders and stride into the Chamber, his chin thrust out, his step purposeful, very much the old lion ready for the fray. It was as if he had suddenly drawn on, like a garment, his public persona.

In Sir Alec Douglas-Home this histrionic element was slight. The inner circle of the Conservative Party which had ensured for him the Premiership in 1963 had paid scant regard to his potential as a television performer. He made no pretence to be one. He went his way, waging exactly the same type of campaign his predecessors had done, leaving his aides to anguish over the inescapable fact that he was certainly not a natural television figure, and that no amount of presentation tricks or camera angles would make him one. Yet Sir Alec was by no means an ineffectual television figure. In the studio he may have been stiff and abrupt and have given the impression that he regarded the questions as slightly offensive, if not to himself then certainly to the office he held. But in the field he came over differently, particularly when facing the hecklers who during this Election pursued him everywhere. The lean, upright figure who stalked from his car through noisy crowds to speak in a market square or on a building site had the assurance of a colonel checking his troops under fire, a man of courage and cool-headedness if not always a master of the deft answer. This was certainly true of the uproar, verging on a riot, which marked Home's meeting in the Rag Market in Birmingham a week before Polling Day. It was covered by OB cameras, and the presence of their scanners and vans and lighting trucks may have drawn in crowds of would-be trouble-makers. Only the fact that he had the microphone, whilst the crowd had only their voices, enabled him to get his message across to the viewing public, if not to the audience in the hall.

The most difficult question which arose during the campaign turned on the great unspoken question of race: Enoch Powell had not yet thrust the issue of immigration to the fore, and all the leaders avoided it carefully. But in the Midland constituencies it was not to be avoided. In particular in Smethwick the Tory candidate was giving voice to the resentment felt by many whites at the influx of coloured immigrants into their area. Every canon of news demanded that we should cover this development, and so I agreed that we should include Smethwick in the list of constituences on which we would present special reports. Once this news reached Transport House the Labour leadership reacted with vigour. A senior official told me that they saw our action as highly irresponsible. It could stir up racial feeling in a most dangerous way. The BBC, I was told, had had similar plans for 'Panorama' but, on Sir Hugh Greene's direct instructions, had cancelled them. I thought this was no way in which to confront a key issue in a democracy. If immigration was a matter of deep concern in a constituency, and yet was to be classed as one which could not be openly argued at the time of an Election, we were inviting people to seek non-democratic ways of sorting out their problems. I became more convinced than ever that we must cover Smethwick. We could not, I knew, go ahead with a balanced constituency report unless the Labour candidate took part. I told the Labour Party that if Gordon Walker refused to do so, ITN would have to announce that that was his decision. We had already made approaches to the other parties. The fact of Labour's ban could not be kept secret.

Such a ban would have done great harm to Gordon Walker's already threatened hold on the seat. Transport House saw this, and yielded to our pressure. Alastair Burnet went to Smethwick and on Saturday 10th October, five days before Polling Day, we presented a report on the constituency which neither avoided nor stressed the racial issue.

Throughout the campaign we once again worked closely by the clock, totting up our coverage figures every morning, and keeping the screen time of the parties within justifiable distance of one another. Once again when the parties and the press, and the now greatly-widened ranks of the academic researchers probed our work, they decided that by and large it had been fair.

For the Results programme on Election Night we had in the studio a small but knowledgeable team of commentators. Alastair Burnet was flanked by William Rees-Mogg of the *Sunday Times,* and John Freeman, Editor of the *New Statesman.* Since Burnet was about to return to *The Economist* we had assembled the next Editor of that paper, the next Editor of *The Times* and the next Ambassador in Washington. Robert Kee chaired their group, and Hugh Berrington of Newcastle University added expert psephological expertise. Kenneth Harris stood by in another studio to interview victorious or defeated candidates, peers, experts and others with something apt to say. Amongst those he interviewed were the Beatles, who chorused, 'Don't take our money away, Mr Wilson.'

Once again we built a temporary newsroom in the basement studio of Television House. When I visited it just before we came on the air on Election Night the scene on the crowded floor was as bright, under the lights, as on a sunny New Zealand beach. Our secretaries and typists were as radiant as actresses; the teleprinters chattered in their corner; cameramen and other technicians waited by their equipment; the short-sleeved journalists were already busy at their desks. At the long curved central desk Burnet and his colleagues radiated a quiet confidence, looking more like a group of dons at a Senior Common Room table, or experts in a Whitehall conference room – settings into which they could readily have fitted – rather than men about to come under the scrutiny of millions.

I was sure that we would deliver a good programme – and we did. What unfolded on our screen until the small hours of that night, and throughout the long drama of the next day, until Labour scraped into power by a margin of half-a-dozen seats, was television news at its best, swiftly presented and clearly explained. It was certainly the best live broadcast which Independent Television had mounted to that date, and even in these technologically more advanced days the recording of it merits study. It sustained its quality up to the final moments when, on the Friday afternoon, our camera outside Buckingham Palace picked up in a dramatic long shot Sir Alec Douglas-Home's car in the traffic in The Mall, as he made his way to offer his resignation to the Queen. An alert cameraman filmed him later leaving, as defeated Premiers are wont to do, by the garden gate at the rear of No.10, just before Harold Wilson swept up to the front entrance. In the new Premier's entourage that bustled into the corridor of power behind him was to be glimpsed the tall figure of Marcia Williams.

The viewing figures showed that even if we had not yet completely turned the tide which flowed the BBC's way on great public occasions, we had done much to stem it. The audience on Election Night was split only marginally in favour of the BBC. J. D. S. Haworth, writing in *Contrast,* an admirable early venture into the professional discussion of television, observed that it is 'curious how, at times like the Election, viewers switch over in droves to the BBC for the "traditional" portentousness of Dimbleby and Co. For the first time, however, there was not much to choose between the two channels. If anything ITN had the more consistent sense of urgency.'[1]

34

The Battle for Time

Throughout the period of the General Election I had been engaged in a struggle to secure a major increase in time for our bulletins. I was able to build upon the stronger position which ITN had secured within the network as a result of the report in 1962 of the Pilkington Committee. ITN had been the only part of the independent television system for which the Committee had praise. It had damned the programme companies and the Authority, but of news it wrote: 'Our general conclusion is that the country is well served by the national news bulletins of the BBC and of ITN. The selection and presentation of both services is fair and objective. For the television news services, a particular but important part of the field of television broadcasting, competition has worked well. Each of the two services is good in itself; each is different from the other in style and approach. Hence they offer the viewer a worthwhile choice and stimulate one another.'[1] The report went on to endorse my claims for a second nightly news bulletin, set about 11 p.m., and for a fully financed and properly scheduled weekly ITN news programme.

This praise, and these proposals, were endorsed by the Government in a White Paper, and by many speakers in both the Commons and the Lords. The Television Act 1963, which greatly increased the powers of the Authority over the companies, put into legal form the requirement which Aidan Crawley had wrung out of the ITA in 1955, that there should be an adequate and irreducible minimum of daily time for news. This became law, together with the essential corollary that such news should be adequately financed. All companies became members of ITN, instead of the first six who had until then operated the company on behalf of the system as a whole, a change which could help offset the domination of the major companies.

I was confident, too, that we had rebuilt the staff to the point where we could take a major lengthening of the bulletins in our stride. Early in 1963 David Nicholas had taken over as Deputy Editor. A newcomer from Oxford, Gordon Honeycombe, had strengthened our newscasting team. Though Nigel Ryan left for a time to try his hand with Television Reporters International, a premature attempt to establish an independent production company, his place was filled in the autumn by another Reuter's man, Sandy Gall, a tall Highlander whose rugged looks made him the very prototype of a front-line reporter. New young reporters were coming through – the brave Michael Nicholson; Richard Lindley, alert and sure-footed, who was to make his mark with ITN before following the well-beaten track to 'Panorama'; Alan Hart, another man of courage who, as Editor of a paper in Nyasaland in his twenties, had slept at night with a revolver under his pillow; Gerald Seymour, who could write good copy and was soon to show that he could write best-selling novels; John Edwards, who had been a teacher in a tough secondary modern school; and Julian Haviland, an Old Etonian who came to us from the *Evening Standard.* They were all new to television; they all came through to the top in it; and they all gained their basic training on the seventh and eighth floors of Television House, established now as the barrack square for a new generation of television journalists.

We had, too, a Chairman upon whom we could rely as an ally in a drive for more time on the air. In 1963 that post was held by the Managing Director of Television Wales and the West, Alfred Francis. A tall, enigmatically benign Liverpudlian who had been a writer, impresario and theatre manager, he headed a company which was not engaged in networking, and therefore had no built-in antagonism to ITN occupying more time on the air. He admired our professionalism – the first time I had heard that word used as a term of praise, which in itself was a sign of changing times, for the older ideal of the gifted amateur had persisted into post-war years.

In the summer of 1963 the ITN Board had put its mind to the future of the news once the new Television Act came into force. In July they accepted my arguments for a two-tiered bulletin, and adopted a plan for the main news at 9 p.m. to be supplemented by a further fifteen-minute bulletin at 11 p.m. This proposal was formally submitted to the Network Planning Committee which was being created as the instrument through which the ITA could exercise its new powers to guide and shape programme policy.

The NPC did not come into operation until early 1964, so the ITN Board proposal lay on the table for some months. This delay was important, for those were the news-crowded months of 1963, the experience of which caused me to change my mind about the two-tiered bulletin. It seemed to me no longer the best way, now that satellites were coming into regular use, to present the day's news. What we needed, I was now convinced, was nothing less than a full half-hour nightly news programme. In the United States the network news shows had been lengthened to half an hour in the autumn of 1963. After some early difficulties, they had quickly established themselves with the viewers. On ITN, on the other hand, the total time allocated to news bulletins in 1963 was no greater than it had been in 1956.

In the interval the supply of visual news had greatly increased, and the means of getting it to the screen had greatly improved. We now had electronic links with the ITV stations throughout Britain, and could draw on the best of their local news programmes. This was a valuable reinforcement, for regional news was one of the most successful areas of ITV programme-making. Eurovision now linked us not only to all Western European television stations, but to several Middle Eastern ones as well. Within a year regular contact was to be established with the countries in the Soviet bloc who were grouped in the Intervision system. To this was now added the vital, if intermittent link of the transatlantic satellites.

The need for more time not only to report the news, but to explore it in depth had also increased. No one body within ITV had responsibility for ensuring that all main issues were satisfactorily examined. 'This Week' and 'World in Action' chose such subjects as interested them. 'Roving Report' did others. But through the gaps between these programmes many important stories continued to slip. John F. Kennedy's campaign for the American Presidency in 1960 had, for instance, been only cursorily treated. I sought for ITN the time and the responsibility to plug these gaps – and a half-hour news was the best way to do it.

I argued my case for a half-hour nightly news in detail, and on paper, to the ITN Board, with an eye to its reaching not only the desks of the Managing Directors of the programme companies, where the real power within the companies was held, but also those of the members of the ITA, now housed in new premises above the crowded shopping thoroughfare of the Brompton Road. In particular I placed hopes on it coming to the notice of Lord Hill, who had become Chairman of the Authority in July 1963.

The ITN Directors were divided in their views. Some favoured the half-hour format, others thought it impractical. In any event the final decision did not rest with them, but with the Managing Directors and the Programme Controllers of the companies. So the Board contented itself with putting forward three possible courses of action to the Network Planning Committee. One was for a half-hour of news, to go out not later than 10.30 p.m.; another was for the 9 p.m. bulletin to be lengthened to eighteen minutes; and third was for a two-tiered bulletin pattern, with a quarter of an hour of news at 9 p.m. followed by another quarter of an hour at eleven. For good measure they recommended that 'Roving Report' be better financed, and freed to cover in depth any news, at home or abroad.

Of these choices, they believed that the choice would fall on the two-tiered bulletin or, as the parlance of the trade had it, on the networking of 'Dateline', which was by then firmly established in London as the second leg of our evening news coverage. So strong was the assumption by the companies that the Authority would ensure that 'Dateline' was networked that the ITN Board instructed us to draw up the budget for the year 1964-65 on the basis of a two-tiered bulletin, with the 9 p.m. news supplemented by an 11 p.m. bulletin.

When, therefore, early in August 1964 I was invited for the first time to attend a meeting of the Network Planning Committee, I went confident that the two-tiered bulletin would be authorised for the autumn, giving us at last scope to treat daily news fully. It would not be the full half-hour which I was sure we must have in due course, but it would bring us a big step nearer to that goal. We would gain not so much the traditional half loaf, but a whole loaf in two halves, which in time could be brought together to form a half-hour news.

At the NPC Cecil Bernstein was in the chair, and the Granada Conference Room was crowded with the Programme Controllers and Managing Directors of all the ITV companies. Bernard Sendall, the Deputy Director-General, headed a group of ITA officials. On the wall a big abstract painting in pale greys and yellows reflected Sidney Bernstein's taste, and conveyed that sense of his presence which seemed to linger in all Granada offices – though this one lacked the ritual linotype of Thomas Barnum.

When the meeting came to consider the ITN Board's proposals, there was a swift decision against a half-hour news. It had no backers among the companies. Then Cecil Bernstein put the alternative, the networking of 'Dateline'. Oppositon to it was at first muted, only two companies spoke against the idea. Granada protested that it would cut across their own late night news-in-depth programme, called 'Scene'; Tyne Tees, where Arthur Clifford was now Programme Controller, feared damage to their late night local news. I took this as a more or less ritual protest, even though it invoked the sacred name of regionalism.

The meeting looked towards Bernard Sendall, awaiting the ITA's ruling. He replied with the quiet deliberation which was his hallmark. The Authority would like to see more time for national news in the late evening, but hoped this could be done without regional news being cut back. This fell short of the definite ruling that 'Dateline' must be networked which I had expected, and which the ITN Board had prepared for. It was clear than Sendall was not armed with any firm brief to require this. My assumption that the networking of 'Dateline' was cut and dried, already agreed behind the scenes between the Authority and the major companies, was manifestly not valid. The battle for it had still to be fought.

The company representatives around the table saw that as quickly as I did. In a moment the flood gates were open. Controller after controller moved in to list the difficulties which would follow this drastic extension of time for ITN. They knew that if the word 'news' rang loud in the ITA's ears, so did that of 'regionalism'. Suddenly, in that long sunlit room, I felt this chance for ITN to pioneer a new phase in television journalism, to use more fully this new technology to inform and interest the public, slipping from my grasp. The nightmare of yet another generation of newscasters, reporters and executives moving across to the BBC recurred. I marshalled my arguments as quickly as I could, but to a ring of closed, increasingly adamant faces. The most I could get was a statement that it was the Authority's hope that all companies would take a 'Dateline'-type programme – a formula which left open the possibility of the companies doing this for themselves, something which would deny ITN the essential element of a two-tiered bulletin, that the second segment should be fully networked from ITN.

All was not completely lost. At least the controllers agreed that 'Roving Report' should be given the status and the finance of a true weekly news report, free to cover the news at home as well as abroad. Even this decision was, however, flawed by a rider that the companies need not network it simultaneously. This would be bound to reduce its impact, and was an invitation, readily accepted in the event, for the programme to be tucked away very late in the evening or early in the day.

A month later I was summoned again to the NPC to hear the outcome of the ITA's hope that the companies would carry 'Dateline', or a programme like it of their own making. Sendall had worked hard on our behalf, but in the face of the companies' opposition the result was at best patchy, with many companies prepared to take it only one or two days a week, which rendered it useless as a news programme, as distinct from a current affairs item. Of greater concern to ITN however was a proposal from Granada that ITN should hand over to other companies film material, or interviews, or other national and international news which had not found a place in the main ITN nine o'clock bulletin. These would be used by programme companies in late-night programmes of their own making. Even more explicit was a proposal from Tyne Tees, who wanted access to ITN material to allow them to present in the late evening what amounted to a national news bulletin, produced from a regional standpoint.

These proposals would have undermined the very foundations of ITN's position as the sole supplier of national and international news programmes to Independent Television. They would have reduced us, so far as the late evening period was concerned, from being a programme-maker to being a mere news agency, a supplier of raw material for others to turn into bulletins. We could find our news, much of it politically sensitive, being put out in a context over which we had no control. However strenuously the companies might strive for fairness and accuracy in their presentation of our material, they were not staffed to provide the up-to-the-second scrutiny which the broadcasting of national and international news entailed. If they did hire large enough staffs for that purpose, the temptation – and the pressure – to utilise these staffs to put out all their own national and international news, and not just these late night bulletins, would be formidable. We could find our right to be the sole source of such news for Indpendent Television being eroded – and on that right depended the money and the time on the air we needed to do a good job.

This was part of a carefully argued case I was later to put to the ITN Board and the ITA. But on that afternoon in Golden Square I had to react immediately to a proposal of which I had no forewarning. I did so with some vehemence. The failure of the Authority to give a clear ruling in favour of the networking of 'Dateline' meant that I was now battling not just for a widening of our daily news time, but for the very survival of ITN's basic position. When Lew Grade joined in the argument, making plain that he saw no case at all for any extra time for news, I hit back with more vigour than tact. The New Zealand upbringing of my generation, rooted as much of it was in the acerbity of competing Presbyterian divines, is not the best training for the English style of argument by quiet understatement. Over the weekend I realised that courtesy as well as common sense dictated that I should ring Lew Grade and take some of the heat out of what I had said. I was sitting at my desk on the Monday morning drafting one or two sentences to express this, when the telephone rang. It was Lew Grade.

'I've been thinking about the meeting on Friday,' he said. 'You know that I always speak my mind, but I want you to know that there was nothing personal about it. Nothing personal at all. Mind you, I haven't changed my mind about news late at night. But there was nothing personal in what I said.' It was no wonder that in two and a half decades in the contentious world of broadcasting, Lew Grade made a multitude of friends.

'I have been sitting here for the last half hour working out how I could put the same point to you,' I replied. 'So I will just borrow your words and put them back to you.'

But if these personal relations were restored, and indeed strengthened, the underlying problem was still unresolved. It was now remitted to the highest level, to the Authority's own Programme Policy Committee, presided over by Lord Hill in person. Two months were to elapse before that august body assembled, because we had other matters on our minds. The General Election was under way, and by the time we gathered at Brompton Road on 11th November we were into the new era of Labour rule.

I went to the meeting with three clear aims. I must first of all, to adapt Harold Wilson's later phrase about the unions, keep Granada's and Tyne Tees' tanks off my lawn. I must hold on to what we had already won – the up-grading of 'Roving Report' into a weekly news programme, which we had entitled 'ITN Reports'. But, above all, I must secure the two-tiered news, in the form of the networking of 'Dateline'. That was the only way in which we could make the major breakthrough which presentation of news on televison now demanded. It was clear that the idea of a half-hour news was premature. But a two-tiered bulletin would be a major step towards it.

It was the first time that I had been in the ITA's new Conference

Room, with its big, functional, oval table, sensibly making for discussion rather than confrontation. Lord Hill sat with his back to the windows, through which the grey autumn sky showed above the Knightsbridge roofs. He was flanked by Sir Robert Fraser, Bernard Sendall and other Authority officers.

The first two battles quickly went my way. Lord Hill ruled firmly against any idea of ITN providing material of national and international news for other companies to put out. We were to remain the sole supplier of national and international services. The half-hour weekly news, 'ITN Reports', was confirmed, though the companies were still not required to show it simultaneously. It was enough if it was shown within twenty-four hours of its release – a dangerous concession, as what is hot news on Monday can be very cold turkey on Tuesday.

The Chairman then asked Sir Robert to set out the Authority's ruling on extra time for daily news. As with everything that Fraser wrote or said it was reasoned, stately, carefully and elegantly phrased, urbane and judicial in tone. There must be a late night in-depth programme on week nights. Companies could either produce their own or take 'Dateline'. It all sounded very reasonable. Those two virtues, news and regionalism, could go forward hand in hand. But with each measured sentence it became clear that ITN had lost the battle. The Authority had either misunderstood the issue, or they had shirked it. The question was not whether time should be allocated in all areas for a nightly news in-depth programme, which the companies could make for themselves if they wished; it was whether ITN should have extra time for a second nightly news programme to enable the news of the day to be more fully presented. That issue had got lost on the way, obscured by the holy cow of regionalism, or had been dodged because it involved a head-on clash with the companies which the Authority wished to avoid. Whatever the reason, the battle for the two-tiered bulletin had been lost. The outcome was a patchwork, with some companies taking the ITN late programme, others doing their own, and yet others taking ITN's irregularly – and almost all of them transmitting it deep in the night, treating it as something to be got out of the way before the prologue. ITV had failed to grasp the opportunity opened by the new technology and by the public interest – in both senses of that phrase.

The only option open to us was to renew the fight for the half-hour news – even though that would be all the more difficult now that the companies had won their fight against the networking of 'Dateline'. I would have to go back and rally a staff who had glimpsed wider horizons ahead, who had shared my belief that with Lord Hill at the head of the Authority we would be at last getting proper elbow room to do our job. We did have, however, one real gain. We now had the weekly news-in-depth programme which Crawley had sought from the earliest days. We could use this to experiment with the fuller and longer treatment of news which a half-hour news would demand, and to train our staff for such a programme.

As a consolation prize, the meeting allocated a further minute of time to the present 8.55 bulletin. I might have secured more, had I battled for it, but I could see little point in doing so. I did not want to creep ahead with extensions to our present pattern, but to make a major leap forward. Only with much more time could we develop new editorial methods to match the new technology – as indeed was to be vividly shown in the early days of 'News at Ten'. Until we did that we were better off with a bulletin of twelve to fifteen minutes in peak hours, within which we could be sure that we could hold the audience by our present techniques. Moreover, if we edged our way forward minute by minute, we might well have got stuck around the twenty minute mark – as proved the fate of the BBC News – unable to make the major breakthrough which only a sudden doubling of time could bring. Indeed when the first counter-attack against 'News at Ten' came in 1968, twenty minutes was the reduced length proposed by the counter-revolutionaries. It would be better to concentrate on making a success of 'ITN Reports' and then to renew the fight for the full half-hour news – for which an opportunity would open up in two years' time at the latest, when the companies would be concerned about getting their franchises renewed. Such were the thoughts with which I sought to offset the sense of numbing disappointment which beset me as I moved out from the ITA offices into the crowded Brompton Road. Put not your trust in princes – or in Authorities.

35

'ITN Reports'

We got away to a good start with 'ITN Reports'. We had opened an office in New York, and had won over Peter Woods from the BBC to be our correspondent there. He secured an interview with the Duke of Windsor, the first the Duke had given at any length to British television. Gerald Seymour sent us from the Borneo jungle a thoughtful as well as a vivid account of the Gurkhas in action in the 'confrontation' with Indonesia. We followed this a month later with the first close-up photographs of the surface of the moon, taken by the American moon probe, Ranger VIII. Videotape of these pictures was due at London Airport only half an hour before 'ITN Reports' was scheduled to go on air. In normal circumstances no dispatch rider could get the tape to Kingsway within that time. We were, however, on the eve of the official opening of the new M4 motorway from Heathrow to Chiswick. The road stood empty, cordoned off, in readiness for the ceremonial tape to be cut the next morning. John Cotter got police agreement for our dispatch rider to use it. Escorted by police cars, he made a race track of the motorway, moving on through the streets to Kingsway just in time to give us an exclusive which, in those early space days, was of absorbing interest.

To the pressure of getting this new programme under way had been added that of the coverage of the last illness and the death of Sir Winston Churchill. We had responsibility not only for reporting these events, but for preparing a major full-length documentary on Sir Winston's life. The task of making such programmes about famous people, to be held in readiness for showing when they died, had been laid on us in 1960, even though within the BBC such work was put in the hands of those regularly engaged in making major documentaries. The profile of President Kennedy, shown on the night of his death, had been one of these. It was a sensitive task, for the pressures of war had made the British at that time a closely integrated people, and the lives of those who had led the country in that struggle were interwoven at one point or another with the lives of us all.

This was particularly true in the case of Sir Winston Churchill. The film which we presented on the night of his death on 24th January 1965 lasted nearly two hours. The final version – for we took over earlier versions prepared by Rediffusion, and by ABC – was the work of Bob Verrall and myself, with commentary by Brian Connell, and was completed in a long weekend of work in a freezingly cold hired cutting room above a fish and chip shop off Long Acre. The critics placed it at least on a par with the BBC's film of Sir Winston, for which Sir Laurence Olivier had spoken the commentary. The influential journal *Television Today* declared that 'both channels did wonderfully well. ITN's version seemed to have the edge with intimacy and humour. Sir Winston was always a rebel with a puckish sense of humour, and somehow the ITV version put across the Churchillian chuckle, whereas the BBC's effort was more solemn.'

In 'ITN Reports' we at last had time in which to allow the cameras to tell the story. Items which in the bulletins had to be cut back to two or three minutes could run for ten, twelve or even fifteen minutes. We could now cover big stories properly in television terms. This was particularly important, for by 1965 the Vietnam war presented a major challenge to the new journalism. Since the previous August American troops had been in action in Vietnam. But the complex nature of the fighting, the fact that the war was one of battles on a hundred different guerrilla fronts, and not just a straight frontal clash as had been the case in Korea, had not become plain to the public. 'ITN Reports' enabled us to put it in this wider setting, as well as to bring through its drama and its horror. Jon Lane for 'ITN Reports' captured memorably the scene of the US Marines in full battle order splashing ashore at Da Nang to protect that key air base against the Vietcong. Sandy Gall travelled the length of Route 19, the main lifeline of South Vietnam, and demonstrated vividly the wide grip the Vietcong had on the countryside. A month later he gave the British public the first pictures from within an American helicopter gunship, as this new war machine roamed above the rice paddies, where tiny black figures in the combat pyjamas of the Vietcong could be seen running for cover under stabbing bursts of tracer fire.

In America another big story, the civil rights struggle, could also be properly covered. Peter Woods reported from the midst of it, being filmed walking in the front rank of the Freedom Marchers moving on Selma, Alabama, and interviewing Dr Martin Luther King as he led the column towards a cordon of State police. From Stanleyville, where yet another Congo revolt flared, Sandy Gall sent back film of scenes which were to become typical of African fighting – long dirt roads (for the wars were chiefly for the roads linking the scattered towns), with the bush crowding in on either side, suddenly revealing huge men in camouflage uniforms, draped with bandoleers, advancing against each other. Gall was seized by the rebels and taken to Stanleyville airport to be expelled. He was led through the airport building, the floor of which was covered with prisoners lying in rows, hands tied behind their backs, awaiting execution. From one row he heard a voice calling, 'Sandy, Sandy.' It came from our Kenyan stringer, an East African Indian called Mohinda Dillon. By fierce arguing Gall got Mohinda freed and put on the aircraft with him. Three months later, when Belgian paras landed in Stanleyville to evacuate the remaining Belgian settlers and doctors and nurses, Gall and Mohinda were with them.

One story gave us a foretaste of a problem which was to dominate news coverage in the Seventies. The IRA, who had for some years lain very low – so low that they seemed no more than an historic relic of a bygone era of violence in Ireland – surfaced briefly when they blew down some telephone poles in protest against a private weekend visit Princess Margaret made to the Republic. We made contact with them, and they offered to allow us to film a training camp near Dublin. So quiet were conditions in Ulster that, by covering this story, we seemed to be doing no more than mark the end of the time when the gun dominated Irish politics.

Sandy Gall went off to Dublin, met an IRA contact, and, blindfolded, was driven with the camera crew by a circuitous and baffling route to a farmhouse in the countryside, where a handful of men described as IRA volunteers assembled tommy guns and crouched around outbuildings in a mock attack. I was therefore surprised when, after the programme was shown, a Special Branch officer came to Kingsway to ask if I would make a copy of the film available to Scotland Yard. The IRA, he pointed out, was a prohibited organisation and we were open to the charge that we were withholding information that could be of value in enabling police to prevent crime.

I accepted certainly the fact that we had a duty as citizens to help prevent crime. Yet I had also a duty to protect Gall and the camera crew. If the IRA were as dangerous as this police officer believed them still to be, they might well take reprisals if we acted not only as newsmen, but also as police informers. I opted to protect our staff and refused to make the film available. Even at that time it was not an easy choice; it was to become a hideously difficult and continuing choice for my successors in later years.

In May 1965 Early Bird, the first satellite available for commercial use, carried us truly into the satellite age. Unlike Telstar, with its chancy twenty-minute periods of transmission, Early Bird – *La Matinuelle* the French technicians called it – was available for eighteen hours a day. At £3,000 an hour it was too costly for us to use regularly, but we now had the reassurance that satellite transmissions would be available for big occasions. For the first time round-the-world television – or at least transatlantic television – was possible on a regular basis.

Early Bird provided such a clear argument for increasing the length of the news that I took the opportunity in June 1965 to renew my campaign for a half-hour news. I proposed to the Board that we should combine 'Dateline', 'ITN Reports' and the bulletins into a half-hour news to be shown at 10 p.m. I had a further reason for doing so. The BBC had decided to move 'Tonight' from the early evening slot it had occupied since 1957 and place it at 10.15 p.m. This would give the Corporation – if they cared to use it – an excellent outlet for late news. They were already experimenting with longer news bulletins on BBC 2. They could race us, if they chose, to presenting a half-hour news on BBC 1.

As I expected, this plea fell on deaf ears. The ITN Board neither endorsed it, nor opposed it, but merely authorised me to submit it to the companies through the Network Planning Committee. The NPC's reply was a firm 'No'. All I secured for my pressure was agreement by the ITN Board that we should make three pilot half-hour programmes. We drew up our plans to make these as soon as we had completed our preparations for the further General Election which was clearly imminent.

36

Election '66

The General Election of April 1966 followed so closely on the heels of the 1964 contest as literally to seem to be déjà vu. One of the main contestants, Edward Heath, was a newcomer to star status. But otherwise there was a sense that this was a re-run, rather than a fresh take.

The most remarkable televison coverage of the campaign came during Harold Wilson's meeting in the Rag Market at Birmingham, where Sir Alec Douglas-Home had been howled at, if not howled down, in 1964. The Prime Minister's speech there on 16th March was planned to run from 8.30 p.m. to 9.30 p.m., a span which straddled, by accident or design (one never did know with Harold Wilson and his entourage) the time in which our main bulletin went on air. I decided to carry a segment of the speech live in the bulletin, and stationed myself in our VTR recording and editing room to select it. When the Prime Minister took up his place on the platform in Birmingham it was clear that the meeting was already in a turbulent mood. He began slowly, lingering over the sentences of his written speech, certainly not reading swiftly through the earlier passages – as he could often do – before coming to the key points. This leisurely approach stimulated the hecklers, and for the next twenty minutes we were treated to a virtuoso performance by a remarkable televison political performer, as Harold Wilson varied his replies from scorn to wisecracks, from derision to apparent indignation, seeming deliberately to tease the audience. He was certainly in no hurry to get on to the main parts of his speech. The reason was not hard to guess. He was playing the audience along, playing for time until 9 o'clock, warming them up as the compère of an entertainment show warms up his audience, until he was ready to come in. And come in he did, right on the stroke of the clock which marked the start of our bulletin. As the second hand on the big clock on the recording room wall moved towards the opening minute of our bulletin, and our titles came up on the screen, Harold Wilson's whole manner changed. He dropped the attitude of the jesting debater, and, almost as if he had changed his very garb, became in a flash the serious statesman. By the time we had switched over to the live feed from Birmingham, and millions of homes in Britain had joined me in this ring-side view from the Rag Market, the entertainer had been replaced by the political leader. Gravity now marked his features, as he set out the core of his argument swiftly and vigorously.

The crowd in the Rag Market, which had by then passed from heckling to uproar, with Conservatives shouting at Labour supporters, and students shouting at them all, were taken by surprise, and for a moment silenced. But within a minute or so they were back on the attack. At home the audience saw the Prime Minister seeking to expound his policy to the country, being shouted and yelled at, but battling on in the face of uproar, steadily putting his message across, pausing only to deliver an occasional riposte. It provided some of the most remarkable television ever seen in a news programme. Now you could indeed 'See It Happen on ITN'. I let it run for four and a half minutes and then cut away for the rest of the bulletin.

The BBC did not show the meeting live. Their hierarchy, I was told, had ruled against it on the grounds that, by allowing live material into a bulletin, one had lost editorial control of its content. That seemed to me an excessively purist approach and certainly did not deter the BBC fourteen years later from putting out live coverage of the siege of the Iranian Embassy in London, or during the Falklands war broadcasting direct the news of the sinking of HMS *Sheffield* from the Defence Ministry.

The test must surely be whether we could reasonably assess in advance what the material was likely to be and judge its newsworthiness. The two earlier occasions on which we had used live material in a bulletin – the first arrival of President Kennedy in London, and the breakthrough of the final section of the new St Bernard tunnel under the Alps – had passed that test. It was a reasonable assumption – and one which proved true – that a major setpiece speech by a Prime Minister would be equally newsworthy.

For Election Night we adopted the same basic pattern as in 1964, though this time we had two computers on the job, both installed in the Scene Dock of Studio 9, alongside the area where the newsroom had been set up, and where the commentators faced the camera. Alastair Burnet, who had continued to appear before the cameras for

'This Week' after leaving ITN for *The Economist*, was again in charge of the programme on the air. David Nicholas, having got 'ITN Reports' well under way, took over the producing of this Election programme, as he was to do triumphantly during the next four Elections.

This was the first General Election since 1950 in which Richard Dimbleby did not head the BBC team. He had died of cancer three months earlier, Churchill's funeral having been the last great occasion on which he had presided at the microphone. But Cliff Michelmore, well known for his work as the compère of 'Tonight', filled the central role admirably for the BBC, where he was flanked by those two ITN graduates, Day and Trethowan.

In the outcome the battle on the night between us and the BBC was very even. Once again Alastair Burnet was at his skilful best, switching from area to area and person to person with deft, brief remarks that gave the whole programme form and point. He sustained this task without any apparent fatigue or flagging right through the next day, when his work was the more difficult because, with the result long decided, there was none of the cliff-hanging suspense of 1964. When at five o'clock in the afternoon of the second day Burnet finally signed the programme off the air, the team in the studio – the cameramen, recordists, journalists, telephonists and studio hands – spontaneously burst out clapping, emerging from the shadows around their cameras and desks in this tribute to a true professional.

The incident of the 1966 Election which caught the headlines, and bulks large in the academic studies of the campaign, occurred not in the studios of Kingsway or of Television Centre, but on the train from Liverpool to London on the morning following Election Night. The BBC had put electronic equipment on to the train which would enable them to transmit live an interview with the Prime Minister. But he refused to give them an interview, though he readily gave one to John Whale and the ITN crew who were also on the train. The reasons for the Prime Minister's attitude to the BBC throughout his period of office, and afterwards during the row about 'Yesterday's Men' have been frequently analysed, but still remain obscure. I was sorry at the time, and remain sorry, that they took the shape of this refusal to share out his interviewing time between both organisations. We wanted any scoops we could get against the BBC, but we wanted them to be on a free-for-all basis. As it was, John Whale's interview would have stood up to any competition, shot at the breakfast table with a bottle of HP Sauce well in view, and full of sharp, clear questions.

37

A Half-Hour News?

By the spring of 1966, with the General Election out of the way, we were well placed not only to bid for a half-hour news, but to produce one. Nigel Ryan was back after his spell with Television Reporters International, and was editing with verve and style 'Reporting '66', as we had renamed 'ITN Reports'. David Nicholas had emerged not only as a natural leader of journalists, but as a producer capable of imparting a Welsh gusto and flourish to the programmes he made. We were also financially and technically much stronger. Hodgson's careful planning had enabled me to use the leverage provided by the Pilkington Report, and by the 1963 Act, with its requirement that ITN should be adequately financed and equipped. The money allocated to ITN had been doubled since 1960, and the staff increased from 202 to 231, an increase which had taken place almost entirely at the sharp end, in reporters, cameramen, recordists and engineers. We now had eleven sound camera teams, nearly double the level of 1956. We were still tightly budgeted, with no scope for extravagance, but that was a useful discipline.

We had too a valuable ally in our new Chairman, James Coltart. With Roy Thomson now absorbed in his newspaper empire in Gray's Inn Road, Coltart had a freer hand, as Chairman of Scottish Television, to give rein to his love for news and for enterprise. I soon learnt that I could open my mind to him about our strategy for gaining a half-hour news. It was based on the belief that we could not rely on the Authority forcing the companies' hands on our behalf. Not only had Fraser sat silent when I had raised the issue with the Board in June 1965, but he had done nothing to prevent both 'Reporting '66' and 'Dateline' from being pushed further and further out of prime time, until both were now seldom seen until well after 11 p.m. Our best hope was to bide our time until the programme contracts came up for renewal early in 1967. There was a chance then that at least some companies might be prepared to earn brownie points with the Authority by allowing us to try our hands at a half-hour news, if only for an experimental period. There was also the chance that Lord Hill might then intervene on our behalf. But if we were to carry out this plan we had in the interval to lie low, and not press our case too hard. If we moved prematurely we could alert the companies to this tactic, and forearm them against it.

It was therefore with no enthusiasm that I learnt that Alastair Burnet intended to advocate the introduction of a half-hour news in a speech he was to make, as Editor of *The Economist,* to an ITA Consultation on News and Current Affairs due to be held at Brompton Road in January 1966. This seemed to me likely to rouse every current affairs producer to the danger that ITN might be allocated time which was at present available to them, and to clarify and harden the oppositon of company managements. Research figures produced for the Consultation also seemed to tell against our case. Lord Hill had now a new head of information and research, Sir Harold Evans, who had been for many years public relations adviser to Harold Macmillan at Downing Street. Evans had conducted a survey of viewers which had shown little desire for longer news bulletins. Of those questioned 83 per cent liked the main ITN evening bulletin at its present length of just under fifteen minutes. Only one-third wanted it lengthened to half an hour. It was pleasant to have confirmed that on every night of the week ITN bulletins commanded a higher audience than did the BBC News, even though under the BBC counterattack the general ITV audience had been steadily declining.

Once the issue had come up for public debate it was clear, however, that we must make our case with all possible force. My forecast of the attitude of our current affairs colleagues proved accurate. They were unanimously hostile to the idea of a longer news. Tim Hewat of Granada declared contemptuously that ITN was incapable of producing a good half-hour news programme. My reply, which stands in the ITA files as the first detailed public argument for 'News at Ten', was that we could do it, and that the imperatives of journalistic and technological development demanded that we should do it. I was not deterred by Sir Harold Evans's statistics. One of the symptoms of the decline of the *News Chronicle* had been the hours spent by senior executives poring over the results of Gallup Polls which had asked the public what sort of newspaper they wanted. The public does not know, and cannot know, what it wants until some Editor offers it to them.

Sir Robert Fraser's summing up confirmed my impression that we could look for little help from that quarter. He said nothing in support of the half-hour news, and laid stress on a point made by a regional News Editor of 'the danger of a surfeit of news and current affairs in the late evening if a half-hour bulletin were introduced at ten o'clock'. The consultation ended with the prospect of a half-hour news further away than ever.

For the next three months planning for and covering the General Election took up all our spare energies. It was not until May that we were in a position to return to the attack on the half-hour news. We did so by experimenting with a pilot programme. Our first attempt was not a success. We simply extended the length of the programme without extending the length of the items within it, the longest of which ran to no more than two minutes. The result was scrappy.

We tried again, using the material available on Derby Day. This time we varied the pattern, putting ten minutes of hard news first, and then using Bosanquet and the 'Dateline' team to provide a segment of news in depth before we rounded off with more hard news – the first time Gardner and Bosanquet had presented a programme together. I showed the programme to the companies, who thought little of it, and to the Authority, whose officials found it 'a powerful piece of viewing'. It was to prove powerful enough, indeed, to win over Sir Robert Fraser to the idea of a half-hour news. He viewed the programme in August, decided – with the eye of an old Fleet Street hand – that it was a workable format, and agreed that a half-hour of news around 10 p.m. was the goal at which ITN should aim.

This modification in the Director-General's attitude from the position he had adopted at the January consultation may also have owed something to the change which was taking place in the climate of competition between ITV and the BBC. For the first time since ITV had come on the air a fundamental shift was under way in the pattern of viewing. Week by week Independent Television's grip on two-thirds of the audience, which for years had seemed unassailable, was beginning to slip. Competition from the BBC was steadily strengthening. BBC 2 had got over its teething troubles and the Corporation's schedulers were using their two channels with skill in

The story which won world attention for ITN: Robin Day interviews President Nasser of Egypt, June 1967.

The first use of a satellite for news: ITN reports from New York via Telstar, 30 July 1962.

Sandy Gall reports from the battle zone in Vietnam, 1965.

Jon Lane films for ITN the landing of American Marines at Da Nang, South Vietnam in May 1965.

Monday July 3rd 1967

HALF HOUR NEWS

ALASTAIR/ TRAILER

Which brings us to the end of this, the first News at Ten. Our aim is to bring you every weekday evening a half-hour news in depth, at a peak ~~visual~~ viewing hour, a new venture in British television. For television itself is now better equipped to cover the world's news than it was when the old, short news bulletin was devised. We know it means asking you to develop a new viewing habit at 10 o'clock every evening; but we mean to make it worth your while. Goodnight.

The first 'News at Ten' newscasters: Alastair Burnet and Reginald Bosanquet (*above*), and Andrew Gardner (*right*), with the closing words of Alastair Burnet's script on the opening night of 'News at Ten'.

The story which got the half-hour news truly under way: the Argyll and Sutherland Highlanders re-occupy the Crater district in Aden.

Election Night, October 1964: 'television news at its best'.

Both Geoffrey Cox's successors learnt their television journalism with ITN. Nigel Ryan (*above*), Editor 1968–77 and David Nicholas (*left*), Editor 1977—

The 1962 Telstar programme won the Producers' and Directors' Guild Award.

The first landing on the moon, July 1969, viewed live on television: the supreme example of television's ability to let people 'See It Happen'.

the battle for ratings. Subtly, BBC 1 was moving over to more popular ground. In the face of this pressure the programme companies had begun hectically to reshuffle their schedules, and the Authority had begun to take a harder look at their programme pattern. Indeed the ITA had decided that the time had come, if not to brandish, at least to hold aloft the big stick which the Television Act of 1963 had given them. They were worried not only by the persistent erosion of the viewing figures, but by a sense that the ITV programme pattern seemed increasingly stale in face of the wide choice offered on the two channels of the BBC. In light entertainment, once a field dominated by the companies, the BBC now held the lead. In situation comedy, with shows like 'Steptoe and Son' and 'Dad's Army' established as national institutions, the BBC was showing more polish and originality. In the summer of 1966, therefore, after making a carefully documented survey of programme strengths and weaknesses within ITV, the Authority called on all companies to take a fresh, hard look at the make-up of their schedules between 7 and 10.30 p.m., with a view to securing within these times a wider range of programmes, to give more variation from the standard fare. It was by far the strongest document of the kind that the ITA had ever put out to the companies, and was regarded as so confidential that only two copies were made available to each company. Coming just six months before the franchises in their areas were due to be advertised for re-allocation, it must have made worrying reading for the Managing Directors and Programme Controllers.

As the autumn of 1966 wore on I could not, however, detect any major change resulting from the ITA action. What was apparent was a considerable re-scheduling of their existing programmes by the companies as they sought to resist the BBC's pressures. This led to a demand that the main evening news should go out at different times in different parts of the country, with some areas taking it at 8.50 p.m. and some at 9.25 p.m. I was able to resist that, and keep to a unified time at 8.50, but it was hardly an augury for a longer news in peak hours.

In November a further obstacle to a half-hour news at 10 p.m. emerged. Sir Robert Fraser had made his first visit to the United States since the American networks went over to the half-hour format. He liked their half-hour format, but even more he liked the hour at which it was transmitted, which was in the early evening, ranging (according to the time zones of that wide continent) between 6.30 and

7 p.m. On his return he urged John McMillan to advocate to his fellow network controllers that ITN should mount half an hour of news at 6 or 6.30 p.m. John McMillan in his turn urged this on me, and on the Network Programme Committee.

The prospect was a great temptation, because at an early evening hour we could work out the production problems which a longer news would pose without the full spotlight of peak time attention on us. But the facts were against it. By 7 p.m. in New York and Washington most of the main news of the day is in. Congress does not sit in the evenings. In Europe, five or six hours ahead of America, the day is over, and the news it has yielded has reached American newsrooms. The reverse is true in Britain. News from America, copious in those days of space development and of the Vietnam war, is barely on the way by 6 or 6.30 p.m. British time – early afternoon in America. Much other foreign film has not yet been cleared through London Airport. At Westminster Parliament has still four hours of news-making ahead of it.

If we were to make our major news effort early in the evening we would, moreover, throw away one of the advantages of broadcast news – the capacity to fill the gap between the evening and the morning papers. Above all, a half-hour news at 6 or 6.30 would not solve the biggest production problem of all, that of attracting and holding journalists of the highest calibre. Few of them would see it as offering an outlet of status. So on paper and in discussions with Sir Robert and with John McMillan I held strongly to my view that a half-hour news must be placed at 10 p.m.

At least this debate had cleared my mind on timing. Any earlier good time, around 9 p.m., would increase our production problems, and would be gambling with the peak hour audience. Ten o'clock was still a good viewing hour, yet if anything went amiss we would not have jeopardised the viewing figures for the evening. Anything later than, at the most, 10.15, would invite a switch to the BBC, who had by now moved their news to 8.50 p.m. Our campaign, therefore, became one not merely for half an hour of news, but for half an hour at ten.

In taking this as our objective, I knew that we were proposing not just a change in television schedules, but in the viewing habits of the British people. In the early television years viewers had accepted television news as not only a late, but a movable feast, because radio was then still the main broadcast news medium. The nine o'clock news on sound was the centrepiece of broadcast journalism. But as the radio audience ebbed away, and news on the air came to mean television news, the public had come to expect – and to get – the main bulletins on BBC Television and on ITN around nine o'clock. A change to news at ten o'clock would mean asking the public to sample not only a new programme, but a new pattern of evening viewing.

Meanwhile time was slipping dangerously away. There were only a few more months in which the companies, with their contracts at risk, would be open to persuasion about a longer news. In mid-December I decided to play my final card, and appeal direct to Lord Hill. At the same time I submitted yet one more paper to the companies arguing the case for a half-hour news, and made a further pilot programme. This was given the working title of 'News at Ten'. Its film content was registered that evening under that name, the first time 'News at Ten' appears in the records of ITN.

Charles Hill had shown himself consistently friendly towards ITN even if he had let slip the chance to give us the two-tiered bulletin in 1964. He had been one of our strong supporters during the early days when he was still Postmaster General, and when he had told me, 'I like my news with sauce.' He readily agreed to meet, and invited me to dinner at the Reform Club. I found him waiting in the main hall of the Reform, that hall which had seen the start of two remarkable journeys, one fictional, one only too real. From it Jules Verne had sent Phineas Fogg on his bid to travel around the world in eighty days. It was here too that Burgess and Maclean in 1951 had foregathered for their flight to Moscow. This December evening it was – as are most London clubs in the evenings – half deserted. The table where we had coffee was well away from any other diners, so I was able to unfold my plan frankly. ITN was now in good shape for a half-hour bulletin. If we got the chance, we could do the job. Would the Authority now rule that we could have half an hour of time at 10 p.m. on weekdays, at least for a trial period of thirteen weeks – the quarter of the year into which television programming is divided?

Lord Hill's reply chilled me. It was not practicable for the ITA to impose a programme change like this on the companies out of the blue. So long as all the companies were opposed to a half-hour news, it would not be realistic for the Authority to seek to drive through such a drastic plan. If, however, the companies were divided, with some in favour of a half-hour news and some against it, the ITA could rule in favour of those who wanted it.

I could see no chance of any such division. There might be a chance that Scottish Television, out of loyalty to their Chairman who was also our Chairman, might agree to the experiment. But all the others, including ITN's good friend John McMillan, were opposed to half an hour of news during the main viewing hours. I felt as if a great door had been quietly but adamantly closed in my face. Charles Hill's personal standing with the companies was high. In his three years at Brompton Road he had done a remarkable job of public relations for Independent Television. He had repaired much of the damage done to ITV's reputation by Pilkington, largely because he demonstrated that he genuinely liked ITV programmes, and watched them. By visiting the companies one by one, and by insisting on meeting the programme-makers and the technicians, he had improved morale within the system itself. With the power to renew – or take away – the franchises upon which the very life of the companies depended, he was at the peak of his power. If in these circumstances he felt it impracticable to rule that ITN be given this one new chance, then the prospects of a half-hour news were bleak indeed.

A month earlier the ITA had put out the advertisements for the new television franchises. They had made one major change in the geography of the system. The Northern region which, by their ever skilful public relations Granada has got widely referred to as Granadaland (much to the fury of Howard Thomas, whose ABC served the same area at weekends) had until now comprised Yorkshire as well as Lancashire and Cheshire. Under the new contracts Yorkshire would be a separate area. The Midlands, where the week had also been divided between ATV and ABC, would be held by one contractor for seven days a week, and a new contractor would be offered the London Weekend franchise, at present held by ATV. These proposals had brought a spate of reports in the papers about groups forming to bid for the contracts. Lord Goodman, who then seemed to be on every public body and in every public print, had one group; Aidan Crawley was forming another. Tim Hewat was reported to be working with the *Yorkshire Post* in yet a third. A fourth consortium, organised by Telefusion, the radio and television relay company which operated in the North, was deemed by the newspapers to be an outsider against whom the odds were long. Three of the groups had sounded me out about joining them, but I had been so absorbed in preparing to secure for ITN at last its place in the sun – or, to be more accurate, in the mid-evening starlight – that I had given them little thought. But that evening, as I digested Hill's words on my drive towards Hampstead, I decided I had better get into a consortium. Clearly the prospects were bleak for any real extension of time for the news, the extension essential to carry ITN into the new phase which both technical development and public interest demanded. Two weeks later I told Telefusion I would join their group.

What I did not know, however, was that within Brompton Road forces were at work which, though this was not their main aim, were to undermine the companies' united front against a half-hour news. Sir Robert Fraser and his Deputy, Bernard Sendall, had had a fairly dusty answer to the paper they had circulated in August calling for a major shake-up in the schedules, and for an improvement in programme quality. There had been some stirrings of new work in children's programmes, and an effort had been made to revitalise comedy. But drama series tended more and more to have a mid-atlantic flavour as the companies, spearheaded by Lew Grade's ATV, sought to offset their increasing costs by sales to America. No new serials had come through to flank the old favourites of 'Coronation Street' and 'Crossroads'. 'The Frost Programme' had been phenomenally successful, but even so only two small stations – Border and Anglia – took it outside the London area. At Christmas the BBC once again dominated the viewing hours. Certainly the fresh, hard look which the Authority had called for four months earlier had not brought results. Throughout the autumn the viewing figures had continued to drift downwards, and the BBC's reputation with the critics and the informed public to edge steadily upwards. Members of the Authority were becoming increasingly sensitive to implications that they were not exerting the new powers Parliament had conferred on them.

Most importantly, Fraser had hardened his attitude. He had been sincere in his faith in the public taste, and had incurred much harsh criticism in the early years for defending Independent Television on the ground that the public liked it. Now that this public support was ebbing, he was prepared to follow the logic of his position, and insist that the companies take action. Bernard Sendall provided him with the means to do so.

Sendall had worked closely with the companies in planning the programme schedules, through the Network Planning Committee, over the previous two years. Prior to that he had had, ever since the start of the system, considerable daily programme experience. He now drew up proposals for a major shake-up in the weekday programme pattern, involving better timings for drama, documentaries and for 'This Week' and 'Word in Action'. As a key element of this new schedule he proposed a half-hour news programme at ten o'clock. For the first time since ITV came into being the news was seen as the central pillar around which the evening's viewing was to be built, not as an irritating extra which had to be fitted in somewhere. This pattern Fraser decided to put to the companies not as a requirement – at least in the first instance – but as a proposal.

Fraser and Sendall were too shrewd and too experienced to precipitate a head-on clash. They by-passed the formal machinery of the Network Planning Committee, where all the companies would be present in full array. Instead they called to Brompton Road the three key men of the weekday networking companies – John McMillan of Rediffusion, Cecil Bernstein of Granada, and Lew Grade of ATV. Around the circular table in the corner of his office Fraser unfolded the scheme, and invited the networkers to adopt it of their own volition. If they did so, that would be ideal. If not, then the Authority would have to try other courses of action.

The three men who faced Fraser and Sendall across the table were realists. No doubt they sensed an added note of steel in Fraser's approach. They knew too that their own ground was weak, not only because their contracts were soon to be at stake, but because the schedules they had devised themselves were not holding the audience. Within a few days they had accepted the plan in principle. They did not disguise the fact that they found it unpalatable, but they yielded to *force majeure*. On one point, however, they sought a modification up to the last moment. This was on the length of the ten o'clock news. They argued strongly that this should be only twenty minutes. A longer time would take the flexibility out of the late evening programming, putting the audience at risk. The advertising agencies disliked the idea of half an hour of news. Revenue could be lost. If the longer news failed to hold the audience, even more revenue would be lost. Lew Grade in particular opposed the idea. 'I resisted "News at Ten" – and I was wrong,' he said with his customary forthrightness to a House of Commons Committee four years later.[1]

On 1st March the ITA was able to write to the other companies telling them that the networkers were devising the summer schedules along the lines proposed, and asking that all companies shape their own plans for the summer to conform. In this letter the length of the ten o'clock news was not definitively set at half an hour. The

Authority stated that it was hoping that the new schedule would 'provide for a newstyle news occupying the whole of the 10 p.m. to 10.30 p.m. period' but that depended 'upon proposals coming up from the Editor'.

On the same day Fraser called me to Brompton Road and told me that we were to be asked for a longer news in the summer at 10 p.m., and I should have my proposals ready for the ITN Board the next week. He questioned me closely as to whether I was sure that half an hour, and not twenty minutes, was the right length. I do not know whether the networking companies' opposition had caused him any last-minute doubts, but I was able to reassure him we had none.

Wednesday 8th March saw the final decision taken. At a special meeting of the Standing Consultative Committee, the main liaison body between the Authority and the Managing Directors of the companies, the new schedule was adopted. The exact length of the longer news at ten was left to be settled by the ITN Board. That afternoon the ITN Board met, and accepted my case for a full half-hour bulletin with little demur, particularly after I had shown myself willing to see a break for commercials half-way through it. There were good technical reasons for this. I knew that mounting a half-hour news programme in its early stages would be full of snags, editorial and technical. A commercial break half-way through would give us a chance to sort out any problems. It took only a few minutes for the critical decision to be taken, and the directors were able to turn their minds to advising me how to go about making the new programme. The long battle to win the time for 'News at Ten' was over. What loomed now was the battle to win the audience for it.

38

Creating 'News at Ten'

We had only three and a half months in which to prepare the new programme, months in which we had to keep our existing service running at full blast. We could not halt operations for a week, or even a day, in order to organise the changeover. We could – and did – halt 'Dateline' for a week before the new programme was due, and cut out two of the final issues of 'Reporting '66'. But the daily bulletins would have to continue unbroken. It was rather like changing over a production line from making Minis to making a new saloon car without interrupting the flow.

This did not worry us greatly. There is no way in television in which you can tip-toe into experiments. There is only one end in television, the deep one. The longer you stand shivering on the bank, the worse you are likely to fare. You can only dive in and swim your hardest. I knew that the Napoleonic maxim which had guided me in the past – *On s'engage et puis on voit* – would apply with even greater force in this development.

We were certainly not lacking in advice, both private and public. Two points were repeatedly emphasised from within the companies and in particular from Sir Robert Fraser. The new programme must be markedly different from the existing mid-evening bulletin and it must be built around a strong central personality. In a feature article in *The Times,* Clive Irving stressed the need for a major anchor man to execute the role which Walter Cronkite for CBS, and Chet Huntley and David Brinkley for NBC carried out in the United States. Irving listed only three figures in British Television as being capable of undertaking the task – Robin Day, Alastair Burnet and Robert Kee. It was an influential article – so much so that one leading commentator, whose name was not included by *The Times* on its list, considered suing for libel simply because he had been left out. It would have provided an interesting case had it come to court.

Since the central part of my argument for a half-hour news had been the need to keep with ITN broadcasters of stature, and since two of the three men listed by Irving had been brought into television and had come through to stardom with ITN, we hardly needed to be taught this basic fact of our trade. Nor did I retort that anchor men do not exist ready-made, standing like tree trunks around which the ivy and clematis of a daily news show can grow and proliferate. Major newscasters are created and developed to full stature by the news programmes in which they appear. They need daily exposure to the public, and to the flow of news, as surely as crops need the sun. Walter Cronkite was as much a product of the CBS early evening news as he was in due course to make it his own show. When I first had contact with him late in the Fifties he was the newscaster of a much lesser news programme, the CBS news at 1 p.m. Only his skill at handling the special programmes at the conventions and on election nights had indicated the potential he so rapidly developed once he had star billing in the early evening. Huntley and Brinkley, then at the peak of their fame for NBC (Cronkite had been promoted to counter their grip on the audience), had not come together as a team because someone had spotted them as two established performers. They emerged because NBC decided to run a programme with one newscaster in New York and one in Washington. On air the two men had proved naturally complementary in style and in approach to the news: the stalwart Huntley the essence of reliability, the swift, wry Brinkley the embodiment of the informed commentator. I was confident, therefore, that even if we did not immediately find the right man for the job, we could find one who would grow into it.

The two ideal candidates, Burnet and Day, had both left us, and were so strongly established elsewhere that there was no hope of attracting them back into a venture the long-term future of which was uncertain. Clive Irving's third man, Robert Kee, who was to do a distinguished job launching ITN's 'News at One' in the early Seventies, was fully committed on other programmes and in any event might have seemed too much up market, to have a shade too much of the senior common room about him for our mass audience at that stage of television's development. Ludovic Kennedy was not going to be tied down in a studio year in and year out. Robert Robinson, still at that time a relatively new face on the screen, seemed to me a likely contender, but he decided the role was not for him. Ian Trethowan was firmly settled into the BBC, where attractive executive prospects were opening before him. We clearly had to look in-house, within ITN itself, for our talent.

I was sure that a combination of either Gardner and Snow, or Gardner and Bosanquet, would quickly come through as a highly effective team. Peter Snow, however, made clear that he did not want to continue as a newscaster. He wanted to report in the field, and above all to develop techniques for clarifying and explaining complicated news stories and news situations – something he was to carry to a fine art. That left us with Andrew Gardner and Reginald Bosanquet. I had no doubt at all that they would measure up to the task, but I had equally no doubt that to the companies and to Sir Robert, who was taking an almost hourly interest in our proceedings, they had the defect which attaches to prophets in their own countries.

I decided that we must flank this home-grown team with a major figure until the programme was safely launched. So I asked Alastair Burnet if he would present the new programme for the first crucial three months trial period. It seemed a preposterous idea to put to the Editor of the major intellectual weekly of the day. But I knew that Burnet had a Scottish lust for work, and that his talents gleamed the brighter under pressure. To my delight he agreed to broadcast the programme on Mondays, Tuesdays and Fridays. On those days he would be flanked by Andrew Gardner. On the other two nights Gardner and Bosanquet would form the team.

This formula met the doubts of the industry and provided us with the necessary big name for our advance publicity. To support this team, and to strengthen our hand on the early evening bulletins, we were lucky to find Leonard Parkin, an excellent correspondent, at that moment footloose and restive in the BBC. He was just back from a stint in Washington, and was too forthright and too straightforward a reporter to find favour with the trendy producers of 'Twenty-Four Hours' and of the other cult BBC programmes of the time. He gave a quick 'Yes' to our invitation, so bringing into ITN a man whose steady and stylish contribution has been of great value ever since.

The title for the new programme suggested itself. 'News at Ten' admirably told the viewers exactly what the programme offered and had the further great advantage, by stressing the hour of transmission, of publicising the fact that we were not only offering a new style of programme, but also that there were other times than the sacred hour of nine o'clock when news could be acceptable.

The other main point which we were adjured to observe by those who wished us well – and those who wished us ill – was that the new programme must not be merely the existing mid-evening bulletin extended to double its length. The half-hour news must be something original, different, clearly distinct from the prevailing pattern of the bulletins.

This was an easy aim to define. How it was to be achieved was more difficult to say, and I resisted many pressures to forecast our methods. These could be devised only by experimentation on the air. I decided we would start with a formula along the lines of the Derby Day dummy run, with an opening segment of hard news, followed by at least one item of news in depth – a 'Dateline' in miniature – with other, more extended news reports to complete the programme. This amounted to amalgamating the existing bulletin with a mini 'Dateline' and a mini 'Reporting '67', and would serve to get us under way, provided we were ready to modify it swiftly as changes suggested themselves.

When on 9th May 1967, just six weeks before we were due on the air, the ITN Half-Hour News planning committee held its first meeting in my white-walled office on the seventh floor of Television House, the first task we faced was to find a title sequence which would underline from the outset that this was a new type of news programme. We tried a number of designs based on still pictures, including some of the first views of the earth from outer space which the American space explorers had taken. We tried some specially shot film sequences. None seemed effective. I decided therefore, at the risk of appearing traditional, perhaps even old-fashioned, that we could not do better than use a shot of the Westminster Clock Tower at the moment Big Ben struck ten p.m. This would have the double effect of demonstrating that the news was coming from the heart of the nation's capital, and of underlining the fact that it came at the new hour of ten o'clock. By filming the tower from downstream of Westminster Bridge, an angle seldom used before, we secured a sequence with a fresh look about it.

This also enabled us to use the chimes of Big Ben as part of our opening sound sequence. We experimented with these one afternoon in the studio, bringing a recording of them up under the final frames of the film of the clock face. It became at once clear that we could not utilise all ten strokes of the bell to establish the hour. A pause of at least a second intervened between each stroke, leaving a gap which, on the air, seemed much longer. At the most, we agreed, we could accept two or three of these 'bongs', as Diana Edwards-Jones quickly termed them. She was experimenting with a first cut of the filmed title sequence, and a recording of the bongs, whilst Andrew Gardner in the studio was intoning at intervals the opening sequence which was due to follow the titles: 'Good Evening. Here is the news' followed by half a dozen potential headlines: 'The *Torrey Canyon* is bombed; more border raids around Gaza; trade figures worsen; the West Indies win the toss and pile up a big opening score.' A misunderstanding by the sound mixer brought up Gardner's words in the midst of the bongs. Diana's swift ear noticed that the gap between one bong and the next fitted almost exactly the time needed for a news headline. She got Andrew Gardner to trim the words, and fit his speech to fill each gap with a headline. It worked admirably. I was listening on the monitor set in my office, and the outcome seemed so exactly right that I sprinted up the stairs to the control room and agreed the pattern then and there. It is a technique which has lasted to this day, providing, with the interweaving of bell and words, an admirable sense of emphasis that is free of portentousness, as well as being an economical use of time. One of the enduring hallmarks of 'News at Ten' had come into being.

This called for a change in the title music. 'Non Stop', with its jaunty cheerful vigour, did not fit into this more formal scene. We tried many alternatives, including themes specially composed and specially recorded. None was right and almost in desperation, close to the day of our first transmission, we settled on 'Arabesque'. It seemed to me over-emphatic, bordering on the strident, and many viewers reacted against it when it was first used. I wanted indeed to change it after we had been on the air a month, but feared that if we did so we could appear to be losing our confidence in our product. So it remained – and remains to this day, when, perhaps because we live in harsher and more strident times, it now seems to match the hour.

To make the studio set look different we helped ourselves to a device the BBC had utilised during the General Election, the Eidophor projector. This enabled a television picture to be thrown, enlarged, upon a cinema screen at the back of a studio. It could show not only still pictures, but also film. We could use this to bring the opening sequence of film stories up on the screen behind the newscaster, before filling the screen with them. This would not only be a new method, but also would interlock closely the work of the newscasters with the film they were introducing.

When we had tracked down one of the rare Eidophor projectors in Britain, we came up against a problem which was to dog us throughout the early months of 'News at Ten'. Our studio on the eighth floor at Kingsway was too small. It provided only some 1,100 square feet of floor space, and – because it was on the top floor right under the roof – was just over ten feet in height. There was no way in which the Eidophor projector could be fitted into this space. We had to beam its pictures around a corner, using mirrors to carry its images from the scene dock which lay at the back of the studio. This involved the use of a huge magnifying lens, for which Europe had to be scoured. And no rehearsals of the Eidophor were possible until two days before the programme went on the air, because key elements of the apparatus had been booked for Billy Graham's crusade at Earls Court. But it was there, and working on the night. Our chief engineer Bill Sweeney and his engineers knew their jobs.

The next problem was temperature. The low ceiling meant intense heat from the studio lights. Air-conditioning could cope with the heat engendered by a quarter of an hour bulletin preceded by about twenty-five minutes of rehearsal. But a half-hour programme, with all its complexities, needed an hour's rehearsal. This cooked the studio to such a heat that the temperature had reached the nineties before transmission time had been reached. The dry runs which we carried out in the closing week of June, mounted in the mornings or late evenings (for the regular bulletins had to go out as usual in the early and mid-evening) showed newscasters glistening with sweat, brought production assistants close to fainting and had cameramen's sweating fingers slipping on the controls. Nor did the weather hold out any hope of relief. Sustained hot weather was forecast for the first ten days of July – and the forecasters were to prove right.

There was no time to enlarge the air-conditioning. The roof could not carry the additional weight of new plant. Bill Sweeney came up with the suggestion that we use a mobile refrigeration plant, of the type trundled out to cool down aircraft on the tarmac of airports of hot countries. The vehicle could have been parked in the yard, eight floors below. But this proved impractical, for it meant that a hole would have to be cut in the studio wall – and that was not on. The only realistic answer was to bring trays of ice into the studio and blow the cold air from them with electric fans. This we did. People coming into the studio to be interviewed on this new and revolutionary style programme would stare with disbelief when they were ushered to a chair backed by a series of ice trays which made the place look like a storage room in a fishmongers.

Soon after the half-hour news had been decided upon I sent Nigel Ryan and David Phillips, a producer who had originally joined us as a sub-editor, to New York to study the American half-hour news shows. They came back convinced – as was David Nicholas – that the key to the success of 'News at Ten' lay in the use of integrated film packages to cover the news. This style of coverage, which for a decade and a half has now been the norm for television news, opens with a shot of the reporter, set against a background which establishes that he is on the scene of the story, whilst he speaks to camera the introduction to his story. He continues his report in words which serve as commentary to the filmed scenes which follow, and which are interwoven with any interviews he has conducted. The story is rounded off with a closing passage from the reporter, once again filmed in the heart of the story's setting. In 1967 this technique was widely used in news feature programmes, but only rarely in news. We relied mainly on the technique devised in the early days, under which the commentary which held the report together and conveyed the main facts was written, not by the reporter in the field, but by a scriptwriter in the office, and read over the film by an unseen voice in a commentary studio. The reporter might provide a filmed into-camera opening and closing sequence, and would do any interviews necessary. But he would not be responsible for the final wording or the final shape of the report. This pattern was technically simpler to prepare than a fully integrated, on the spot report. It took less time, and so enabled a reporter to cover more news in a day, as he could move on to other locations or to other interviews whilst the finished story was being completed back at the studio.

The integrated news package had two major advantages. It was a smoother, more artistic, more finished job. Each story formed a compact little television programme in itself, readily watchable. It gained also both unity and authority from having only one voice on it, that of the reporter, instead of two – the reporter and the studio commentator. It was manifestly the work of the journalist at the scene, conveying the same authenticity as does an outside broadcast. It also represented a significant shift in the roles of the journalist and the film technician, tilting the balance in favour of the reporter as against the film editor. In an integrated news package the editor cut the film to fit the reporter's words rather than the scriptwriter writing words to match the film. By allowing scope for such news packages, the half-hour news widened significantly the function of the reporter in television – and made it essential for television news organisations to gather much more of their own news, instead of relying extensively on the agencies.

But we could not go over to this new technique at a stroke. It called for more camera teams, more editing units, more reporters – in short, for much more money. The most we could do was to employ the method in a special unit I set up under Nigel Ryan to supplement our other coverage.

It was a crowded spring and early summer, for in parallel with these preparations we had been carrying through a merger between the ITN syndication service and the film news service of United Press

International, the first of the international newsfilm agencies. This brought into being UPITN, which quickly established itself as one of the two main world-wide agencies providing news on film, and soon, news on videotape – delivered by satellite – to television stations throughout the globe. These negotiations involved a meeting in New York in May. I journeyed there through Washington, where Eric Sevareid arranged for me to talk with President Johnson in the White House, a stimulating reminder that television journalism was not only a matter of planning and schedules, of conferences and arguments, but was concerned with people, with power, with the deep shifting currents of history.

39

Close-Up on a President

Visitors to the White House took a different route in 1967 to the one I had known as a wartime diplomat. You no longer went through a side hall where the press corps waited, free to talk to those who came to see the President. Now access, no doubt for security reasons, was through a side door from the closed, guarded roadway between the White House offices and the big grey building which used to be the State Department. I waited in what I was told was the Fish Room, so named because Franklin Roosevelt had had tanks of tropical fish in it, and because both Ike and JFK had hung on the walls stuffed swordfish which 'their wives wouldn't allow them to keep at home'. Now one wall held a painting of the signing of the Declaration of Independence, and another a painting by Remington of two Pony Express riders helping a third under attack by Indians. It was one of the many pictures in the White House which portray scenes from the American West, a reminder that this was a real experience, not just a subject for movies.

The President was in a small back room, seated on a big black leather chair which tilted back, with three small television screens behind him, and a telephone with many buttons. On one wall were coloured photographs of the past five Presidents, including Johnson as a slim, young Congressman alongside Franklin Roosevelt. It seemed an odd, cramped place for an interview, a fact which I attributed at the time to the need for security, but to which the Watergate revelations provided later a better clue. No doubt it was equipped for taping, so that a record of our talk would exist. It seemed filled by the massive figure of the President, his eyes wide-set, warm and yet also hard, eyes that were studying, wary, watchful throughout our talk.

What was the main aspect of American policy in Vietnam he wished the British public to know? He gave two answers. A desire to halt aggression, a desire to fulfil their treaty obligations. 'We have forty-one treaties to help defend other countries, ranging from Nato to Panama. If we break one, who will trust us to keep the others?' (Earlier Dean Rusk, the Secretary of State, had told me, 'If there were fourteen enemy divisions in Sussex, I would want to do something about it. But we can't dishonour our alliances in the Far East and honour them in Europe.')

But Lyndon Johnson's mind soon moved from foreign policy to what he termed the 'communications media' – the single word 'media' had not yet become quite established. 'You are answerable to nobody, elected by nobody, yet you take upon yourselves great power.' He paused only to exclude the British media – 'I don't know how you work things there' – before he went on to attack the American networks and the press for irresponsibility, lack of attention to truth. It ceased to be a conversation, and became a long, passionate monologue.

He leant forward as he talked, swinging round in his chair, his hands clasped. From time to time he sipped root beer from a patterned, buff-coloured glass. What came through was an immensely stubborn sense of character, of a strong if limited mind, a hard man hard pressed. I had seen the same look of baffled strength on the faces of infantry brigadiers in the midst of hard, ugly battles in the mountains of Italy. When I pointed out that all the media, but television in particular, were for the first time this century reporting a war in which their own country was engaged without being subject to censorship, and that we could take no other guide than giving the news as it came, he listened intently. One point I made caught his attention. It was a new fact to him that in the film records of World War II, and of Korea, you will hardly ever see a sequence which shows our own troops being killed or wounded, and few even of the enemy dead. Vietnam was the first war ever fully portrayed on the screen. He came back to this fact again in our talk, and I noted that a month or so later it found its way into a speech he made in Chicago.

Did he want British troops in Vietnam? 'I'm not going to tell Harold Wilson how to run his own affairs, when he comes to see me next week. I'm not like Lester Pearson, who comes here and makes a speech on my doorstep against the bombing of Hanoi, or like Douglas-Home who comes here and sells buses to Cuba. They can run their own affairs. But they ought not to leave us alone to resist aggression. We will continue along the road as our conscience dictates. Why do you keep on attacking me in your media for this? It is the only action we can take. Even if we were to go down, we would have done the right thing. I am only trying to do what Churchill did – and he's the man I most admire.'

When he discovered I was a New Zealander, the President's manner warmed. New Zealand was the first overseas country in which he served in the Navy in the war. He turned thankfully from the problems of the present to other days. 'Hell, I've got a photograph of myself in Auckland somewhere – here, come with me,' and he strode into the formal Oval Office next door. It was much larger than I recollected from the evening early in 1944 when I was called here to take my farewell of President Roosevelt before I returned to the Army in Italy. Its long windows looked out over the White House lawns, green in the steamy sunshine. A print of a young naval Lieutenant Johnson, on an Auckland beach with the unmistakable outline of Mount Rangitoto behind him, was produced. It had already been packed, ready to send to a Senator. 'Find another one for him. This one should go to a New Zealander,' the President told his secretary, and he wrote a greeting to me across it. 'Now come and see the dogs,' he said.

The Presidential beagles had been in the news recently, after Lyndon Johnson had been photographed lifting one of them up by the ears. Was this cruel, or did the dogs feel no pain, merely enjoying such handling? In their enclosure in the gardens the four small beagles and one big white collie yelped and barked with excitement as we approached. 'You see, I still have some friends left,' the President commented, only half in jest. Marines and plain-clothes men were suddenly, though discreetly, apparent among the trees. The dogs tore madly into the Oval Office, where the President fed them vitamin tablets as big as a new penny. Well over an hour had passed – twice the time allotted originally for the talk. When I left his huge figure loomed above me. 'Try to tell the British the truth about us,' he said, but without too much hope in his voice. I felt I was leaving a lonely and isolated man whom, I noted when I got back to my hotel, could not hide a sense that 'he might think that he might fail'. Outside in the street the anti-war protesters with their placards paraded slowly up and down opposite the White House railings, where a week before we had filmed demonstrators chanting, 'Hey, hey, LBJ, how many kids did you kill today?'

40

Run-Up

The news which we had to continue to cover whilst we made our preparations for 'News at Ten' was big news. Francis Chichester (soon to be Sir Francis) sailed round the Horn in wild seas, and reached the approaches to the English Channel on the final stage of his single-handed voyage around the world. The BBC got the first pictures of him off the Horn, but we countered by winning the contest to secure the first live coverage of his yacht in home waters. It was a contest which led both the BBC and ourselves to charter ocean-going vessels and aircraft capable of relaying pictures from far out at sea. It also brought on to David Nicholas's expenses one of the strangest items ever to be listed on a journalist's expenses sheet – the cost of 300 tons of gravel as ballast for the Dutch coaster we had hired. As Peter Black wrote, 'Such competition sounds daft to the outsider, perhaps, but competition is the way journalism works, and it is the best way there is.'[1]

In the same Western Approaches the giant Liberian tanker *Torrey Canyon* ran aground, and had to be bombed and set on fire by the RAF to check pollution spread by its oil. And on 6th June the Six Day War broke out between Israel and her Arab neighbours. At any time this would have been a heavy burden for us. In the circumstances it was particularly so, but it had the merit of providing our reporting teams with valuable experience of the integrated package technique.

A week after the war ended, and only thirteen days before we were due to mount the half-hour news, we held our first dry run of 'News at Ten'. We recorded it hard on the heels of the mid-evening news. It was a hot night, the studio was stifling, and the outcome was not impressive. We had one more trial run that week, followed by three the next week – on the Wednesday, Thursday and Friday nights – before we were due to go on air. With each we got more grit out of the works, though the problems of preparing double the amount of material within the one extra hour before transmission proved formidable. But the Eidophor had at last been installed, the title sequence was distinctive, and the dual newscaster format worked well. By the Friday evening I was confident that we had a programme which looked different, which looked good and which provided a framework within which we could widen and deepen our treatment of the news. What we needed now above all was a good spate of news to carry us through our opening days.

I noted with relief that the BBC showed no desire to try to pre-empt us in a move to half-hour news. Their only action was to put 'Twenty-Four Hours' directly against us, apparently confident that in Cliff Michelmore they had a star who could outshine any we could offer. J. D. S. Haworth, of *Television Today,* who had close contacts with the BBC, interpreted this as meaning that 'both BBC News and "Twenty-Four Hours" have sufficient respect for ITN to await "News at Ten" with unease, but this unease is tempered by a delight that Geoffrey Cox had seemingly decided to take such risks, committing himself so fully to a gamble whose failure could have done the BBC much good'.[2]

As we came closer to D-Day, interest in the press grew steadily and my commitment became increasingly public. I found myself having to deploy to the press the arguments I had for so long used in private in favour of the half-hour news. I summed up our aims as 'trying to prove that the news of the day can fill half an hour either by its sheer dramatic quality or because it can be more readily assimilated if it is presented with analysis at the time'.[3]

The journalistic trade press took us seriously. The *UK Press Gazette* saw 'News at Ten' as 'a frontal assault on morning newspaper readers'. The *World's Press News* said 'this could be the biggest competition newsmen on the dailies have had to face since television started'. And *Television Today*, under the headline 'Sir Geoffrey's Revolution', commented that this development 'represents the most daring upheaval in the organisation of television reporting ever seen in this country'.[4] The *Yorkshire Post* chided me for 'grandiose generalisations' when I said we were out to change the viewing habits of a lifetime. I was well aware that I was giving hostages to fortune by the claims I had made, but we needed every bit of publicity we could get to attract the substantial audience which alone could mean success.

41

Defeat – and Victory

What we needed above all on Monday 3rd July was a real flow of news. Yet when we gathered for the morning's conference, with 'News at Ten' for the first time featuring on the film list, I knew that the luck which had helped us so often in the past had deserted us. After the big stories which had crowded the schedules for weeks, the list was drab and threadbare. The main story was a negative one. A strike of freight services on the railways, called as a protest against containerisation, had been called off. This was important news, but was neither exciting nor visual. The Middle East was quiet. Fighting which had flared up on the West Bank of the Jordan, and had given us some vivid film twenty-four hours earlier, had flared down. The most on offer was an interview with King Hussein of Jordan, who was in London to see Harold Wilson. He had been frequently interviewed of late, and allowed himself to say little. An interview with an Egyptian commander on the Suez Canal produced little more. Wimbledon alone offered some excitement, with Roger Taylor from Sheffield bidding to be the first Englishman for many years to get through to the semi-finals. If we were not faced with making bricks without straw, we were likely to be making them with at best a few scattered whisps. I was thankful that Nigel Ryan had two in-depth pieces under way – a report by John Whale on the Montreal Exhibition, Expo 67, which the Queen and Duke of Edinburgh were due to visit, and a report by

John Edwards on how the Israeli seizure of Jerusalem had destroyed at a stroke the considerable and lucrative tourist trade which the Kingdom of Jordan had developed when its territory included the Old City.

This news list would have been meagre enough for a shorter bulletin. For 'News at Ten' it was scanty rations indeed. But at least we had no major late-breaking stories to interrupt rehearsal. In sweltering conditions – for it was not only a hot but a humid evening – Alastair Burnet and Andrew Gardner steadily coped with delayed film and with studio cameras which played up in the heat. Julian Haviland recorded an into-camera report on the progress of the Bill to legalise homosexual practices between consenting adults – a significant measure, no doubt, but not one to sit easily in a peak-time programme, even in our new-found progressive age.

The studio, despite its ice trays, was like the hot room of that disappearing institution, the Turkish bath, when I went in five minutes before transmission to wish them well. In the control room Diana Edwards-Jones was volubly undismayed. I went back to my office, switched on the monitor in the corner, saw the commercials come and go, and heard for the first time on the public air our new theme music. Then the titles came up, and the camera zoomed in across the Thames to the clock-face of Big Ben and I heard Andrew Gardner's steady, confident voice announce the headlines between the strokes of Big Ben. For better or for worse, the half-hour news was launched.

But only just. As the programme unfolded, it seemed often off key. There were several technical hitches, with film slow in coming up, a wrong map displayed, a still picture which failed to materialise. But these were minor errors. Its central flaw was that it lacked shape and personality as a programme. The individual stories were efficiently done, as well as could be expected on a night of thin, dull news. Burnet and Gardner worked well together and the two-man technique was both new and strong. The commercial break fitted in naturally, providing a sorely needed pause for getting the second half into shape. Yet these adequate pieces did not add up to an adequate whole. The programme lacked pace, lacked flow, lacked an integrated style. Though I could not put my finger on these defects at the time, I knew that at the end of that long day when the final caption came up, and the cameras caught Alastair and Andrew instinctively turning towards each other in the studio – an action which was to become a hallmark of the programme – that we had not got it right. But we had got it on the air, and that in itself was a great achievement. I hid my anxieties and spread my congratulations and thanks around the weary technical crews, the weary newsroom and the remarkably unwearied newscasters. Yet I went home a worried man.

The papers the next morning gave me grounds for that worry. They were unanimously critical or disappointed. The *Yorkshire Evening Post* found us 'an unimpressive adversary for the BBC's "Twenty-Four Hours" '. *The Times* felt 'that the right balance between the programme's various ingredients had not been struck'. The *Daily Telegraph* pointed out that we had not used the later hour to bring in later news. 'Most of the items had been broadcast by the BBC in their 8.30 news.' Nancy Banks Smith in the *Sun* wrote, 'Every journalist knows that the birth of a new news venture is attended by pangs not comprehended outside the trade. I won't assume to judge "News at Ten" on the basis of one edition. Suffice to say that sober competence rather than excitement prevailed. What I don't understand is how anyone could suppose that the new programme is revolutionary . . . I doubt if its news interleaved with in-depth format will allow it to compete with "Twenty-Four Hours".' The *Daily Express* found the close-up of Big Ben striking one stroke for each headline 'as irritating as it was old-fashioned'. The *Morning Star* declared that there was 'nothing in this new project which had not been done as well as in the BBC late news or "Twenty-Four Hours" '. Others attacked us for the way we 'machine-gunned the headlines over the chimes of Big Ben'; for a 'dramatic over-Americanised introduction'; and for presenting no more than 'a very simple news round-up relieved by a few minutes of commercials'.

It was Peter Black, shrewdly perceptive as ever in the *Daily Mail*, who offered me the first hint as to where the trouble lay – and how it could be cured. 'Nobody does anything for the first time without a nervous edge, and the first edition of ITN's "News at Ten", all the news that is news, screwed up tension almost audibly . . . The overall disappointment was in the lack of momentum and of narrative verve one got from the old bulletins . . .'

The only parts which won praise, I noted, were John Whale's report on the Montreal Exhibition and John Edwards's report on the collapse of the Jordan tourist trade. These were both news packages, integrated picture and commentary pieces, and had the polish and pace which so much else of the bulletin had lacked.

As always, these morning papers lay in their serried ranks on the table in my room as we met for the morning conference on the second day of the programme, with another twelve- or thirteen-hour day ahead of us. From the programme companies, even from those producers who wished us well, there was only an ominous silence. When the day's news and film list was distributed, I knew we were in for another thin day. The only home story of any strength was a White Paper on Road Safety, the epitome of a worthy but dull subject, only very slightly relieved by a proposal that driving lessons should be introduced into schools. We would have to lead on a story which we had organised in advance, an interview which Reginald Bosanquet had recorded in Salisbury with Ian Smith on Rhodesia under sanctions. It was good stuff, but it was another static story, visual radio rather than active television. To be fairly and fully presented, it needed to be set in its perspective. We arranged for a group of three MPs to come in and discuss the issue live on air. Michael Foot was amongst them, which promised that it would be a lively discussion, but once again it was static television, even if we separated it from the interview, and placed it in the second half of the programme – a structure which I suspected had contributed the night before to the lack of momentum which Peter Black had noticed.

When we came to rehearsal time I realised that we had a programme which, with its jerky lack of rhythm, its lumpy disproportion between items, was very similar to that of the first night. Only one item, an on-the-spot report from Sandy Gall, on the Allenby Bridge between Jordan and the occupied West Bank, really held the attention. One home story which had developed during the day had a quirky interest, but had proved hard to cover. The chairman of the Housing Committee at Crawley New Town had been accused of demanding from housewives who sought new homes assurances that they were of good moral character. He suspected apparently that they might use Council property for illicit love affairs during the day. 'Chastity Test on Housewife' was the evening paper headline. But the councillor was on holiday in the Isle of Wight, seemingly out of range of the cameras, and without his version the story had in more senses than one little body to it.

Yet it was to play its part in regaining our momentum. Shortly before transmission Don Horobin arrived eagerly in my office. Southern Television had tracked down the Crawley councillor and could give us an interview with him. We looked at the schedule. The only way we could fit this interview in at that late stage was to scrap the discussion on Rhodesia. In the Green Room, opposite my office, at that moment, Michael Foot, Lord Byers and a Tory spokesman were with George Ffitch, ready to go up to the studio. Was it practicable, let alone courteous, to cancel their discussion at this stage? What kind of impression of this major new programme would they carry back to their colleagues at Westminster if a key issue like Rhodesia was kept off the air to make room for a story of this kind? I hesitated. Don Horobin read my mind. 'I've no doubt which story the viewers would prefer,' he said, fixing me with that intent gaze which had reporters grabbing their coats and rushing out to get the story whatever the cost. It was late in a long hard day. I drew a deep breath and said to Don, 'Well, this is what Editors are paid for.' I walked across the corridor and faced the assembled MPs. 'Gentlemen,' I began, 'I hope you will all one day write your memoirs, because what I am about to say will I am sure merit at least a footnote in them. I am going to ask you to hold over this discussion to make way for an interview with a councillor who imposes a chastity test on would-be council tenants.' There was an utter, chilling silence before Michael Foot burst into laughter, and the moment was saved.

By the time I got back to my room, the second edition of 'News at Ten' was under way. It was free of the technical hitches of the first night, and the chastity test interview certainly lifted the second part. But it was once again jerky and ill-shaped, broken apart rather than linked by the commercial break, and exuding this time, for all Burnet's and Gardner's self-possession, traces of lack of confidence. Wearily we crowded into the lifts, saying little in our dismay, hiding our disappointment as we went our different ways in the hot London summer night.

I was too tired to think further that night, but when I woke in the morning I saw suddenly the reasons for our failure, and a possible cure. We were making a programme with no clear goal. Its task was not, as had been that of the old bulletins, to tell and portray the news of the day. It was not to analyse and probe the main stories of the day, as had been 'Dateline's' remit. It was not required primarily to tell one or more big stories in depth, as did 'Reporting '67'. It was a mixture of all three, and each was blunting and obscuring the role of the others. We were doing this primarily because of a desire to meet the demand, voiced insistently at the ITN Board and by the Programme Controllers of the companies, that 'News at Ten' should be something different from news at 8.55, must at all costs not be just the old mid-evening bulletin writ large. This had obscured our aim. We were guilty of that cardinal sin, which at his wartime planning conferences General Freyberg had always emphatically denounced, the failure to define an objective clearly.

I knew I had to act quickly. So on that third morning of the programme, when the planning conference assembled, I came to the point at once. 'We are getting things wrong because we do not know clearly where we are going. Amidst all the demands for new patterns, we have lost our way. Forget all about the need to make something different. We will go back to what we know how to do well – to tell and depict the day's news. Put out of your minds the question of doing something different. Just make a normal ITN bulletin, at twice its old length.'

I felt a sense of relief sweep the room. It persisted even though the film list was again thin. The new Anglo-French swing-wing aircraft had been grounded; Roger Taylor was virtually certain to be knocked out in the Wimbledon semi-final (as he was); LBJ had been filmed with his grandchild on his launch. These were the best on offer.

But the gods were with us. An hour later an exultant Don Horobin was in my room. In Aden the Argyll and Sutherland Highlanders had made a dawn raid into the Crater district. Alan Hart and our camera team had gone in with them. Hart had what he claimed to be some spectacular film. Here at last was an action lead.

And it was a beauty. Hart had applied the integrated technique tried and tested on 'Reporting '66' and 'Reporting '67', with the added bonus that he had recorded his commentary live, as the action unfolded. He and the camera crew had ridden in one of the foremost armoured cars. They gave us a report which had almost the impact of live coverage, as they captured not only the scene of the action, but also the sound of the clipped orders, the sudden bursts of firing, the shouts in Arabic and Glaswegian as the patrols seized crouching gunmen. The boyish figure of the Argyll's commander, Colonel Mitchell – Mad Mitch – who directed the action, spoke to Hart in the midst of the shuttered streets as this No Go area was brought back under British rule. We let the story run for every second it was worth, cutting it to 6 minutes 24 seconds – an unprecedented length for a story in a regular news bulletin.

It transformed the night's programme. It was for this that we had sought the extra time, to enable us to use television to tell the news as only television can do, and we had done so with clarity and verve. The drama and pace of the story not only gave us a strong opening, but also carried the other heavier items along with it. It made even the problem of the swing-wing aircraft seem relevant and gave point to an otherwise heavy Commons debate on defence. After the break the tennis provided further action, if disappointing action, as Taylor went down to defeat. Princess Grace, on a visit to London, added elegance. LBJ with his grandson was corny, but even a President's grandson can be a scene-stealer. A packaged film report about putting the Crown Jewels on permanent show in the Tower proved palatable as a final item.

When the titles came up at 10.30 against the longshot of Westminster I knew that we had shown what a half-hour news could do. Even more importantly, I knew we had clarified our goal. We were back firmly at our old task of telling the day's news. There were many problems of technique yet to be ironed out. But no one could deny that this programme had been eminently watchable, and eminently informative. We had found our feet.

The next day Aden provided us with another strong story. Francis Chichester began his journey up the Thames in brilliant sunshine. We brought the women's semi-finals at Wimbledon up into the first half of the programme, showing Britain's Ann Jones win her way through to the final by beating Rosie Casals. And another packaged film story, this time from the home front, dealing with hippies taking drugs at the National Gallery, held the attention without difficulty for nearly four minutes.

On Friday, to round off this first week, we had abundant action. Francis Chichester arrived at Greenwich and knelt, with the Royal Naval College as a spectacular background, to be knighted by the Queen; the Israelis patrolled the banks of the Suez Canal, observed by Sandy Gall in a story which matched Alan Hart's for immediacy, if not for drama; John Newcombe won the men's final at Wimbledon. And from Pamplona Richard Lindley caught with deft commentary the atmosphere of the stampede of the bulls through the streets, a scene then still as genuine as when Hemingway had first portrayed it, not yet reduced to a tourist cliché.

These action stories had done much to restore the momentum Peter Black had found lacking. But we had further lessons to learn in pacing a longer bulletin. Early in our second week, on the Tour of France cycle race, one of the few British international cyclists, Tommy Simpson, collapsed and died of exhaustion under the midday sun of mountain road in the Pyrénées. The race was covered by mobile OB cameras of French television, and the moment of his collapse was recorded on videotape. There was no doubt that it merited being the lead story. But the action pictures called for considerable interpretative material, both about Simpson and about the hazards of sport driven to its limits. This could be provided only by studio or film interviews which would inevitably slow down the pace of the bulletin. Could we risk placing this interpretative material in a chunk at the head of the bulletin, delaying the rest of the news, or should we hold it over till later, as we had done with the rail strike on the first evening, and had planned to do on Rhodesia? We decided that the action pictures of the rider's collapse were so dramatic that they could carry the viewer's interest through the interpretative material, and so we kept all elements of the story together. This proved to be the right decision. There was little or no sense of the lead story being top heavy; the impression was rather one of significance being added to intrinsically interesting news. From then on we very seldom separated interpretation from reporting. By doing so we restored – though this had not been our conscious aim – a further element of cohesion, for by taking two bites at the same story we had inevitably put a strain on the concentration of viewers.

We knew, however, that the key to our immediate future lay in using to the full the wider scope for action news which the longer bulletin gave. Not only did this allow us to let people 'see it happen' more adequately, but also longer news stories helped to make 'News at Ten' look and feel different from the older type of bulletin. Big action stories were not, however, easy to come by. Early in our second week we faced the problem that one such story had taken place at almost the extreme limit of our range, and very close to transmission time. During the evening of Tuesday 11th July the agencies flashed the news that Margot Fonteyn and Rudolf Nureyev had been arrested and held by the police of the San Francisco anti-drug squad at a party in Haight-Ashbury, the hippie area of San Francisco. This was the heyday of the Flower Children, and Fonteyn and Nureyev, who were dancing in San Francisco, had been touring Haight-Ashbury when the raid occurred. Strenuous telephoning disclosed that ABC Television in America had camera coverage of the two stars being questioned in the Haight-Ashbury precinct police station. If we had been willing to wait until ABC brought it to New York for their own bulletin, it would have been available to us at a reasonable cost. But the difference in time zones made that too late for 'News at Ten'. The only way we could get the story on time was to pay the high costs of transmitting it by land lines across America and by satellite to London. By all our previous standards, the costs – between £5,000 and £7,000 – were prohibitive. But with the fate of the new programme still in the balance, I agreed to the money being paid.

The result outdid our expectations. Here was the stuff of innumerable American crime serials in real life. In a crowded office, against a background of metal filing cabinets and of desk tops littered with documents and paper coffee cups, a short-sleeved detective asked, 'Noo-ray-eff? Say, how do you spell a name like that? N like Nobody, U like United States . . .?' whilst a cool but concerned Margot Fonteyn waited to be questioned in her turn, until both were released as innocent. John Whale provided good clear commentary. We had it entirely to ourselves. All the BBC could muster was a series of still pictures. The sense of immediacy, of late news of keen human interest being brought to the screen from half-way round the world came through strongly. It transformed what had threatened to be a routine programme of short, run-of-the-mill stories – an investiture at Buckingham Palace, a protest march about school meals, a visit by King Hussein to Nasser – into a news report truly of the satellite age.

We needed this reinforcement. Although we were sure, from the moment Alan Hart's Aden report had reached the screen, that the new pattern would work, and had dismissed the two opening days from our consciousness, others had not. To our rivals, our foes and some of our owners, the disappointing programmes and the bad press of our opening nights had been proof that the experiment of a longer news had gone wrong from the start. Warnings reached me from Jim Coltart, in his role of ITN Chairman, that his phone was busy with calls from doubters in the programme companies. One company had, after the first two poor programmes, called for an early special meeting of the ITN Board, to discuss scrapping the whole project at once and reverting to the older style of bulletin. The forebodings of those advertising agencies who had predicted that a half-hour news would kill the late-night viewing figures seemed to be coming true.

On the Friday evening of that first week, after the programme for the day had been put to bed, the production team and the newscasters gathered round to watch a discussion on BBC 2 of the first week's performance of 'News at Ten'. They heard all but one of the assembled media critics dismiss both the idea of a half-hour news, and

ITN's execution of it. Only Paul Johnson took another view, saying in effect, 'Hold on, they may be on to something here.'

The weekend critics proved also uniformly hostile. Stuart Hood, writing in the *Spectator* with the authority of a former Editor of BBC News and a former Controller of BBC Television, expressed 'a keen sense of disappointment'. Milton Schulman in the *Evening Standard* said that 'News at Ten' had had 'more teething troubles than a student dentist with the palsy . . . ITN had neither the personnel nor the resources to produce a news programme commensurate with their hopes and their ambitions.' The *World's Press News* thought the whole concept 'thoroughly misguided. The programmes were trite compared to "Twenty-Four Hours", ragged compared with the following day's newspapers.' And when on Monday 10th July the *UK Press Gazette,* whose voice was keenly listened to in Fleet Street, devoted a full page to a scornful appraisal of 'News at Ten', I detected even in the stalwart Jim Coltart a trace of real concern. The *Gazette* said that when 'News at Ten' had first been announced newspapermen saw in it a danger. 'It could make hell of first editions and prove particularly embarrassing for London printing times. Then came the show and everyone relaxed again.'

To this chorus of informed disapproval the viewers gave their answer. On Wednesday 12th July John McMillan telephoned me. He had problems enough of his own at that moment, for his company, Rediffusion, had been shot from under him in the reshuffle of contracts, having been reduced to the role of junior partner in London. But McMillan found time to ask me if I had seen the ratings for 'News at Ten's' first week. I had not. 'All five issues were in the Top Twenty,' John said. 'Two of them in the first ten.' When the weekly blue-covered TAM ratings volume came in the next day, with its sharply-outlined black contours on the squared pink or pale blue paper, the proof was there that the public had found the programme eminently viewable. Night after night 'News at Ten' stood out clearly, a peak in the mountain range of the evening's viewing, with audiences ranging from 4.45 million homes to 6.9 million homes. At no time did 'Twenty-Four Hours' reach more than half of these totals. There was one worrying sign: we did not hold the audience evenly throughout the half-hour. There was a falling away after the commercial break. But we had held a far higher audience than that gained by the shows which had previously occupied the slot between 10 p.m. and 10.30 p.m. Far from diminishing the audience later in the evening, we had strengthened it. In programme-making terms, this was a striking success.

I knew that we had won only the opening round in a long contest. We had not yet secured a permanent grip on this segment of viewing time. But we had won the chance to continue the experiment. Audience figures like this would put paid to any early efforts to hustle us back to shorter bulletins, particularly if the trend continued. And it did. The next week four of the programmes were in the Top Twenty, with this time three in the Top Ten. I shared my delight with Coltart. Sendall was soon on the telephone from the ITA to express their pleasure. From the programme companies, other than Rediffusion, I had not one call of congratulations or approval. But their silence was to me golden enough, for it meant that for the time being at least what we had, we held.

42

Now See It Happen

Action news continued to provide the most significant element in 'News at Ten' throughout this early period. It reached a peak in early August in an eye-witness report by Alan Hart of the white mercenaries seizing the Congo town of Bukaville, on the border of Ruanda, in what was to be the last spurt of the long Congo civil wars. Hart was working with one of our best cameramen, Len Dudley, and an equally skilled recordist, Barry Martin. They set up the camera on the Ruanda side of the short bridge which marked the frontier between the two countries, a point from which, with a long-range lens, they could survey, as if from a grandstand, the Congolese hillside opposite. Hart recorded a running commentary as refugees, laden with huge bundles, came slowly across the bridge. Then, with shouts that the mercenaries were coming, the refugees began to run, to be elbowed aside by fleeing Congolese frontier guards, who handed over their rifles to the Ruanda soldiers at the eastern end of the bridge. In this panic a crippled girl on all fours was trying to drag herself across the bridge.

It was a false alarm, and in a few minutes the Congolese troops were furiously demanding back their rifles. But soon, on the white road winding down the hillside, the camera picked up the mercenaries, in single file on the jungle edge, their torsos looped with belts of ammunition, heavy automatic weapons in hand, as they skirmished their way towards the frontier. 'Here come the mercenaries, with Black Schramm's battalion leading,' commented Hart, in the exact style of an outside broadcast. It provided a report of such impact that we decided to run it for thirteen minutes – as long as the whole mid-evening bulletin had been a year earlier. 'These are the rare moments which electrify the electronic embalmer,' wrote Maurice Wiggin.[1] When the story evoked a telephone call of praise from Robin Gill, Lew Grade's chief lieutenant, I knew this aspect of our formula was working.

Action news was, moreover, abundant in that summer and autumn of 1967. With one African civil war ending in the Congo, another even bloodier one was getting under way in Nigeria, where the Federal forces based on Lagos were determined not to let the oil-rich province of Biafra go its own way. Sandy Gall, working with the camera teams of our new ally, UPITN, was soon sending back pictures of this war, as huge black troops in jungle uniform, commanded by elegant officers speaking Sandhurst English, probed their slow and cautious way along yet another series of white, tree-lined roads. And from the United States the long hot summer of black rioting erupted before the television cameras. We began the fourth week of 'News at Ten' with coverage from Detroit, as fires lit up the sultry night air, looters smashed shop windows, and National Guard troops in steel helmets, rifles at the high port, moved along the streets as if in an enemy country. The American networks provided copious film of this, even though, in an effort to help reduce the violence, they had adopted a self-imposed ban against showing live coverage of rioting on their own screens. Soon Newark, Syracuse and Milwaukee were adding their quota to this bitter story.

To get this material to Britain we used the satellite lavishly. John Whale added his own commentary to the American network pictures, reinforcing the sense that our own reporters were on the spot. We had not yet hit upon the device of ending each story with the reporter signing off as, 'This is Sandy Gall, for "News at Ten", Nigeria', or 'John Whale, for "News at Ten", Plainfield, New Jersey'. That simple yet highly effective method of simultaneously reporting the news and publicising the programme was a touch added by Nigel Ryan when he took over the Editorship.

This action coverage involved not only skill but risk. A week before they sent off their block-buster from the Ruanda border, Hart, Dudley and Martin had spent ten hours in a Congolese gaol in Bukaville, accused of being spies for the mercenaries. They managed to throw a note out of the gaol window, which a passer-by took to the German Consul. He got them freed just when a firing squad was forming up to deal with them. In Hong Kong Ernest Christie was roughed up during a street riot. His camera was smashed, and he was saved from serious injury only because he laid out an attacker with a karate chop. In Cairo Mario Rossetti and Alan Hart went in search of the exiled President of Ghana, Kwame Nkrumah. Rossetti was waiting in a car in a suburban street whilst Hart made inquiries when he suddenly felt small cold circles pressing against his temples from either side. A voice said, first in Arabic, then in English, 'Don't move a millimetre.' Two Egyptian secret servicemen, guarding Nkrumah, had come up behind the car. Rossetti's alarm was rapidly mixed with indignation when Alan Hart strolled nonchalantly by, never acknowledging by so much as a glance that he had anything to do with such a suspicious character. But, once round the corner, Hart sprinted off to get the aid of the British Consul, who in due course got Rossetti freed.

A month later what might have been a major tragedy occurred in the Yemen. A plane carrying an ITN crew had to make an emergency landing at a desert airstrip after smoke had been seen coming from the box containing their cameras. In the box were found eight sticks of explosive and eight detonators, which had apparently been placed there whilst the baggage was being loaded. Six of the detonators had gone off without detonating the main charge. This seemed proof that ITN teams bore charmed lives – and indeed, given the constant risks they faced, casualties were few. But a year later Peter Sissons, doing a reporting stint in Nigeria, was shot through both legs in a Biafran ambush. ITN flew a London surgeon out to him, and he came through safely to take a more static but extremely successful role as newscaster of 'News at One'.

Side by side with this action material we carried, particularly in the second half of the programme, a steady element of interpretation and background, often in the form of studio interviews. We persisted with this despite the continuing signs in the graphs that the audience tended to drop away after the commercial break. Material from these interviews steadily began to find its way into the morning papers. This was certainly the case when we interviewed Michael de Freitas, leader of the British section of the Black Muslims. De Freitas, who was later to be murdered in the Caribbean, had hinted in a speech at Reading that Britain might see racial rioting like that in America. Strenuously cross-examined by George Ffitch, he alleged police brutality and injustice in the courts towards the blacks. We countered this with an interview with Duncan Sandys (later to be Lord Sandys) who not only called for a ban on all further coloured immigration, but said that 'steps should be taken to reduce the number of immigrants already here'. This remark, made a year before Enoch Powell's Wolverhampton speech advocating repatriation of immigrants, was widely reported – but roused little reaction. The West Indian Standing Conference did call upon the police to prosecute Sandys, but dropped the demand when it was refused.

The public continued to find this editorial formula palatable. Week after week the ratings continued to be good. During the first five weeks of the programme 'News at Ten' was in the Top Twenty on all but three weekday nights. We had double, sometimes three times the audience of 'Twenty-Four Hours'. 'It is a clear knock-out victory, one which Auntie cannot disregard,' said the *Guardian* on 4th August. Criticism too veered round sharply in our favour. *Variety*, the main organ of American show business, which was by now required reading for every British television executive, headlined its view that 'British Buffola News on TV'. It went on to report that, 'as never before the citizenry has begun to devour news mileage in such volume as to make the TAM Top Twenty ratings look like a guide to video journalism.' This development, it declared, was 'entirely a triumph for the commercial network.' At home the *Northern Despatch* decided that 'ITN seems to have found a formula for making politics and current affairs in general into exciting and dramatic entertainment. This gutsy television may not always look at events in depth, but by golly it makes the viewer aware that these events are taking place.'

Such comments and above all such viewing figures clinched our fate. In mid-August, after only half of our three-month trial period had elapsed, the companies decided that 'News at Ten' would be continued throughout the rest of the year. The very important autumn schedule would be built around a half-hour of news at ten o'clock. Though I sensed that the battle was not finally won (for what television struggle for a place in a crowded schedule is ever final?) it would take now a massive counter-attack to dislodge us. We could turn to the next phase of development, that of ensuring that we had the reinforcements of talent, and of money, to keep up this pace over the months, and then the years ahead.

The viewing figures held up well in the autumn, which was a relief, as we had to carry a good deal of lumpy material from the Party Conferences and from the TUC, even though sharp interviewing from Ffitch and Burnet made these the more digestible. These were the last appearances which Alastair Burnet made as a newscaster for 'News at Ten' in its formative phase, as he had to return to the very full time task of editing *The Economist*. 'News at Ten' was the work of many talents, but Alastair Burnet's contribution was cardinal to its success. Had he not been with us to launch the programme, 'News at Ten' might never have got under way. Not only did Burnet give it style with his authority, his incisiveness, and his subtle and supple use of language, but he made it look and sound new. Though Andrew Gardner and Reginald Bosanquet were the team who, over the next decade, were to embody the half-hour news, the programme companies – and perhaps the public – would never have accepted them as an opening pair.

They proved well matched. Gardner I had always seen as a key man in a half-hour news, with his natural presence, his excellent diction, and his instinctive link with the audience. Bosanquet, with his touch of the Regency buck, was an excellent foil to Gardner, bringing to the programme the sense of a man who had hurried to the studio from the heart of what was then seen very much as Swinging London. I had reservations about Bosanquet as a newscaster over a long period. This was partly because the slight facial paralysis from which he had suffered since childhood continued to reassert itself when he was tired, giving a slur to his words which was the equivalent of a smudged print. But it was also because I valued his skills as a reporter and interviewer, and saw his place as being in the field as much as in the studio. But that first autumn I knew that we must establish the Gardner-Bosanquet combination as the cornerstone of 'News at Ten'. I had expected some criticism from the press and the companies, for this flew straight in the face of their deeply held view that only a single major star could hold the programme together. But such was the momentum of 'News at Ten' by then that the change passed virtually unnoticed, and the partnership was forged which was to carry the programme through its first decade. It was a partnership which, reinforced by Sandy Gall and Leonard Parkin, carried over into this longer news the note of relaxed authority which had been cardinal to ITN's earlier success. Peter Black noted this when he assessed our performance at the end of the year: 'It's the style of "News at Ten" that wins its following. Andrew Gardner looks comfortable, as if he is smoking a pipe. The BBC's disadvantage is that it can do nothing in the news line without feeling the weight of its forebears, all those occasions when the world waited for it to speak.'[2]

This was to prove a remarkably durable quality. Nine years later Philip Purser was noting that 'the newsreader's relationship to the stuff he peddles is of crucial importance. Richard Baker and Kenneth Kendall still handle it with invisible white gloves. On ITN the stout duo of Reginald Bosanquet and Sandy Gall, especially, treat it convivially: even if the heavens are falling there should be time for a quick one before last orders.'[3]

It was a quality further developed by Alastair Burnet when he returned to ITN in 1976, and which has given him, especially during the exacting period of the Falklands war, a stature within British news broadcasting comparable to that won by Walter Cronkite in the United States.

We were able to end the year with the first live news broadcast from Australia, which had been linked to the West Coast of the United States by a satellite in orbit over the Pacific. Prince Charles flew out to Melbourne, on his first overseas public engagement, to attend the funeral of the Australian Prime Minister, Mr Harold Holt, who had been drowned whilst surfing. It was a costly transmission, which came near to being frustrated when we learnt that the RAF plane in which Prince Charles was travelling was running ahead of schedule, and would touch down and pass out of the range of our cameras before the brief satellite pass became available. But the RAF, who were in touch from London with the plane, proved co-operative, and delayed the landing until Diana Edwards-Jones in our control room was able to call over the line to the Air Ministry, 'Cue Royal plane.' Down it swooped, visible on our monitors as it landed in the Australian sunshine twelve thousand miles away.

43
The New Journalism

With the establishment of the half-hour news television journalism in Britain came into its own. Not only did the public now regard us as their main source of news, but we were at last able to supply that news vividly and reasonably fully. Prior to 1967, significant though our coverage had been, we had neither the time nor the technology to do our task adequately. From now onwards we were able to anticipate the front pages of the next day's papers, to be the first as well as the main source of the main news of the day. From now onwards the householder who picked up a newspaper from beside the milk bottles on the doorstep, the worker who bought a paper from the corner shop, would almost certainly have gained a prior impression of its main contents from the screen the evening before. This was the real revolution brought about by 'News at Ten', a development far more significant than the changes in techniques or in timing which had made possible our expansion from a bulletin to a programme.

It was not a phenomenon unique to British viewing. It had already become marked in the United States. Theodore H. White, the American journalist turned historian, in the third of his massive studies of *The Making of the President*, wrote in 1968, 'if one had to locate the precise date of television's breakthrough to dominance in American life, one would have to choose, certainly the fall of 1963 when, on September 2nd, the half-hour evening news shows were established on the national networks – a date as significant in American history as the Golden Spike that linked the Union Pacific and Central Pacific to give America its first continental railway in 1869.'[1]

The value of the half-hour news, and the power of the camera, were demonstrated to the full when in August 1968 Soviet tanks moved into Czechoslovakia. The Czech television authorities, by boosting the strength of their southern transmitter, ensured that their pictures reached across the border to Austria and from there, via Eurovision, to the world. When that link was cut they smuggled some last reels of film out of the country. The pictures of the jeering, weeping, angry crowds shouting protests and abuse at the Soviet troops, or hurling stones and rubble at the tanks; the fires rising from buildings shelled by the invaders; the crumpled bodies of the dead by the roadside provided evidence beyond any doubt that this was an invasion, not the arrival of a welcome ally. One reason why the occupation of Czechoslovakia remains clear in the public mind to this day is the clarity with which television news captured this scene.

Television has also contrived to convey other, more constructive scenes in a way no other medium can match. The supreme example of this was man's first landing on the moon on 24th July 1969. When the cameras could show, live, the moment when Neil Armstrong's boot groped its way down the ladder of Apollo 11's landing module and stirred the grey dust of the moon's surface, they provided a level of reporting hitherto unknown.

We have since then had our own experience, during the Falklands campaign, of warfare being relayed into the homes from which come those caught up in the fighting. The impact of television pictures from the Falklands was cushioned by the partial censorship, whether deliberate or due to logistical difficulties, which the British authorities imposed. The war was over too soon to provide any test as to how our morale would have stood up, day after day, to the portrayal of scenes like those which followed the bombing of the transports at Bluff Cove. My own estimate is that so long as the chances of victory are good, and so long as most people hold the cause to be just, the public nerve holds. This has been the case over the long years of bombing and shooting in Northern Ireland and on mainland Britain. But when defeat seems possible, or victory seems a long way off, or doubts grow about the rights of the conflict, then the terrible reality of war, conveyed with such unique truth by television, can seem too high a price to pay – as I believe occurred in the United States in 1968.

The two main changes which were brought into journalism by television in the mid-Fifties – the use of the camera to show events as they happen, and the use of the probing interview to scrutinise, under the eyes of the public, people in the news – remain the basis of television news today. Technology has changed. The Cine-Voice camera has given way to ENG – electronic news gathering by light-weight electronic cameras. Videotaping has enabled interviews to be more neatly dovetailed into programmes. But the basic development which television added to journalism, that of giving the public more direct access to the events and people who make news, endures.

It does so despite the many problems which visual news has brought both for journalism and for society. For journalists the central problem is to ensure that the razor-sharp instrument of the moving picture is used to convey the truth, to ensure that the camera remains the servant, and does not become the master, of the news. No more misleading adage was ever devised than the statement that the camera cannot lie. It is an instrument which has to be guided and controlled, which can distort, as well as portray the truth. Because the impact of the picture is so sharp, because in Wordsworth's words the eye is 'the most despotic of the bodily senses', pictures can only too easily convey a false impression. They can distort by showing only part of the truth, as happens if they concentrate on a solitary punch-up in what is otherwise a peaceful demonstration. They can distort by their absence. Truthful reporting of the Vietnam war was seriously impeded by our inability to show, except in occasional official propaganda material, any scenes of the war from within North Vietnam, or within Vietcong-held territory. Not only was the cost of the war on that side of the lines not portrayed, but we could give no evidence of what life was like to the people of North Vietnam – and therefore likely to be like for those of the South once the war was lost.

This was even more strikingly apparent in the case of Cambodia. For more than five years the sufferings of its people, like those of neighbouring Vietnam, had appeared every day on our screens, filmed in the sharp greens and blues of those lands. Then in April 1975, as the Khmer Rouge finally captured Phnom Penh, all film from Cambodia disappeared from our screens – and from the consciousness of the West – as abruptly and as completely as if Indo-China were a spacecraft which had passed on to the dark side of the moon. The genocide of the Cambodian people by the regime of Pol Pot, a crime on a par with Auschwitz and Belsen, went unrecorded, and virtually unnoticed until the Vietnamese, to justify their invasion of what had then become Kampuchea, admitted, briefly, some cameramen and reporters.

The same is true of day-to-day reporting not only of countries behind the Iron Curtain, but of many countries in Africa, the Middle East, South America and the Far East. 'A strange situation has developed. Over the Western democratic societies the eye of the camera roves, dwelling to an inevitable and considerable extent on trouble and disagreement. From a large part of the rest of the world comes, in television terms, virtually nothing. May this not be the greatest distortion of all?'[2] Not the least of the achievements of Solidarity during the year of relative freedom it won for Poland was to open their country to overseas television crews, providing the first chance to portray the realities of life in a Communist state.

The best corrective to these problems posed by journalism's newest tool, the moving picture, is journalism's oldest tool, the word. Commentary, investigation, analysis and explanation in words can ensure that pictures serve the truth, can overcome the inescapable fact that things are seldom what they seem, can get at the deeper reality below the vivid surface of the staged demonstration, the organised parade, the specious public speech, the dramatic highjacking. In this task the other main technique pioneered in the Fifties, the probing interview, becomes all-important. The right to ask questions of people in the news, particularly of people of power or would-be power, and to ask these candidly and, through the cameras, before an audience of millions is one of the greatest gains television has brought to journalism, at least on a par with the directness and vividness of the moving picture. As a technique, the interview has weathered the years well. It has survived excesses, such as those when dramatised interrogations before shouting studio audiences brought charges of 'trial by television'. It survives the occasional weaknesses which arise when, in the huge range of daily interviewing which takes place on radio and television, reporters have neither the skill nor the time to press their questions home, and so allow what is propaganda rather than information to get on the air. There are other occasions, more common within the wider scope of current affairs programmes, when interviewers abuse this right of access to public figures in order to grind their own axes rather than to elicit information or clarify issues. But by and large the right to question, established in so many hard arguments in 1955 and 1956, is well used, and has become an integral part of the democratic process in Britain, in the United States, in Australia and New Zealand to a greater degree than is the case in other Western democracies, let alone in totalitarian countries.

Daily news programmes are not in themselves sufficient to carry out the task of putting news into perspective. They need the support of current affairs and news analysis and documentary programmes. Today these exist in abundance, particularly on the BBC, with its two channels, and has increased with the arrival of Channel Four and of

Breakfast Television. Yet it is remarkable how many major issues across the years have slipped through this net, at least to the extent that they have not been made the subject of a full-scale documentary, or a lengthy current affairs report, in which the combined and complementary powers of the picture and the word have been fully deployed. High-rise housing is one of these. During the years when our cities were being transformed by skyscraper housing blocks, no television programme seriously probed, let alone challenged, the rightness or even the practicality of this massive exercise in social engineering. Similarly I believe that a study of programme schedules in the Sixties and Seventies would show that remarkably few, if any, full-scale inquiries were mounted into the widespread changes in educational and disciplinary practices in British schools, or in modifications to the curricula. It took the public inquiry held by the ILEA, at a cost of £100,000, into the nature of the teaching – or lack of teaching – at the William Tyndale Primary School in Islington in 1976 to bring this to public attention. When Angela Pope for the BBC did apply fully the techniques of the modern documentary to portraying a London comprehensive school from the inside, there was such an outcry from teachers and from the authorities that no programme of comparable candour was mounted for years. The 'Kingswood' series of 1982 told us more about the teachers and the problem children than about the average children. Certainly no parent could make a choice between private or state education on the basis of the information provided by television.

Similarly, no full-scale inquiry was launched by the BBC, or by the major ITV companies, into the structure of the trade unions, and of their increasing power in society during the decade after 1964, when their strength was enormously increased by the spread of the closed shop, and of the paying of social security benefits during strikes. Within Independent Television the only documentaries on the subject were two fairly modest efforts from a regional company, Anglia, one of which found its way on to the network only after strong opposition from amongst the other companies. 'I shall show it, but I shall not watch it,' was the disdainful verdict of one programme chief. Similarly the Parliamentary struggle over the closed shop early in 1976 attracted little or no in-depth examination on the air. Broadcasting was directly affected by the degree to which freedom of speech would be endangered if one union were allowed to dominate journalism. The newspapers saw this as a threat to the freedom of the press, and fought to have the media excluded from the closed shop legislation. But the documentary producers walked by on the other side.

Television's failure to get to grips with one major issue, that of Ulster during the years leading up to the troubles, has become a matter of public discussion. There has been a good deal of complaint that television neglected the injustices suffered by Roman Catholics in the North, leaving these as a mass of dry tinder ready to be sparked off by the civil rights marches of the winter of 1968/9. This is true. What is not true is that this neglect sprang, as one senior IBA official has said, from a 'conspiracy of silence'. The issue of Northern Ireland was not probed in the Sixties because it seemed to be a non-issue, a problem which was being steadily lessened by the prosperity of the Sixties, and by the growing, if unpublicised ties between the Republic and Ulster. With a multitude of other problems coming to the fore, such as Vietnam, Northern Ireland did not claim a high place on the list of matters of concern. Nor was television alone in taking this stance. The same was also true of the British press – and to a considerable degree also of the press of the Irish Republic.

There was probably more deliberate calculation behind the attitude of producers towards any full or systematic highlighting of mass Commonwealth immigration in the late Fifties and early Sixties. It was treated in the news and in current affairs, but no doubt owing to a very understandable wish not to arouse racial prejudice, the full scale and the full implications of this change of Britain to a multi-racial society were not brought to the fore by the use of the documentary technique.

This failure – for it is no less – of television journalism owes something to the nature of the medium. Its dependence upon pictures weakens its capacity to convey ideas, or to look ahead to events which have not yet taken visual form. Today it is easy to portray the failure of high-rise housing by filming the graffiti-scrawled walls, the soul-destroying asphalt playgrounds, the abandoned, vandalised blocks awaiting destruction. But to predict such events in pictures is a different matter. The main reason however for the failure lies in a failure of editorial control. The jigsaw structure of ITV leaves no one company or one person responsible for ensuring that all major news is probed as well as reported. Within the BBC the practice of leaving editorial initiative to producers, leaving ideas to come up from below, makes it only too easy for subjects which may not appeal to the producers of the day to be neglected. To plug these gaps for the future

– and for the present – we need to look hard at the criteria which are applied for the selection of material for news bulletins and all other actuality programmes, as well as at the criteria which govern the treatment of items once they have been selected.

Within ITN and within the BBC the treatment of news across the years has been governed by the twin principles embodied in the first Television Act, and long established by practice in the BBC newsroom, those of accuracy and impartiality. The first of these arouses no argument. If you ever had any doubt about its importance you need only station yourself near the switchboard of a news organisation after an error has crept into the football results. Twenty-five years ago impartiality was regarded as equally sacred. In recent years it has, however, come increasingly under attack, as involving artificial concepts of balance, or as being an unattainable ideal, or indeed a delusion. Yet balance, the principle of giving both sides – indeed of giving all sides – is the long-accepted basis on which both Parliament and the Law Courts operate. If impartiality is an unattainable ideal, so too are many other virtues. But that does not make them any the less worth striving for. It is certainly the best compass by which the daily journalist can steer through the maelstrom of events. It continues to be rigorously applied within ITN and, so far as I can observe, within BBC News, even though that is no longer the case within television current affairs or documentaries. In those areas the viewer no longer knows whether to expect from a programme a fair statement of all the arguments, which he sometimes gets, or an opinionated piece of editorialising, reinforced by all the power of film, which he also sometimes gets. Nor is there any guarantee that such editorialising will be offset by a later programme giving the other side of a contentious issue. John Pilger is given air time to argue, against the highly-emotive background of starving children, that blame for the sufferings of the Kampucheans under Pol Pot should be laid at the door of the Americans. Truth is apparently adequately served if within the same series Auberon Waugh is allowed to be rude about the British working class.

Within daily news, however, impartiality makes not only for good journalism but good sense. Certainly when passions run high, when broadcast news is dealing with events which shake society to its depths, objectivity and fairness, which go hand in hand with impartiality, are what the public instinctively seeks from broadcast news. The long years in Northern Ireland have proved this – and it is to the eternal credit of ITN and the BBC News that during those years their daily reports have continued to achieve a high degree of public trust. The short, sharp shock of the Falklands war made the importance of impartiality even more clear. The moment when the news comes under the glare of close and informed scrutiny, the moment when people's lives and their homes and possessions can be affected by the accuracy and fairness of the news, any hint, any shade of editorialising becomes unacceptable. Now that the dust of the moment has begun to settle, it is clear that in this even more acute test of the Falklands both broadcast news services retained the confidence of the public, though the BBC News suffered for the moment some knock-on effects from missiles aimed chiefly at other parts of the Corporation's output.

But impartiality alone is not enough. It is a good guide to how news should be treated on the screen, but is not in itself a guide as to which news should be selected, either for daily bulletins or other actuality programmes. It is not adequate as a touchstone by which News Editors can decide, from the multitude of events that occur each day, those which should be reported, and those which should be given prominence. In other words, impartiality is not a guide to news values. Still less is it a guide to the producers of news in depth and current affairs and documentary programmes, whose power of choice is not hemmed in by the newsman's imperative of immediacy, and who confront a plethora of potential subjects. As a guide to such selection impartiality is a guide only if one gives it the meaning which Samuel Taylor Coleridge attached to it. Looking back on his long Editorship of the *Morning Post* at the height of the Revolutionary War with France, when he was advocating policies independent both of Pitt's Government and of the Opposition, he attributed his success with the public to 'genuine impartiality'. 'By this,' he added, 'I mean an honest and enlightened adherence to a code of intelligible principles previously announced and faithfully referred to in support of every judgement of men and affairs.'

Such a code exists today in the values of Parliamentary democracy and the rule of law. Editors are rightly wary of proclaiming their adherence to any abstract code other than the vague one of pursuing news values, for fear of tying their hands in the task of getting at the facts, and publishing them. This sensible empiricism rests, however, on a freedom of the press and of broadcasting which in turn rests upon our Parliamentary democracy and the rule of law. I believe much would be gained, and nothing would be lost, if Editors were to state openly that these are principles they would be prepared to see 'previously announced and faithfully referred to' in taking their basic decisions about news values. Such an action would not only give journalists a clear compass bearing by which to steer through the maelstrom of daily news, but would provide a rebuttal to those academic critics, such as the Media Group of Glasgow University, who claim that the phrase 'news values' merely hides an underlying support for the Establishment and the powers that be.

Accepting that broadcasters have a responsibility to sustain and support the principles of Parliamentary democracy and the rule of law does not involve suppressing information or censoring news. On the contrary it imposes upon Editors an obligation to give the fullest possible service of accurate news, because such a service is as essential to the political health of society as a good water supply is to its physical health. Reporting and examining defects in the structure and functioning of our society is a clear part of such a service – as are also reporting its successes. Nor does it involve keeping off the air those who challenge the very fundamentals of our democracy and the rule of law. It is part of the duty of the newsman to ensure that those who advocate change, of however extreme a kind, are allowed to state their case. But they must be prepared to do so under questioning, to argue it and not merely to assert it, and they must in parallel desist from using force to overthrow democracy. Democracy is a tough plant, which can stand a lot of rough handling – provided its opponents are prepared to accept the same treatment.

For society as a whole, and not just for journalists, television news has produced problems. Foremost amongst these in recent years has been the proliferation of scenes of violence. These can be not only horrific in themselves, but can result from the deliberate mounting of acts of violence in order to catch the camera's eye – that difficulty which confronted me in my early days in Kingsway with the film of the Algerian ambush.

Suppression of such material is not an answer, for it brings a greater evil in its train, that of weakening of public faith in the truthfulness of the news. It is possible for television News Editors to hold back news without losing that trust, where the time of such a ban is short, and where the public can clearly see that lives are at risk. This has been done in kidnapping cases, and during the Balcombe Street and Iranian Embassy sieges. Bomb scares are no longer reported on BBC or ITN, as they are phoney events depending for their effectiveness on being given credence by the media. In all these cases – as indeed in the war in the Falklands – the public can readily understand why, with lives at risk, they did not get the full story. But where the outcome of such curbs is less clear, where what is gained is some vaguer and more debatable result, the outcome could be merely to allow rumour to flourish, and public confidence in the broadcast news services to be weakened. That confidence is of incalculable value to society. To provide news services which people trust is the most important service television can render to democracy.

44

Facing Facts

In July 1968 I attended my last meeting as an executive of Independent Television News. The medium which others had spurned in 1956, and about whose scope I had then had my own anxieties, had now become a dominant influence in society. The years of the emergence of television news had been the first stage of the cultural revolution of our times, in which this new visual form of communication has modified profoundly the intellectual and artistic climate which had persisted since the days of Gutenberg and Caxton. Within journalism that revolution has brought great gains. The camera has enabled the news to be told more clearly, and for all the medium's limitations, more truthfully. The probing interview had made public figures more directly accountable to the people they govern, or seek to govern. There is no doubt that as a result of television most people today are better informed, and more reliably informed, than they were when the great majority of them snatched their information from the headlines of the popular press. As one form of the media, indeed as the major form of the media, news on television has meant a major advance for journalism.

It is essential, however, if we are to get the best out of this marvellous medium, that it should not be asked to do more than it can. Television does not and cannot offer a complete diet of information. Its rich pictorial content requires the balancing components of the written word and the spoken word. Many stories, many concepts are better conveyed in print or on radio. This is certainly true of abstract but very important news, such as that dealing with monetary theory or with the Common Agricultural Policy. It is also true of much news from closed societies, where the camera, even if admitted, may have its scope so limited that it misleads rather than clarifies. All the main forms of journalism need one another. Each has its strengths, which offset the limitations of the others.

During the Editorship of my successor, Nigel Ryan, ITN forged ahead rapidly. Ryan gave the programme a further polish and style, as well as developing its capacity to combine analysis with reporting. He developed the use of the integrated news package until 'News at Ten' became a deftly-shaped mosaic of such reports. This called for more money and staff, and Ryan showed himself pertinacious and courageous in securing these. He brought into being 'News at One', which had its own strength and identity from the outset. It was during his Editorship, too, that Paul McKee, now Deputy Chief Executive of ITN, and David Nicholas pioneered the use of computerised graphics in a way which has dominated the coverage of General Elections ever since.

During the Seventies, too, the international newsfilm agency UPITN, which Hodgson, Coltart and I had created in 1967 by merging ITN's syndication service with the film agency of United Press International, came fully into its own, ranking alongside the BBC's Visnews as one of the world's two main television news agencies. By the end of the decade UPITN, under the skilled management of Kenneth Coyte, was supplying 170 stations in more than 70 countries with a service delivered around the clock by satellite. Building a world-wide agency was not one of the demands laid upon Independent Television by Parliament or by the IBA; it is not an achievement which, by its nature, attracts the attention which has been won by 'News at Ten', or by ITN's other programmes; but it is no mean achievement.

In 1977 Nigel Ryan went off to wider fields and David Nicholas came forward to fill the Editorship with great distinction. His clearheadedness and courage have carried ITN through the exacting tests of Ulster, of violence in the streets of Brixton, Bristol and Toxteth, and the supremely exacting test of the Falklands. Nicholas has too the right mind and the right character to withstand the new assaults on the integrity of the media.

Some of these assaults, particularly those from within the academic world, raise questions which go to the heart of journalism in a free country, for they challenge the belief that there can be such a thing as objective truth, and that people can be sincere in seeking it. A central tenet of faith with many of the critics of television news is that journalists delude themselves if they believe they can be objective or fair. Whether the journalist knows it or not, these critics insist, he is blinkered in his approach to the news by his background and his experience, or, in short, by his class. Even the most manifestly objective and impartial of journalists is, by this credo, unconsciously a propagandist. This is not my experience of the attitude of those who find their satisfaction in seeking out and presenting the day's news. There are two main types of journalist – the historians and the preachers. The historians' pleasure comes from the hard news, from sorting out the facts, establishing the truth amidst the fog of distortion, of half truths and quarter truths and bald untruths which surround every event. The preachers are the feature writers, the columnists, the editorialists whose pleasure comes in telling people what they should think about the latest news.

'Historian' is perhaps not an exact word for those whose satisfaction comes from turning the passing scene into words or pictures, for it implies a longer view than most of us take. Certainly an interest in history first drew me into journalism, and added greatly to the intangible rewards I got from it. When in November 1936 Franco launched on Madrid the first night air raid on a civilian city since World War I, and the air war which had been so frequently forecast and dreaded had become a reality, I stumbled through the burning and broken streets to send my story to London with a mixture of emotions in my mind. I felt shock and sympathy for Madrileños; concern for what this portended for us all; and a normal ration of fear. Yet I could not stifle a sense almost of exultation at being present when this page of history was being turned. But in due course this sense of history was overtaken by an alternative interest – the sheer pleasure of trying to get the facts right.

A journalist of a later generation has put this view well:

'In the end the reporter's quest is for facts, all the facts, not just the selected facts that would slant a story in a given direction. Facts are in the last resort the humanist's only weapon against which the doctrinaire bully can only attempt outright suppression. The search for facts can be an odd enriching experience. It can also on occasion be dangerous, hilarious, time consuming and oddly unsatisfactory, since the armchair editorialist will philosophise with utter disregard for facts. Statisticians will say that facts can be made to fit any interpretation, and totalitarians will claim that fact finding is a dangerous alibi.

'But the reporter's quest for facts bring rewards of its own, which have only partly to do with being proved right in the end. The truly addicted reporter (and most of the other kind drop out of the game sooner or later) will never tire of joining in the chase, watching the adrenalin flow and bringing all available ingenuity to bear on a situation which, like life itself, is never tidy, finite or simple.'[1]

The war strengthened my pleasure in the quest for facts. As an intelligence officer to an infantry division, it was my task when we were in battle to set out each evening to General Freyberg and his senior officers the information we had gathered about the enemy, and an estimate of their intentions the next day. The keen faces which surrounded me, often drawn with weariness and strain, were of men who were going to base their actions, at least in part, on what I told them. The lives of the men they commanded, and indeed their own lives, would depend upon the accuracy of the information I imparted. What is more, I had to face them the next day, when that information had been put to the test, when tanks or troops or guns whose presence I had not been able to warn them of might have put a whole plan at nought, when my facts had been put to a deadly proof. It was a chastening discipline, but a stimulating one. It developed in me a relish for establishing the truth which is an end in itself. Television, properly used, provides an invaluable new means of achieving that end.

The foundations laid by the pioneers who battled through the early years in Kingsway, and which were maintained in the difficult years of the early Sixties, and then developed and widened into 'News at Ten' and ITN's other programmes, have proved sound. They have been able to sustain what has become not only a great journalistic enterprise, but also an institution which is part of the daily life of millions of people. Building it was hard work, but fulfilling work, and it had a quality which has become more scarce as television has become more powerful and more crowded – it was fun.

Notes

Chapter 2 From Radio to Television

1 Memorandum quoted in Grace Wyndham Goldie, *Facing the Nation* (Bodley Head, London 1977), p. 41

Chapter 6 Seeds to Nurture

1 Kendall McDonald, *Evening News*, 14th January 1956

Chapter 9 News into Pictures

1 Robert Dougall, *In and Out of the Box* (Harvill Press, London 1973), p. 218

Chapter 13 Newspaper of the Air

1 *News Chronicle*, 14th June 1956
2 *Sunday Times*, 16th September 1958

Chapter 18 War on the Screen

1 *The Listener*, 29th November 1979
2 Clark to author, 1975

Chapter 19 'News to Fit the Medium'

1 *Sunday Times*, 11th November 1956
2 *The Listener*, 16th November 1956
3 *Sunday Times*, 4th November 1956
4 *Spectator*, 8th November 1956
5 *TV Times*, 4th January 1957
6 *Manchester Guardian*, 22nd December 1956
7 *Spectator*, 28th December 1956

Chapter 20 Truly Live Television

1 *Sunday Times*, 13th January 1957

Chapter 21 'Roving Report'

1 Fraser to author, July 1959
2 *Manchester Guardian*, 20th April 1957

Chapter 22 The Nasser Interview

1 Robin Day, *Day by Day* (Kimber, London 1975), pp. 193-4

Chapter 23 The Road to Rochdale

1 H. G. Nicholas, *The British General Election of 1950* (Macmillan, London 1951), p. 126
2 *Daily Express*, 23rd February 1958

Chapter 24 New Faces – and New Methods

1 *Yorkshire Post*, 8th July 1958

Chapter 26 Covering a General Election

1 Charles Curran, *A Seamless Robe* (Collins, London 1979), p. 71

Chapter 27 News Specials

1 *Spectator*, 17th April 1959
2 Address at Birmingham University, October 1968, quoted in *The Third Floor Front* (Bodley Head, London 1969), p. 122

Chapter 28 Time Is Short

1 Interview with Eamonn Andrews in 'ITV – This Is Your Life', broadcast 22nd September 1976

Chapter 32 Death in Dallas

1 Theodore H. White, *In Search of History* (Jonathan Cape, London 1979), p. 517

Chapter 33 Television Election

1 *Contrast*, Vol. 4, No. 1, p. 16

Chapter 34 The Battle for Time

1 Pilkington, *Report of the Committee on Broadcasting* (HMSO, Cmd, 1753, 1962)

Chapter 37 A Half-Hour News?

1 2nd Report from Select Committees, Session I, 1971, p. 159

Chapter 40 Run-Up

1 *Daily Mail*, 28th May 1967
2 *Television Today*, 29th June 1967
3 *TV Times*, June 1967
4 *Television Today*, 25th May 1967

Chapter 42 Now See It Happen

1 *Sunday Times*, 13th August 1967
2 *Daily Mail*, 15th December 1967
3 *Sunday Telegraph*, 22nd February 1976

Chapter 43 The New Journalism

1 Theodore H. White, *The Making of the President, 1968* (Jonathan Cape, London 1969)
2 E. R. Thompson, address to IBI, Rome 1960

Chapter 44 Facing Facts

1 Edward Behr, *Anyone Here Been Raped and Speaks English?* (Hamish Hamilton, London 1978) p. 315

Index

Since the activities of Independent Television News and of the author interweave on most pages of the book, detailed page references for them have been omitted.